LANGUAGE IN THEORY

Routledge English Language Introductions cover core areas of language study and are one-stop resources for students.

Assuming no prior knowledge, books in the series offer an accessible overview of the subject, with activities, study questions, sample analyses, commentaries and key readings – all in the same volume. The innovative and flexible 'two-dimensional' structure is built around four sections – introduction, development, exploration and extension – which offer self-contained stages for study. Each topic can be read across these sections, enabling the reader to build gradually on the knowledge gained.

Language in Theory:

- ❏ is a comprehensive introduction to the conceptual frameworks which underpin the study of language
- ❏ approaches theories of language through themes such as gender, race, creativity and cognition, allowing students to investigate language theory in practice
- ❏ is written in a clear, entertaining style with extracts from such diverse names as George Orwell, Donald Rumsfeld and Friedrich Nietzsche
- ❏ provides classic readings by key names including Cixous, Derrida, Foucault and Lakoff.

Written by experienced teachers and researchers, this accessible textbook is an essential resource for all students of English language, linguistics and literature, and philosophy.

Mark Robson is a Lecturer in English Literature at the University of Nottingham.

Peter Stockwell is Professor of Literary Linguistics at the University of Nottingham.

ROUTLEDGE ENGLISH LANGUAGE INTRODUCTIONS

SERIES EDITOR: PETER STOCKWELL

Peter Stockwell is Professor of Literary Linguistics in the School of English Studies at the University of Nottingham, UK, where his interests include sociolinguistics, stylistics and cognitive poetics. His recent publications include *Cognitive Poetics: An Introduction* (Routledge 2002), *Sociolinguistics* (Routledge 2002), *The Poetics of Science Fiction, Investigating English Language* (with Howard Jackson) and *Contextualized Stylistics* (edited with Tony Bex and Michael Burke).

SERIES CONSULTANT: RONALD CARTER

Ronald Carter is Professor of Modern English Language in the School of English Studies at the University of Nottingham, UK. He is the co-series editor of the forthcoming *Routledge Applied Linguistics* series, series editor of *Interface* and was co-founder of the Routledge *Intertext* series.

OTHER TITLES IN THE SERIES:

Sociolinguistics
Peter Stockwell

Pragmatics and Discourse
Joan Cutting

Grammar and Vocabulary
Howard Jackson

Psycholinguistics
John Field

World Englishes
Jennifer Jenkins

Practical Phonetics and Phonology
Beverley Collins & Inger Mees

Stylistics
Paul Simpson

FORTHCOMING:

Child Language
Jean Stilwell Peccei

LANGUAGE IN THEORY

A B C D

A resource book for students

MARK ROBSON AND
PETER STOCKWELL

Routledge
Taylor & Francis Group

LONDON AND NEW YORK

First published 2005 by Routledge
2 Park Square, Milton Park, Abingdon, Oxon OX14 4RN

Simultaneously published in the USA and Canada
by Routledge
270 Madison Ave, New York, NY 10016

Routledge is an imprint of the Taylor & Francis Group

Typeset in Minion and Univers by Florence Production Ltd, Stoodleigh, Devon
Printed and bound in Great Britain by TJ International Ltd, Padstow, Cornwall

British Library Cataloguing in Publication Data
A catalogue record for this book is available from the British Library

Library of Congress Cataloging in Publication Data
Robson, Mark.
  Language in theory: a resource book for students: Mark Robson and
Peter Stockwell.
      p. cm. – (Routledge English language introductions)
  Includes bibliographical references and index.
  1. Language and languages. I. Stockwell, Peter. II. Title. III. Series:
Routledge English language introductions series
  P107.R635 2005
  400–dc22   2004015930

ISBN 0–415–32049–6 (hbk)
ISBN 0–415–32048–8 (pbk)

HOW TO USE THIS BOOK

The Routledge English Language Introductions are 'flexi-texts' that you can use to suit your own style of study. The books are divided into four sections:

A Introduction – sets out the key concepts for the area of study. The units of this section take you step-by-step through the foundational terms and ideas, carefully providing you with an initial toolkit for your own study. By the end of the section, you will have a good overview of the whole field.

B Development – adds to your knowledge and builds on the key ideas already introduced. Units in this section might also draw together several areas of interest. By the end of this section, you will already have a good and fairly detailed grasp of the field, and will be ready to undertake your own exploration and thinking.

C Exploration – provides examples of language data and issues for reflection, and guides you through your own investigation of the field. The units in this section are more open-ended and exploratory, and you will be encouraged to try out your ideas and think for yourself, using your newly acquired knowledge.

D Extension – offers you the chance to compare your expertise with key readings in the area. These are taken from the work of important writers, and are provided with guidance and questions for your further thought.

You can read this book like a traditional text-book, 'vertically' straight through from beginning to end. This will take you comprehensively through the broad field of study. However, the Routledge English Language Introductions have been carefully designed so that you can read them in another dimension, 'horizontally' across the numbered units. For example, Units A1, A2, A3 and so on correspond with Units B1, B2, B3, and with Units C1, C2, C3 and D1, D2, D3, and so on. Reading A5, B5, C5, D5 form a strand which can take you rapidly from the key concepts of a specific area to a level of expertise in that precise area, all with a very close focus. You can match your way of reading with the best way that you work.

The glossarial index at the end, together with the suggestions for further reading, will help to keep you orientated. Each textbook in the RELI series has a supporting website with extra commentary, suggestions, additional material and support for teachers and students.

LANGUAGE IN THEORY

This book arises from a recognition that students of linguistics tend not to know enough about the philosophy of language and critical theories associated with language, and that students of philosophy and critical theory often talk about language without knowing much linguistics. In fact, this observation also applies to many of our academic colleagues, and might be said to have applied to the two authors of this book before we embarked on writing it. For us, writing it has been a valuable learning process, and it is perhaps a book that had to be written collaboratively.

Language in Theory is intended to reflect on various approaches to language: the multiple meanings created by the word 'in' in the title serve to remind us of this. Firstly, the book is concerned with linguistic theories, frameworks, models and approaches, across the range of disciplines addressed by the RELI series as a whole. Just as you will find that sections of this book relate to each other in ways that we have not explicitly made apparent (and that perhaps we are not even aware of yet), so you might find that questions raised in other books in the RELI series are also tackled here, if often in a very different form.

This sense of connectedness is crucial to understanding the purpose of this book. One of the most obvious ways of thinking about the 'in' of our title is to recognise that, to some extent, any and every discussion of language has a 'theoretical' dimension. To talk about theory in this way is not so much to consider the work of specific thinkers, but is instead to begin to identify the structures, values and assumptions that underpin every view of how language functions, whether as an abstract system or as a set of empirical examples (and the ideas of both 'system' and 'empiricism' are themselves related to 'theories'). Books like this one are designed to make their readers more aware of such theoretical underpinnings. In this respect, to flag up, as we do, the notion of *Language in Theory* becomes another way of suggesting that there is no language that could be safely located 'outside' of theory. What, for example, would an approach to language that didn't make *any* value judgements or assumptions look like? Chances are it would be entirely unrecognisable to us. Among the many problems such an approach would face, probably the most intractable would be how, in the absence of any assumptions, it could determine what was and what was not language.

That we implicitly carry around a set of categories, concepts and structures that allow us to make meaning can be seen from a very famous example. Michel Foucault (one of the most notable names associated with Theory with a capital 'T') begins his 1966 book *The Order of Things* by explaining how it was influenced by the Argentinian writer Jorge Luis Borges:

> This book first arose out of a passage in Borges, out of the laughter that shattered, as I read the passage, all the familiar landmarks of my thought –
> *our* thought, the thought that bears the stamp of our age and our geography

– breaking up all the ordered surfaces and all the planes with which we are accustomed to tame the wild profusion of existing things, and continuing long afterwards to disturb and threaten with collapse our age-old distinction between the Same and the Other. This passage quotes a 'certain Chinese encyclopaedia' in which it is written that 'animals are divided into: (a) belonging to the Emperor, (b) embalmed, (c) tame, (d) sucking pigs, (e) sirens, (f) fabulous, (g) stray dogs, (h) included in the present classification, (i) frenzied, (j) innumerable, (k) drawn with a very fine camelhair brush, (l) *et cetera*, (m) having just broken the water pitcher, (n) that from a long way off look like flies'. In the wonderment of this taxonomy, the thing we apprehend in one great leap, the thing that, by means of the fable, is demonstrated as the exotic charm of another system of thought, is the limitation of our own, the stark impossibility of thinking *that*.

(Foucault 1989: xv)

Even something as apparently neutral as a list immediately makes us think about how we categorise the world and the objects and people within it. The strangeness of Borges's taxonomy comes precisely from its impact upon the reader's sense of the familiar. Foucault talks of 'familiar landmarks', 'ordered surfaces' and of an 'age-old distinction'. The structure of the taxonomy is familiar, but its content is distinctly odd. Another way of thinking about this is to see it as, in Freud's terms, 'uncanny', as 'strangely familiar' (see Freud 2003 and Royle 2003). Let's think for a moment about what we just called the difference between the taxonomy's structure and content, however. We know what is going on in this division of the world, we make similar distinctions and classifications all the time, but the principles according to which this particular division is made make no sense. This wouldn't matter so much, perhaps, if it were not for the fact that the whole point of such taxonomies is to allow us to make sense of the world. The categories that the taxonomy uses point to the thinking that lies behind it. If the 'Chinese' taxonomy seems strange, it makes us reflect on what we think of as 'normal', what we think of as the rules by which it seems reasonable for us to play. Breaking these rules makes us more aware of what the rules are, makes us remember that there *are* rules. But it also unsettles us, it can make us think about how these particular rules became the normal ones, and whether such a *normalisation* was justified and rational. The strange makes us reconsider the familiar.

One of the effects of theory on those who encounter it for the first time is to provoke a similarly unsettling sense that the normal rules – our assumptions, values, principles of judgement, and so on – are no longer of much use to us. Many of the insights of theory seem to run counter to 'common sense' or to the procedures for analysing language that we may have been taught. But if we think about the very notion of common sense, and we begin to unpick it, then we immediately have to confront a series of questions, such as: how did common sense become common? How common is it? Are there groups within a culture who might not share in this supposedly shared wisdom? Does common sense change across history? For example, very few of us now would ascribe crop failures to the influence of the devil, but in previous centuries this would have been the most obvious cause. Are there habits of thought that, precisely to the extent that they have become habits, have ceased to involve any real thought? Common sense is often invoked to authorise ideas that have become part of a tradition, that are associated with the status quo, and with conservatism. It is no accident that one of the rallying cries of John Major's 1990s Conservative Government in Britain was 'common sense'.

By contrast with the habitual modes of thought that allow you to come to quick decisions and judgements, awareness of theoretical ideas may often seem to slow you down. Where common sense may seem 'instinctive', the ideas presented by theory can appear decidedly counter-intuitive. Notions that once seemed all too obvious might turn out to demand to be used with some caution. This is another way of thinking about our title. The subject of this book is language, in theory. But language, in the context of theory, may not be quite what common sense would suggest.

It is probably time for us to say something about what we mean here by 'Theory'. While we have so far used the term in a fairly non-specific way, to refer to the structures by which we try to think about language (and the world more generally), Theory has come to mean something much more specific in the Anglophone academic world. Indeed, it means very little outside it, leading to the odd situation that the French, for example, who have since the 1960s furnished most of the world's prominent Theorists, are only just themselves beginning to recognise 'Theory' as a valid category. For many in the Anglophone world, 'Theory' is short for 'Critical Theory', and you will find many books and courses that use this title. A word of warning, however. Critical Theory is also the name for a body of work that emerged from the Frankfurt School, most famously associated with the work of Adorno, Horkheimer and others. When you see Critical Theory used in secondary literature you need to be aware that the term means different things to different people. Some will be referring to the narrower usage (in the Frankfurt School tradition), others will have a wider sense of it (including, alongside the Frankfurt School, what has come to be known as structuralism and poststructuralism, as well as gender theory, postcolonialism, visual culture and cultural studies). In order to avoid confusion, and to make clear that we are using the term in an inclusive sense, we have adopted 'theory', not 'critical theory'.

Theory in the English-speaking world has a particular institutional history, in which English departments have played a dominant role, and it is especially those who work primarily on literature who have led to the rise (and perhaps the decline) of theory. This is partly why many of our discussions in this book repeatedly turn to literature for examples, and to discussion of the particular problems that literature raises for any consideration of how language works. The turn to theory was in part a turn towards a broader set of concerns than was conventionally allowed to literary studies. Theory seemed to offer a rationale for a strong interdisciplinarity, in which it was permissible for literary critics to draw upon material from philosophy, history, political science, sociology, art history, anthropology, psychoanalysis and a range of other disciplinary traditions. What made such an apparent eclecticism seem plausible was

in part the odd history of these disciplines, especially in their European manifesta-
tions, which had led to an emphasis on structural questions, inspired by a certain
reading of the work of the Swiss linguist Ferdinand de Saussure. By one of those
academic ironies that litter our history, many literary critics found themselves
learning about linguistics as a result of their new-found interest in, for example, the
structural anthropology of Claude Levi-Strauss. Students of language may thus find
much that is familiar (if strangely, uncannily familiar), even if they are new to the
texts that have come to be identified as theory.

This book is also concerned with language in use – that is, how language is used in
thinking about language. Discussion of language must always itself use language, and
so it is important to form an understanding of how language relates to itself in critical discourse. Most of the critical thinkers discussed here are very concerned with
questions of style, aware of the degree to which form impacts on content. How an
argument is presented is often as important as what is being 'said'. We hope that
reading this book will lead you to think further about the ways in which you go on
to write about language, as well as giving you some new ways of approaching your
analyses of language.

Although the book is concerned with language in theory, throughout we have tried
to offer practical examples and circumstances to allow you to think about language
more accessibly. We are concerned with language as a system and concept, with
language as being representative of ideas, but we are also concerned with the material
expression of language. Even though this is a theoretical book, we have tried wherever possible to illustrate our points with real examples of natural language occurring
in the world around us. The exercises and questions that we set also invite you to
find and work with such examples for yourself. Here, also, there is a theoretical
dimension to this choice. One of the standard distinctions made is between 'theory'
and 'practice'. Theory tends to come off badly in this comparison, prompting statements of the form, 'That's all very well in theory but does it work in practice?'. Like
so many of our conventional binary oppositions, this one doesn't actually stand much
scrutiny. Every practical use of language is always already in relation to theory, susceptible to description in systematic terms, or used in accordance with a set of
pre-existing principles. *Language* is, we might say, always *in theory*.

There are nine strands across this book, beginning with social and communal issues
and moving towards individual and interpretative issues, broadly speaking:

1   Gender
2   Race
3   Society
4   Performativity
5   Intention
6   Cognition
7   Creativity

8   Figuration
9   Interpretation

These strands are arranged according to the standard RELI series design, with four sections taking you from introductory ideas (A) to complex understanding (B), offering practical thinking exercises (C) and readings with issues to consider (D). You can read the book alone, but many of the discussions will be more interesting if you are part of a discussion group. There are general discussion points provided at the end of each section B unit: these are often intended to be challenging and to open up wide-ranging discussion and thinking – they draw on the combined material from the unit in A as well as B. The discussion points in section C are intended to be more data- or example-driven. After each reading in section D, there are also suggested issues to consider. In all of these activities (which are marked as such in the margin), there are usually no right or wrong answers; indeed, we would find several of the questions difficult to answer ourselves. To develop your thinking, you will need to read further and deeper, and we have included a section on further reading at the end to suggest where your studies might go next; these are also arranged by the theme of the strands.

The glossarial index indicates where terms are used in the book. Rather than offer a decontextualised definition, this feature shows the term used in context. All work referred to in the book is collected in the references at the end.

CONTENTS

CONTENTS **CROSS-REFERENCED**

ACKNOWLEDGEMENTS

Perhaps more than any other sort of book, this book is the product of collaborations. The ideal reader we want to create, the philosopher–linguist, does not even exist as an ideal author yet, so we have drawn on the work and thinking of many others in creating *Language in Theory*. Firstly, we must thank our colleagues at the University of Nottingham, where the peculiarity of the School of English Studies is its unique strength. In particular, the following people have influenced the book, whether they were aware of it or not: Svenja Adolphs, Robert Cockcroft, Val Durow, Sarah Grandage, Matt Green, Craig Hamilton, Peter Howarth, Louise Mullany, John McRae. We are especially grateful to Ron Carter, who in many ways is the closest to an ideal reader we could imagine, and has made many suggestions throughout the writing process. Rob Pope, Claire Kramsch and Andrew Merrison read initial sketches and made perspicacious suggestions that focused our minds on the different sorts of readers who would use the book. Thanks to Louisa Semlyen, Christy Kirkpatrick and the *RELI* editorial team at Routledge for the vision to see the potential of unusual projects and the skill to bring them to fruition.

Several of the practical exercises and some of the phrasing in the book first appeared in workshops and seminars at the British Council, Buenos Aires, at the University of Helsinki, the Vrije University Amsterdam, Lancaster University, and at the Poetics And Linguistics Association (PALA) conference at Bogazici University, Istanbul. For these opportunities and the discussion of ideas, we are grateful to all our colleagues and their students, particularly Isil Bas, Michael Burke, Jonathan Culpeper, Mary Godward, Rod Lyall, Bo Petterson, Merja Polvinen, Elena Semino, Mick Short, Paul Simpson, Gerard Steen and Peter Verdonk.

Joanna Gavins read the draft, the final draft, and the final final draft while giving birth and looking after her and Peter's daughter Ada: thank you.

D5 Reprinted from 'What is an Author?' in *Textual Strategies: Perspectives in Post-Structural Criticism*, by Michel Foucault (ed. Josué V. Harari). Copyright © 1979 by Cornell University. Used by permission of the publisher, Cornell University Press.

D6 From *Philosophy in the Flesh: The Embodied Mind and Its Challenge to Western Thought*, by George Lakoff and Mark Johnson. Copyright © 1999 by Perseus Books Group. Reproduced with permission of Perseus Books Group in the format of textbook via Copyright Clearance Center.

D7 From 'Common Language: corpus, creativity and cognition', by Ronald Carter, in *Language and Literature*, 1999, Vol. 8, No. 3. Reprinted by permission of Sage Publications Ltd.

D8 From *The Critical Difference: Essays in the Contemporary Rhetoric of Reading*, by Barbara Johnson, pp. 97–102. Copyright © 1981 Barbara Johnson. Reprinted with permission of The Johns Hopkins University Press.

D9 From *Total Speech: An Integrational Linguistic Approach to Language*, by Michael Toolan, pp. 169–79. Copyright © 1996 Duke University Press. All rights reserved. Used by permission of the publisher.

Section A

INTRODUCTION:
KEY CONCEPTS IN
LANGUAGE IN THEORY

A1

GENDERED LANGUAGE

Simone de Beauvoir famously claimed that 'One is not born a woman; rather, one becomes a woman'. This immediately draws the distinction between biological sex and the social construction of expectations, behaviour, patterns of thinking and economic role that is *gender*. That language use is partly determined by the gender of speaker and hearer is apparent in numerous sociolinguistic studies that appear to show that men and women use language differently. Early studies suggested that the performance of femininity includes such patterns as:

❏ over-hesitancy, including pausing, stuttering, 'um-ing and ah-ing', and uncompleted sentences which . . . slow . . . and . . . trail . . . off . . .
❏ non-assertiveness, including the avoidance or hedging of phrases that er, you know, sound overly fluent or too, ahm, confident, and the use of a rising intonation that invites agreement and support?
❏ self-reference in subject matter, and a tendency to personalise by using first person pronouns, inclusive and intimate 'we', and possessives
❏ avoidance of swearing and other taboo forms
❏ superpoliteness, including a (hmm, yeah) high degree of (sure, yep, mmm) positive and supportive backchannel
❏ non-interruption (especially of men) in conversation.

(Notice, too, how this brief list is largely expressed as negatives from the male norm.) Though these recorded differences seem to correspond directly with the dimension of social power rather than gender, the fact that women often find themselves in socio-economically less powerful situations can explain their tendency to use such patterns (and, of course, vice versa). Nevertheless, repeated use of these features has led to an identification that there are such things as *genderlects*.

Debates have raged over the question of whether these customary patterns of language have become so fossilised that language itself can be seen as inherently sexist, man-made and male-oriented. Language thus seems to treat masculine features as the norm and feminine features as eccentric or 'other'. Language usage then becomes part of the ideological apparatus that sustains gender, and language use itself must be regarded as being *phallocentric*, capable only of offering expression to masculinity and unavoidably denying women a public voice of their own. In this view, women are forced to use patterns of expression that are both alien and alienating.

From the wider angle, such a view challenges the traditional and perhaps popular perception that language is simply an open set of choices, from which speakers can select words and grammatical structures to express themselves sufficiently. In the traditional perception, language simply expresses a codified representation of the world as it is: language is a plain tool that mediates either the world or personal identity. Instead, we might say that language is subject to the same pressures of ideology that reflect social and economic conditions. Language *constitutes* reality and identity, and the constraints of language limit the expression of realities and identities that are seen as non-normative. The practice of language, in other words, carries dominant social values along with it. The experience of women (and other decentred groups) is denied expression as a result.

A contrary view to this would argue that there are elements of *essentialism* in the argument. First, the position presents language as a single, essential object that can be monolithically characterised in rather simple, unitary terms. The claim that language itself is sexist appears to give a personality to language, objectifies it, and thus makes it appear controllable. Instead, you might conceive of language as a set of communicative events occurring in a huge number of permutations every day and throughout the past. The variety of language, imagined like this, makes it seem complex, fluid and subject to a vast number of conflicting and complementary pressures which ensure its fine-grained texture, stylistic variety and almost infinite capacity for creativity. Language, then, displays a resistance to control by any single group (even a very powerful one).

Second, and similarly, the former view presents all femininity as a single, unified, non-variant object. All individual women – from all cultures, of all ages and from all historical periods – are reduced to one sense of femaleness, that has essential and easily definable qualities and boundaries. This does not seem very satisfactory, either. Even more depressingly, it would offer no possibility either for the expression of an individual woman's experience, nor any means of discussing it or even thinking about it.

Some sociolinguists and feminist writers have instead offered a more functional view of language, focusing on the uses to which language is put. This involves separating out the user of language from the set of possible choices available in all utterances. For example, several fieldwork studies seem to indicate that women are rather conservative in their speech, selecting choices that appear politely old-fashioned, and even *hypercorrecting* their accents to a more socially prestigious form when they are in a self-conscious situation. (Women, for example, seem to adopt a higher-value 'telephone' voice more readily than men.) It has been suggested that this is because women are more aware of their projected image or social *face* than men, or are more socially 'insecure'. Studies even seem to show mothers teaching their boy and girl children differently when it comes to correcting their accents: girls are 'corrected' towards a nationally prestigious pronunciation, while boys are left to use the local variety that is actually spoken by the rest of the family.

However, rather than seeing these patterns as inherently and essentially 'womanly', it is important to recognise the ideological and political factors involved. The women who hypercorrect tend to be those in a certain upper-middle-class position that places them into roles in which they need to present several 'faces', as appropriate to the direction of the social stratification in which they find themselves. From this perspective, these women seem to possess particular 'multicultural' language skills that other groups may lack. Notice, too, that the traditional sociolinguistic explanation of women's difference here is the thing that is rather sexist, not the language of women itself. It is easy to reverse the description to present the 'genderlect' as a positive skill which others are missing.

Similarly, research into the close-knit social networks of especially urban working-class women reveals that it is women who generate innovations in language use and then maintain those variations. Women with very dense social networks are often at the forefront of language change, whether it comes to accent variation, or innovations in word-choice, phrasing or grammatical patterns. For example, the introduction of the American English 'Can I get a sandwich?' rather than the traditional British English 'Could I have a sandwich?' seems to have been led by young professional women in London. Similarly, the spread through the 1990s and early twenty-first century of the 'uptalk' rising intonation across the English-speaking Western world (and which has even been observed crossing into other languages), was first observed in the UK being used by this same group. The pattern is now common across the country and has even spread to young(ish) men.

This perspective on language – originating largely out of feminist interest in the workings of social power and ideology – can be extended into a view of all language use, including women's usage. The crucial factor is not so much gender, primarily, as the particular sort of community in which you find yourself. These groupings are effective in patterning language use, of course, only if they are also partly defined functionally, in terms of the social practices that they enact. It seems, then, that the *community of practice* is the crucial social factor in determining language, including the determination of patterns that constitute gender.

Gender, then, is a matter of linguistic performance in a social context. Femininity is performed, or perhaps we should talk of 'femininities' being performed, since there are and have been a range of gendered identities available for performance. Being 'ladylike', having a 'girlie' chat, 'bitching' about a work colleague, being 'motherly', and so on, are all made manifest through particular patterns of language. Their practice also reinforces and adjusts these (and many other) femininities so that the relationship between language and social role must be regarded as a two-way process. Language constitutes gender, and the performance of gender continually acts to pattern language. The combination of this social practice and language pattern is better termed *discourse*, and this integrated notion will become more important as we progress through this book.

THE LANGUAGE OF 'RACE'

Many people see the language that they speak and write as a fundamental part of their identities. Differences between languages are often said to lie behind differences in national character, suggesting that language both shapes and reflects the identities not only of individuals but also of regions and of whole cultures. The view that there is a natural link between the linguistic culture into which someone is born and their own sense of self lies behind the idea of the 'mother tongue'. Most people are aware of accents and dialects within their own language, and will make judgements based upon their perceptions of them. Within the English language, we might think most obviously of the differences between, for example, British English, American English and

Australian English. Yet even the notion of British English becomes more complicated if we take into account the differences between the English-language dialects and accents of England, Ireland, Scotland and Wales. These can be further sub-divided by region (Northern, Southern, Geordie, Cockney, Highlands, and so on).

Such identifications can range across and within languages, and in multicultural societies linguistic variations also mark the impact that migrant communities have had on those cultures. So, for example, British Asians will often speak a language such as Punjabi or Bengali at home with their families, whereas they will speak in *Standard English* when at work or school. Immigrant communities frequently retain linguistic and other traces of their 'origins', in order to help preserve a connection with the culture of the country from which they or their families have migrated. In areas of high migrant density, these languages may become more widely spoken than any other. Thus the state of California has considered taking Spanish as its official language, despite being part of a supposedly English-speaking country. As a result, the English spoken in such areas is marked by its co-existence with other languages.

It should already be apparent, then, that connecting language use to any idea of 'race' can present enormous problems. Part of the difficulty stems from the word 'race' itself. You will have noticed that we have repeatedly placed it in inverted commas. Henry Louis Gates, Jr (1986: 402–3) explains the thinking behind this: '"race" is a metaphor for something else and not an essence or a thing in itself, apart from its creation by an act of language' and, he continues, '"races", put simply, do not exist'. Language is seen to be productive of racism through its part in forming the category of 'race'. Gates argues that racism is not just a matter of how people behave, it's about how they think; it's a question of the assumptions that people make and the value judgements that they base on those assumptions. Language can betray those patterns of thought, even when there is no intention on the part of the speaker or writer to make a racist comment. For this reason, 'race' is a fundamentally linguistic matter.

The category of 'race' is most frequently used to denote a person's skin colour. But does it make more sense to categorise people on the basis of their skins than on, let's say, their hair colour, or the colour of their eyes? Here, language is not pointing to objects in the world in a neutral manner, it is instead acting in accordance with a decision about what is important in judging an individual or group. The same kind of thinking informs all of these choices (skin, hair or eyes). It is not that one would be a better choice than another. 'Race' is not something that a person can be said to possess, and cannot be seen as part of her or his 'nature'. A classification imposed from outside, it's a matter of perception, not expression. Would we be happy with a theory of language that suggested that people with brown eyes have a different relation to language than those with blue eyes?

Whether we accept the use of the category of 'race' or not, there are strong historical reasons for exploring the link between language and identity. Part of the reason that many people connect personal identity to language is attributable to a cultural inheritance that is bound up with experiences of colonialism and racism. Not only is language use potentially marked by 'race', but some would also argue that taking into account the ethnicity of the speaker or writer when we read is essential. So 'black writing', for example, demands a certain kind of reading, it's not just a question of style or subject matter.

So far, we have considered the use of language as a form of expression. It is also necessary, however, to think about the ways in which language can be used to represent 'race'. A famous example of the attitudes expressed towards other languages (and the people who use them) during the nineteenth-century expansion of British colonial power is a comment made by politician, literary critic and historian Thomas Babington Macaulay, in his famous *Minute on Law and Education* (1835):

> I have no knowledge of either Sanscrit or Arabic. But I have done what I could to form a correct estimate of their value. I have read translations of the most celebrated Arabic and Sanscrit works. I have conversed, both here and at home, with men distinguished by their proficiency in the Eastern tongues. I am quite ready to take the oriental learning at the valuation of the orientalists themselves. I have never found one among them who could deny that a single shelf of a good European library was worth the whole native literature of India or Arabia.
>
> (Quoted in Said 1983: 12)

There are many things to note about this passage. It begins with an admission of ignorance, a confession (though without any shame) that Macaulay doesn't have any knowledge of the languages on which he passes judgement. Separating the content from the languages in which texts are written, he relies on translations. Turning to experts, it seems that the people he chooses are not oriental but instead 'orientalists', that is, Europeans. The final point seems to involve a fairly random choice: any shelf of European works, no matter which texts you choose, are worth the entirety of Indian or Arabic literatures. For Macaulay, teaching Indians the English language is the only way to make them useful to a British administration in India. They are allowed, as he states later in the *Minute*, to remain Indian in 'blood and colour', but they must speak and think like Europeans.

Such suggestions that other languages are either valueless or meaningless are also to be found in literary texts. Joseph Conrad's *Heart of Darkness* (1899), a novella which deals with the colonial encounter, contains a passage in which the protagonist, Marlow, is travelling on a boat. Observing the figures on the bank, Marlow says:

> The steamer toiled along slowly on the edge of the black and incomprehensible frenzy. The prehistoric man was cursing us, praying to us, welcoming us – who could tell? We were cut off from the comprehension of our surroundings; we glided past like phantoms, wondering and secretly appalled, as sane men would be before an enthusiastic outbreak in a madhouse. We could not understand because we were too far and could not

remember because we were travelling in the night of first ages, of those ages
that are gone, leaving hardly a sign – and no memories.

(Conrad 2000: 1984)

While Marlow registers his own inability to interpret what he sees honestly, the way
in which he phrases this incapacity is revealing. What he suggests is not that he isn't
in a position to judge. What he calls into question is the idea that *anyone* could make
sense of this spectacle. In other words, he proposes that the man's actions, gestures
and words are meaningless. But there is an obvious answer to Marlow's question 'who
could tell?'. The 'prehistoric' man himself knows exactly what he is doing, and presumably so does anyone else who is either from within or sufficiently familiar with his
culture. Marlow makes the colonial gesture par excellence, in that he claims that his
position is objective. Like Macaulay, he suggests that *no one* could be found who
would disagree with his judgement. What this reveals is that those who belong to the
culture of the 'prehistoric' man don't count, their knowledge is outside of history.

LANGUAGE AND SOCIETY

In this unit we will be examining the relationships between forms of cultural expression such as language and literature and other aspects of social existence, including
economics, history, institutions and modes of social organisation. In particular, we
will need to think about how language plays a part in forming us as 'subjects' within
society.

From the outset, we have to recognise that one of things at stake here is the definition of what it means to be human. One of the earliest texts in political philosophy
tries to provide such a definition:

Nature, as we often say, makes nothing in vain, and man is the only animal
who has the gift of speech. And whereas mere voice is but an indication of
pleasure or pain, and is therefore found in other animals (for their nature
attains to the perception of pleasure and pain and the intimation of them
to one another, and no further), the power of speech is intended to set forth
the expedient and inexpedient, and therefore likewise the just and the unjust.
And it is a characteristic of man that he alone has any sense of good and
evil, of just and unjust, and the like, and the association of living beings
who have this sense makes a family and a state.

(Aristotle 1995: 1253a1)

This is a passage from Aristotle's *Politics*. While there is much to be said about this, what is primarily of interest for us here is the connection that Aristotle makes between the faculty of 'speech' and the possibility of distinguishing between good and evil, just and unjust, and so on. Non-human animals are capable of feeling and expressing pleasure and pain, but only human animals are capable of making value judgements about these experiences. Further, it is the fact that such judgements may be held in common that founds institutions such as the household and the state. Speech founds politics itself (see Rancière 1998, ch. 1). This is partly what lies behind Aristotle's famous description of man as a 'political animal'. Speech is not simply one faculty among others.

This concern with the linguistic expression of ideas and values such as goodness or justice is important because it allows us to think about why people behave in the ways they do. As Terry Eagleton puts it:

> One can understand well enough how human beings may struggle and murder for good material reasons – reasons connected, for instance, with their physical survival. It is much harder to grasp how they may come to do so in the name of something as apparently abstract as ideas. Yet ideas are what men and women live by, and occasionally die for.
>
> (Eagleton 1991: xiii)

What Eagleton is referring to, of course, is the realm usually called politics, but which also encompasses religion and philosophy. The realm of abstract ideas can have as much, if not more, of an impact on our behaviour than biology or genetics. The things we hold most dear, notions of family, freedom, faith, love (of a person, a deity, a nation, and so on), and which might lead us to kill or even to die, are more than just the product of an instinct for self-preservation. Such ideas are often fostered, sustained and strengthened by language. The various discourses that present values to us, our own or those of others, form the matrix through which we interpret the world, and provide us with the terms of reference for our decisions. This, after all, lies behind the emotive public speech, behind propaganda, and behind advertising for everything from political parties to charities. Such forms of address aim to work by activating a set of responses that manifest attitudes we have already internalised.

In thinking about the relationship of language to forms of social interaction, we need to think about the concept of ideology. Ideology was for some years a very unfashionable term, being associated with an unsubtle form of classical Marxism. Like the 'class struggle' or the 'proletariat', ideology was too clearly associated with an era which – with the fall of the Berlin Wall, the disintegration of the Soviet system, the 'end of history', the emergence of globalisation and 'the third way' – was felt to bear little relation to the political terrain of the late twentieth and early twenty-first centuries. Much of the criticism of the concept of ideology came from within leftist thought itself, and this combined with liberal, humanist and right-wing pressure to cause the term to lose favour. Several commentators noted, however, that just as the term began to lose academic currency, forms of explicitly ideological thinking took hold across the world (including religious fundamentalisms, nationalisms, aggressive market capitalisms, as well as liberation theologies, environmentalisms, anti-capitalisms, and so on). In recent years, inspired in large part by the work of thinkers such as Slavoj Žižek, ideology has again become a key term in critical discussions of language (see, for example, Žižek 1989 and 1994).

Probably the simplest (some would say crudest) version of ideology is one which suggests that it is a form of distortion. We cannot see the world 'as it really is', the argument goes, because of the operations of some power (ideology) which makes us see the world in a particular, and erroneous, way. Ideology is thus seen as a kind of misrecognition or mystification. This emphasis on seeing is crucial, since ideology is often associated with a particular 'image' or 'view' of the world. What this version of ideology also suggests is that the problem is to do with us, it is a matter of how we see, rather than a question of how objects *really are* in the world. As such, there would always be the possibility of achieving a true sense of the real world, if only we were able to change our perception.

One of the most powerful reworkings of the concept of ideology is to be found in the work of Louis Althusser (1994). Althusser refuses the easy separation between appearance and reality that more straightforward notions of ideology presume. Rather than being a distortion of reality, ideology for Althusser is a fundamental part of the experience of being human. Althusser's own phrase – 'man is an ideological animal by nature' – rewrites Aristotle's idea of man as a political animal. In other words, we are only able to recognise ourselves as humans at all through ideology, because it is ideology that makes us human. There is no mystification, then, ideology is not false perception but perception itself.

A key distinction that Althusser (1994) makes is between what he calls a Repressive State Apparatus and an Ideological State Apparatus (ISA). The former works explicitly in terms of violence, through force (including the police and the armed forces), whereas the latter works through ideology. One is primarily public, the other may be largely private, including ideas such as the family.

Central to Althusser's version of ideology is the idea of 'interpellation'. As a Marxist thinker, Althusser is interested in the ways in which capitalist societies maintain themselves by processes of 'reproduction'. Thus capitalism, on this view, works through various mechanisms (repressive or ideological) to produce the kinds of people that it needs to function, and at the same time reproduces the structures through which this reproduction of subjects is enacted. For Althusser this occurs through a kind of calling or hailing which makes us recognise our place within a society. This is what he calls interpellation: 'The existence of ideology and the hailing or interpellation of individuals are one and the same thing.'

This question of point of view is, however, where one of the strongest objections to this conception of ideology comes in. How would we know that the position we occupy is a demystified one? How could we ever be secure in claiming that we stood outside of ideology and that we could therefore point at it in an objective and neutral way? If ideology really is a matter of how we see, then it could never be a case of simply stepping to one side in order to see round the obstacle to clear sight – we are the obstacle. As several critics have noted, there is no more ideological statement than the one which claims that it is not ideological. As we noted at the beginning of this book, everything, not just language use, presupposes a theory, whether it is made explicit or not.

PERFORMATIVE LANGUAGE

What is the relationship between language and the world? This is a big question, and it is one that is asked in several different guises throughout this book. One answer is that language refers to the world, it indicates and describes it. For good or ill, the language at our disposal also shapes the ways in which we think about both objects and people. We have looked at this in the units on, for example, gender, 'race' and society.

We might also want to consider how language impacts upon the world in more direct ways. One way of thinking about this is to consider what is called *rhetoric*. It is common now to think of rhetoric as somehow empty. When we say that a speech is rhetorical, that it's 'just rhetoric', this usually implies that it has no worthwhile content. This is a long way from its traditional meaning, however. Rhetoric aims to persuade, to make the hearer or reader feel or think something. As such, it acts upon the world. Not all language refers to a pre-existent situation; some forms of language-use make things happen. One aspect of this will be the focus of this unit.

In *How To Do Things With Words*, the philosopher J.L. Austin argues that there are statements that are best understood as *performative*, or *illocutionary*, linguistic acts (Austin 1976). Examples of the kind of statement that he is referring to here would be 'I now pronounce you husband and wife', 'I name this ship the *Anonymous*' and 'I promise that I will be there'. Other examples would include declaring war, betting and verbal contracts (even if they aren't worth the paper they're written on). In focusing on how words make things happen, or are a form of happening in themselves, Austin elaborates what is known as *speech act theory*.

One of the first distinctions that Austin makes is between performatives and what he calls *constative* utterances. A constative utterance is descriptive, it involves saying something about something. Constatives tend to be statements of fact ('That man is bald'; 'I am reading this book'; 'A constative is a statement of fact'). But performatives don't do this. Instead, by saying something you are doing something. When someone says 'I declare war' or 'I bet you fifty pounds', the action is completed in what they are saying, no further act is needed. For this reason, constative state-ments can be judged as either true or false, either they are accurate descriptions or they are not. In the case of performatives, however, there is nothing to judge them against. All you can say is that they make something happen or they don't.

How does this work? For a start, say out loud 'I name this ship the *Anonymous*'. Did anything happen? Chances are (and it would be very unfortunate if we were wrong here), you aren't currently standing in front of a brand new ship with a bottle of champagne in one hand and this book in the other. A performative utterance, then, depends upon a particular situation or context if it is to be operative.

Performatives may fail if certain conditions are not met. Austin calls the things that stop performatives working *infelicities* (the utterances are somehow 'unhappy'). There are some very basic rules. First, a convention must exist which will allow the operation of the utterance. In the case of marrying, there must be a marriage ceremony in which this form of words is recognised and accepted. Second, the circumstances must be right. If you say 'I now pronounce you husband and wife', you must have the necessary religious or civil authority for it to be binding. Third, we must follow the procedure correctly. 'I now pronounce you husband and wife' only works at the end of the ceremony, after the vows have been made. This is the significance of the 'now'.

As Austin points out, there are all sorts of ways in which infelicities may occur. There may not be a convention in operation for what you are trying to do. The example he gives is an attempt to divorce simply by saying 'I divorce you'. As is so often the case, we move quickly from marriage to divorce. In most if not all countries, an attempt to divorce in this manner would not be accepted. Equally, proposes Austin, the object may cause problems as well as the circumstances: 'consider the case in which I say "I appoint you Consul", and it turns out that you have been appointed already – or perhaps it may even transpire that you are a horse' (Austin 1979: 238). Here there is nothing wrong with the statement itself, nor with the convention by which consuls are appointed. A performative must also receive consent. If you offer a bet and no one accepts it, then it isn't a bet. All of these are examples of what Austin calls *misfires*.

There is also another way in which performative utterances may be infelicitous. This concerns the question of intention (see also Unit 5). Utterances such as promises, oaths, and so on, depend upon a certain seriousness. If you say 'I promise to . . .' then you should genuinely mean to commit yourself to a course of action. If you don't make a sincere promise, then there is an infelicity, but it is not strictly a misfire. The convention for promising may exist, the form of words may be right, but without the appropriate intention this is not a true performative.

What this raises is the whole issue of seriousness. Austin famously refuses to allow utterances on the stage or in poetry to be counted as speech acts at all:

> a performative utterance will, for example, be *in a peculiar way* hollow or void if said by an actor on the stage, or if introduced in a poem, or spoken in soliloquy . . . Language in such circumstances is in special ways –

intelligibly – used not seriously, but in ways *parasitic* upon its normal
use – ways which fall under the doctrine of the *etiolations* of language
[meaning that language becomes sickly]. All this we are *excluding* from
consideration.

(Austin 1976: 22)

Much has been made of this exclusion of literature from serious language use (see,
for example, Johnson 1980a, Felman 2003, Fish 1980 and Miller 2001. Further
discussion of the problems that arise from this may be found in Unit B4).

Let's stick with the main question at hand here. How can we tell the difference
between a felicitous and sincere speech act, and one which is (for a variety of possible
reasons) infelicitous? John Searle proposes that we can remain 'neutral' on the question of whether a promise is sincere or insincere. All that is required is that instead
of insisting that someone making a promise has the intention to perform the act
which the promise entails, we instead recognise his or her responsibility for the intention (Searle 1969: 62). But should we remain neutral where promises are concerned?
The answer to this question is one that should concern us, not least because certain
performative utterances have taken on a great deal of social significance.

In particular, the promise has an importance that goes way beyond its linguistic
classification. Promises are crucial to many of our social interactions, on both a
formal and informal level. However minimally, we need to be able to believe that
the promises people make may be trusted. This is as true of the hope offered by
political assertions of good intention as it is of the assurances offered by friends and
teachers. We tend not to promise people things they do not want ('If you continue
like this, I promise you you will fail the exam'): such promises are more likely to be
taken as threats or warnings.

Friedrich Nietzsche recognises the centrality of the promise for a consideration
of morality, describing human beings as animals which are 'entitled to make
promises' (Nietzsche 1996: 39). In Nietzsche's discussion, the main problem faced
by humans as promising animals is forgetfulness. Only humans are capable of
promising, because only humans have an appropriate faculty of memory, but this
memory may only be maintained through effort. In pursuing this link between
promising and morality, Nietzsche is following Immanuel Kant.

For Kant, to offer a false promise is fundamentally irrational. Kant asserts that
since one must always act in accordance with the *categorical imperative* – 'I ought
never to act except in such a way that I could also will that my maxim should become
a universal law' – a contradiction cannot be avoided if one chooses to make a false
promise (Kant 1998: 15). This contradiction arises since if it seems prudent to
promise without any intention of fulfilling that promise in order to avoid a difficulty, then this takes on the status of a maxim which others may follow as a universal
law. Your decision to make a false promise would provide an example to others, and
thus no promise would be trustworthy. To decide to make a false promise is consequently irrational, since it would end up cancelling out all promises. Such irrationality
cannot be used as a foundation for moral action.

Here, then, is another sense in which we can see language impacting on the world. This allows us to think about performativity in two ways. Firstly, there is the utterance. Declaring war, betting, swearing an oath, and so on, are performative rather than constative. They are a kind of act, rather than statements of fact. But, second, as acts they have effects. Such effects are not necessarily limited to the specifics of an individual case. The broken promise is a classic example. How many times can someone break a promise to you before you refuse to believe any other promise offered? Does this affect the way in which you treat promises made by others? As Kant proposes, an individual instance is quickly taken for a law.

LOCATING INTENTION

Where does meaning come from? In other words, who decides what a word, sentence or text means? This question about a person (*who* – speaker or hearer, author or reader?) might become a question about space (*where* is meaning generated?) or else about time (*when* does a sentence become meaningful?).

Let's think about this series of questions a little more carefully, and lay out some of the most common answers:

Who?

Speaker
Here's the obvious place to start. A word, sentence or text means whatever the person who speaks or writes it wishes it to mean. Meaning is thus a matter of intention or will, and the aim of communication or interpretation is to recover this intended meaning. In this respect, the speaker or author takes on the role of the classical oracle, or of God. This suggests that meaning is subjective. In ordinary conversation, this is why we accept people correcting our interpretations of their speech ('That's not what I meant, I meant . . .'). It is also what allows people to claim a special right to speak on a particular topic, as if their experience, the fact that it is they who are saying something, makes it more true.

Hearer
The opposing idea. You can say whatever you like, but if I hear something different, then that is what your sentence 'means'. My responses or actions will be determined by what I heard you say, not what you wanted to say. Thus the person who hears gives a sentence meaning. This also suggests that meaning is subjective, since every hearer may come to a different conclusion about what something means.

Author

Writing does not function in exactly the same ways as speech, which is why we have separated 'speaker' from 'author'. While, in conversation, it is possible to refine or correct a misapprehension of meaning, writing functions in the absence of one or both parties. In some respects, that's what writing is for (think about letters or emails). As we write this book, no reader is present (other than ourselves). When a reader reads it, we are not likely to be present. Despite these absences, it is common to think of the author as the one who 'puts' meaning 'into' a text. But, if the speaker is in a god-like position, in writing, as James Joyce's (1977: 336) character Stephen Dedalus puts it: 'The artist, like the God of the creation, remains behind or beyond or above his handiwork, invisible, refined out of existence, indifferent, paring his fingernails.' This, then, is closer to the absent God of Kierkegaard (or Woody Allen). As such, meaning is not subjective for the reader, it is objective, since every reader should find the same meaning in a text (the one the author put there).

Reader

The role of the reader is, as in the relationship between speaker and author, complicated by distance and absence, and is thus not the same as the hearer. A reader cannot ask an author for clarification, and must instead work upon and with a text. Freed from an omnipotent author, however, the reader can offer a response. As such, differences between readers (in terms of age, class, gender, ethnicity and so on) may emerge. In fact, if we emphasise the reader, then the author simply becomes another reader, no more in control of her or his text than any other reader.

The community

Within most societies there are individuals who are given authority to decide what things mean. We might think of obvious cases such as judges, jury members and censors. Historically, most religions have also nominated people to interpret scripture and to provide an 'authorised' reading. These individuals, then, are often associated with institutions and with ideological functions (see Units A3 and B3). Reading communities can also gather authority and power to themselves, of course, simply by being large: if a sufficiently large number of people decide on the significance of something, then it could be argued that their perception constitutes what it means. Most people believe (falsely) that electricity – with its currents, plugs and outlets – works like water, and they act as if this were true.

The choice that we make in answering 'who creates meaning?' corresponds to a set of answers to the question of where meaning happens:

Where?

The speaker's mind

If the speaker determines meaning, then this meaning is generated by what the speaker wishes to say. This is perhaps indicated in one of the French verbs for 'to mean', *vouloir dire*, which literally means 'to wish to say'. Meaning is thus produced as a conscious choice in the mind of the speaker. Even a slip of the tongue, which might appear to be an involuntary utterance, can be attributed to the speaker's unconscious desires (as in a simple psychoanalytic interpretation). It is still possible to think of this in terms of intention.

The hearer's mind

Just as the speaker intends a meaning, so the hearer's interpretation will be the product of how he or she processes an utterance. As such, meaning is generated in the mind of the hearer. Again, this may reveal unconscious as well as conscious mental processes. Psychoanalysis is particularly concerned with extreme forms of these processes, such as paranoia, in which someone projects a set of over-interpretations onto the things that he or she sees and hears.

In the text

Writing, distanced as it is from both writer and reader, confronts us first of all with itself. The meaning of a text is somehow *in* the text. We are only aware that an author tried to say something because of the text – why, then, do we need an author at all, if the only way of recovering authorial intention is through the text?

In language

There is no private language. Words only mean anything because we have seen them before, or because they can be translated into words with which we are familiar. This is how dictionaries work. It follows that the language we use is always already shared. In speaking or writing, we activate these common meanings. Roland Barthes, in a famous essay called 'The death of the author', proposes that 'it is language which speaks, not the author' and that 'the text is a fabric of quotations, resulting from a thousand sources of culture' (Barthes 1989: 53). All writing is a form of quotation, and meaning is generated not by author or reader, but instead through their relationships to language itself.

In metalanguage

Another way of thinking about the role of dictionaries is not so much as description but as prescription. Dictionaries give us an authorised sense of usage. Equally, there are other forms of authority over language, institutions that tell us what certain words or statements mean. We might think here of law, of linguistics, of literary criticism, or of religious exegesis. Metalanguage (as in all these examples) is language about language.

In contexts

All meaning is, to some extent, bounded by the context in which it appears. Words change meanings over time and in different social and cultural situations, can have different senses in different parts of the world, or may have technical connotations that can only be recovered through a careful reconstruction of the context in which they occur.

Let's follow this through to thinking about when meaning occurs:

When?

Thought
Meaning happens at the point when the thought or intention occurs in the mind of the speaker or writer.

Expression
Meaning is generated when the thought or intention is spoken or 'put into words' (although this phrase might suggest that there has to be something which can be 'put' somewhere).

Reception
Only at a point when it is heard does the meaning of a word or statement occur. While there are several variations on this idea, the simplest is that there is a kind of meeting between the mind of the speaker–author and of the hearer–reader in which they both have the 'same' idea. This is easiest to think of in terms of conversation, in which hearing and responding happen quickly and in which apparent misapprehensions can be negotiated.

Interpretation
Is hearing or reading sufficient, or is it actually a question of understanding? We might be able to take in a sentence in a conversation immediately and to respond appropriately, but can the same be said of a poem? Interpretation implies a delay, a process, rather than a simple reaction. (We say more about this in Units A9 and B9.)

In repetition
This is more complicated. If we accept that a wholly original word or sentence would be incomprehensible (literally meaning-less, since no meaning would be assigned to it), then it follows that the meaning of an utterance must already have been established, prior to its use on a specific occasion. It is only because the utterance is to some extent a repetition, and because it is repeatable, that it is meaningful. Imagine trying to use a dictionary that, each time you consulted it, gave a different meaning for a given word. Meaning exists, then, in a combination of past and future.

A6   CONSCIOUSNESS AND COGNITION

What is *the mind*? The way that you answer this question largely determines your view of how language works, as well as providing an indicator of your fundamental beliefs. Any answer to the question commits you to a view about relationships between language and thought, the mind and the brain, language and reality, perceptions and the body, cognition and reference, and every possible permutation of these concepts.

Through the ages, a distinction has often been drawn between the mind and the body, a basic *dualism* that implies further distinctions between reason and emotion, soul and flesh, spirit and corporeality, the higher faculties and bare earthy necessities. Though traceable back to Plato, the mind/body distinction is most famously captured in René Descartes's 1637 formulation, 'I think, therefore I am', so that it is often referred to simply as *Cartesian duality*. Here, the basis of existence is in the mental faculties rather than in bodily sensation. Language, of course, belongs to the mental side of this dualism, which makes it easy to see language as an internal cognitive system that simply represents the objects of the external world. The mechanism by which this representation is made is called *reference*.

Understanding reference from a dualist perspective is reasonably easy: words denote objects, that is, they are descriptions of those objects in the world. We can draw the relationship very plainly:

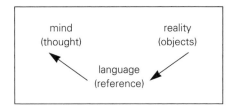

In this view, objects in the world are thought about through the mediation of the language system. Language is simply referential; descriptive of the world 'out there'.

Of course, this becomes much harder if the things that are being thought about are not 'out there': things like abstractions or generalisations ('liberty', 'society'), lies, fictions and imaginary objects ('unicorns', 'Jane Eyre', 'Superman'), hypothetical or conditional objects ('if I were rich', 'when I imagine'), and whether non-nouns can be said to 'refer' or not ('run', 'and', 'into') in some sense. In order to preserve our diagram, we might want to think of the world that is being referred to as one bounded *possible world* among many. Our *actual world* is just one of all the worlds which are possible, and linguistic statements about this world are judged for their referential value if they appear to our thinking as being true or reasonable statements about that world. Statements about unicorns, wishes or fiction are similarly referential in their own possible worlds: exclaiming, 'It's not a bird or a plane, it's Superman!' has a truth-value in that world in which New York is called Metropolis.

This view does not even commit you to being accurate and correct. If Peter sees a weather balloon and mistakes it for a flying saucer, and he shouts to Mark, 'Look at that alien spaceship!', he has still successfully referred to the object attributionally even if he has not been descriptively precise.

Thinking about the relationships between the mind and the material world in these ways has preserved our sense of reference in the diagram, but at the cost of forcing us to reverse the directions of the arrows. In other words, language in this view is no longer simply *descriptive* of the world but is *constitutive* of it. Our conception of the world is pointed towards language rather than directly at the world. At this point, we might as well redraw the diagram with the world (whether real or possible) bracketed off and accessible only through language. In fact, we can go even further and say that, in this view, there is nothing beyond the integrated linguistic mind on the left of the diagram. If we abandon the mind/embodied world distinction, we have adopted a variety of *monism*.

The most well-known form of monism is to make no distinction at all between the mind and the brain. This variety of monism is *materialism*, which argues that thought and language are simply emergent properties of the material lump of brain. There is no ghost in the machine; the machine (that is the body, or at least the brain part of it) simply thinks it is aware of itself as a natural consequence of its condition. You can claim that reality is out there, but the fact that we only have language to think about it means that it doesn't really matter that reality is objective; or you can argue on a principle of *idealism* that all objects in fact only exist by virtue of an observing consciousness – all phenomena are therefore mental constructions, including our means through language of gesturing towards them.

These positions can even be blended so that you can argue there are some objects that exist independently in the world (like books, cars or large groups of people) and another category of objects that only exist when mediated through an observing consciousness (literature, traffic, society). The former are *autonomous* objects and the latter are *heteronomous* objects. This useful distinction (from the perspective of *phenomenology*) introduces two crucial concepts to the discussion so far: *reception* (about which more in A9) and *consciousness*.

Consciousness, which we can gloss briefly as self-awareness, shares many of the same problems we have discussed. You can begin to make your own sense of consciousness explicit by considering how you would answer the following two questions:

❑   What happens to consciousness when you are asleep, anaesthetised or dead?
❑   Could computers ever develop machine consciousness?

Consciousness can be seen as a phenomenon of the mind, or as an emergent property of the material brain, or even simultaneously as a determinant and consequence of our linguistic ability: as a product of rhetoric. Consciousness has come to the foreground of modern thinking about mind, body and language largely through the psychoanalytical sense of *the unconscious* mind.

In Freudian psychoanalysis, the representation of the world to the individual takes place in symbols, images and language in general, with associations and significances often worked through without the person being aware of those processes. The workings of the unconscious can only be seen indirectly by their effects on dreams, outward behaviour, and 'parapraxes' such as slips of the tongue, mistakes and accidents. Because of this, the unconscious is as much part of a theory of language as forming a theory of subjectivity, and in fact early psychotherapy courses were based on verbalising war traumas and were hailed as 'the talking cure'.

The language of psychoanalysis – from counselling therapy to pop psychobabble – informs much of our modern conception of the mind and how we express (or repress) ourselves. It has influenced the language directly, as well as being substantially a theory of language and mind, of course. Fundamentally, the unconscious mind is produced when there is a conflict between basic instinctive needs and drives (the *id*), which form themselves into a sense of personal identity (the *ego*), and our sense of restraining external social factors, rules and conventions (the *super-ego*). The tension produced by this conflict would be distressing if raised to consciousness, so it is blocked from conscious awareness in a process of repression, forming the unconscious mind.

In this conception of the mind, we have a conscious view of the shared social world and its conventions (including its language), alongside an unaware sense of the associations and significances of the world which might only emerge indirectly through dreams and verbal accidents. Language, then, is a window into the unconscious.

In the later development of psychoanalysis under Jacques Lacan (see 1968, 1977), Freud's scheme is valued more for its poetic and creative qualities. Lacan reads Freud metaphorically rather than literally, and shifts the status of many Freudian statements about the body and sexuality onto the symbolic plane. Crucially, Lacan asserts that the unconscious is structured like a language, and therefore we exist in the realm of the Symbolic. He argues that the social rules of the world imprint themselves on the mind through language. In other words, social strictures determine linguistic forms, and the form of language constitutes the world and sets the parameters of personal identity. Language socialises us, in this view.

Though individual symbols in the language system (signifiers) stand in an arbitrary relationship with the objects they represent (signifieds), the realm of the Symbolic in which we all psychically exist means that we are 'spoken by language'. In this view, individuals face anxiety in the constant awareness that the terms by which all things (including ourselves) are understood are always arbitrary and shifting, and we have no means of recovering the pre-linguistic childhood state of the Imaginary world.

This view regards language as ineradicably metaphorical, and binds its conception of the processes of thought into the metaphorical domain as well. Certain authoritarian privileged signifiers (such as the authority of masculinity in our society, or religious and social morals) appear to pin down meanings temporarily; these moments of fixity are only illusions of permanence, though through their operation they create historical and cultural periods of repression and control over groups regarded as marginal. Analysis (both in the therapeutic and linguistic senses) offers a means of raising these processes to conscious awareness.

CREATIVITY IN LANGUAGE

Creativity has long been regarded as one of the defining features of human language. Birds, dogs, bees and ants might have modes of communication, but they seem to be built out of fixed patterns for conveying limited messages. Even though urban sparrows seem to have variable 'accents' in different cities, we might perceive this variation as an accidental wandering away from the correct copy, rather than the result of a poetic sparrow passing on its novel voice to admiring flocks elsewhere.

Clearly, there are factors implicit in our contemporary understanding of creativity, even in this brief comparison, and it is important to remember that earlier ages understood creativity differently from us. We seem to require creativity to have novelty and uniqueness. We seem to want creativity to attach to an inspired individual rather than simply be a factor arising from the dumb forces of historical change. In short, we seem to want creativity to be special, rare and (therefore) valued. Creativity has to be deliberate and intended, rather than accidental or mistaken. A slip of the tongue or inarticulate mangling of a sentence is not commonly regarded as creative, though its results are sometimes indistinguishable from genuine creative acts. The formulation 'genuine creative acts' presupposes authenticity on one side and productivity on the other.

The creativity inherent in language is demonstrated in Chomsky's famous sentence, 'Colourless green ideas sleep furiously', offered originally as an example of a well-formed though semantically odd sentence that had not been produced before (though now it has become so famous it has largely lost its creative power by repetition). The example perhaps became so famous because it is strikingly deviant: 'green' contradicts 'colourless'; ideas are not typically colour-coded; only organisms not abstractions can literally 'sleep' and do so 'furiously'. This is without considering any of the metaphorical ways these pieces of deviant language could be resolved.

Creativity and newness – in the form of noticeable deviance – seem closely related. The following intriguing sentence opens Jeff Noon's short story, 'The Shoppers':

> In the first shop they bought a packet of dogseed, because Doreen had always wanted to grow her own dog.
>
> (Noon 1998: 7)

Where Chomsky's sentence is syntactically well-formed but semantically deviant, Noon's sentence is creatively odd at the cognitive level: we don't recognise 'dogseed' as an element in our experience, and we know that dogs are not grown in this way. The newness of creative language has even been seen as a defining characteristic of verbal art, as 'defamiliarisation' or 'estrangement' in the terms of the Russian Formalists in the 1920s. Crucially, it was language which was the transforming medium, changing ordinary objects and concepts into artistic creations by linguistic or cognitive deviations from the expected norm.

Deviation requires, of course, a sense of a norm from which to deviate; similarly, creativity requires an established set of parameters against which to be measured. Creativity must thus be seen as a feature which necessarily acts on a material such as language. Verbal creativity is highly valued in its spoken form in songs and speeches and in its written form as literature. Of course, many of the stylistic patterns evident in these types of discourse are also found in everyday language, where jokes, echoing, puns and other textural effects are apparent in newspapers, advertising, family conversation, friendly banter, graffiti, promotional flyers and internet chat.

Though the newness of deviation seems always to have been associated with creativity, striking deviance seems to be a post-Romantic quality attached to the notion. It arises alongside the idea of imagination (or Imagination, for the Romantic poets), which is equally concerned with intentionality. That is, it is hard to conceive of imagination without thinking of an object that is being imagined, or which the imaginer intends to imagine. Imagination is inherently creative in this sense since it by definition brings about the object imagined, and it is also by implication wilful and deliberate.

Furthermore, the imagined object does not have to exist. In fact, we might even suggest that the most common objects that are imagined are non-existent objects: that is, objects that are either not part of the inventory of the actual world, or are at least not present in the here-and-now of the imaginer. Thinking about real objects is simply thinking, rather than 'imagining', and would probably not be regarded as creative. Nevertheless, because imagination brings a necessary object, it seems that imagined objects always share at least some of the properties of the experiential world. It is difficult to see how we could imagine something that was utterly alien – not a thing or state or process. It is more probable that we apply actual world principles by default unless the imagined object deviates from our experience in a way of which we are consciously aware. Imagination, in this case, assumes a correspondence with possibility: only that which is possible can be imagined; the impossible is unimaginable.

Thinking about imagination places creativity squarely within the mind of the individual. It is also a post-Romantic stereotype that creativity inheres in individuals: think of the image of the lone creative genius producing his masterpiece (it is typically a masculine product). The notion of genius itself flows from this conception of creativity. Genius implies the origin and source of creativity, encouraging a perception of creativity as an individual responsibility, rather than creativity being an emergent property of social forces acting on individuals. The notion of 'genius' closes off any desire to measure, analyse or account for creativity: it is simply the ineffable and mystical power inherent in gifted individuals.

Of course, even without admitting the asocial ideology of this persistent view, it is possible to recognise that creativity can often be a result of co-creation. Throughout this book we have taken a view of language as interactive discourse and as social practice, and we must recognise that creativity is also a collaborative act. In fact, this book itself is a result of co-creation: you might be able to discern two distinct 'voices' in the style of the writing, which we have not tried to disguise.

The practice of language itself is even a creative act. Speakers and writers create texts; hearers and readers create meanings out of those texts. The receptive process is usually not as passive as the term suggests, either. Readers and hearers *use* the discourse they encounter to generate new ideas and to respond to that discourse. Hearers typically answer the speaker in front of them, in ways which are linguistically appropriate but not usually simply an echoing of the original utterance. In other words, verbal response to texts is stylistically creative in taking the meaning of the speaker, adapting it and reshaping it in order to create a new meaning derived from the first.

This means that the notion of *originality* in creativity depends on choosing a point of origin. Since all verbal objects arise from previous objects, a sense of creative originality must have an artificial line drawn behind it, with the creative moment being located in the inspired instant of genius. Genuine originality is rare in language: most discourse is echoic or allusive, dependent on the receiver recognising familiar patterns and drawing down certain sorts of knowledge. Creativity as simply the reframing of knowledge tends to be downgraded: words denoting this sort of creative practice include 'craftiness' or 'cunning', with their disparaging shades and connotations. Of course, even the highly valued forms of creativity depend on these sorts of workaday creativity, if they are to be read at all.

The creative function of language is not simply necessary for the transmission of information; much talk is *phatic* – that is, concerned to establish and maintain social relations. People talk, gossip, chat, shoot the breeze, chew the fat, and pass the time of day simply for its own sake, creating new utterances again and again. In this sense, creativity is the ubiquitous social glue that offers the main motivation for language performance in the first place.

Furthermore, as Derek Attridge (2004) argues, creativity falters if it remains wholly private. The product of creativity needs to be *accommodated* within the surrounding culture if it is to be perceived and valued: it then becomes an *invention*, publicly recognised and available for interpretation. It also becomes available for intertextual practice, for imitation and echoing, and in the process may also lose some of its sense of originality, its sense of 'otherness' (which is deviance again). Attridge argues that prestigious literature retains a *singularity* if it persists. He acknowledges the continuities between everyday creativity and prestigious verbal art, though he also draws attention to the placement of value on literary art as a matter of ethics. In responding to language, readers have a 'responsibility' to the singularity of the experience.

A8　　　　**FIGURES**

What is a figure? And what is a figurative use of language? These are deceptive questions. We can all tell when language is being used in a figurative way, and no doubt everyone is familiar with some of the technical terms (such as metaphor, simile, metonymy, and so on) used to describe this happening. To say that 'My love is like a red, red rose' is clearly not to offer a 'real' description of someone. And often we use figural statements to express things that can't be described in a realist way. For example, someone might say 'My love is as deep as the ocean'. Chances are we all know what this person is trying to say. But does love actually have a depth? Can it be measured in this way? Is this 'better' than saying 'My love is as shallow as a puddle, but has the surface area of Greenland'? If so, why?

To go much further than simply pointing at figures or tropes (which we'll discuss in a moment) quickly becomes much more complicated. Figurative language tends to be associated with rhetoric. Rhetoric, from classical times to the present, involves the use of language to create an effect on the hearer or reader, and its primary function is persuasion. The question of whether one figure is better than another can thus be answered by asking which one 'works' best, in other words, which is most persuasive. One answer to this is to say which strikes us as most true. Because of this emphasis on truth, philosophers have been interested in rhetoric from the start, and many of the characterisations of rhetoric to be found in early philosophy are still with us.

First, let's think about what a trope or figure is. A trope is literally a 'turn' or 'swerve' away from a 'normal', 'ordinary' or 'proper' use of a word. This is the distinction that is often made between the 'literal' sense of a word or phrase and its 'figural' meaning. The roots of this approach lie in the Greek word *tropein*, which means to turn or swerve. (We are using all of these quotation marks, sometimes referred to as 'scare quotes', in order to point out that all of these terms need to be thought about and can't be taken 'at face value', to use another figure.) The Roman rhetorical theorist Quintilian (1953: 3.8.6) described a trope as 'the artificial alteration of a word or phrase from its proper meaning to another'. This artificiality is often picked up on, and is to be found in the roots of the word 'figure' as well, from the Latin *figura*, which means something 'made', 'shaped' or 'formed'. For Plato, it is precisely this level of artifice that makes rhetoric untrustworthy. In the *Gorgias* (Plato 1989: 459b–c), rhetoric is criticised because its purpose is to persuade, and therefore rhetoricians need only concern themselves with what is effective. But that which is most persuasive is not necessarily the most true. Politicians, journalists and advertising executives have been exploiting this fact for centuries.

What is important is to think about this connection between language and truth. Rhetoric is commonly divided into three parts: *inventio* (the rules for finding your subject matter), *dispositio* (the rules for arranging your material) and *elocutio* (the rules governing the presentation or performance of your discourse). In this classical organisation of rhetoric, figurative language would fit in to the final section, *elocutio*. In English usage, this is the origin of the idea that language is a kind of clothing for ideas, that language is merely what surrounds thoughts. In other words, the same thought could be expressed in different words without any alteration in its fundamental meaning.

But is this true? The most obvious place to look for an objection to this idea is towards literature. Literature, and particularly poetry, employs figurative language in ways that are striking, memorable and to some extent irreplaceable (see section B5 for a discussion of this in terms of translation. This overlap is not accidental. 'Translation' and 'metaphor' are related, both stemming from the Greek *meta phorein*, to carry across or over. This is clearest in the modern German word *übersetzen*, 'to translate', which means to carry or ferry across). The language used in literature isn't really derived from an ordinary or normal description. In this context, the distinction between literal and figural meanings is very hard to sustain and, in fact, quite a lot of literature is precisely about this problem. Let's think about one of the most famous examples:

> Shall I compare thee to a summer's day?
> Thou art more lovely and more temperate.
> Rough winds do shake the darling buds of May,
> And summer's lease hath all too short a date.
> Sometime too hot the eye of heaven shines,
> And often is his gold complexion dimmed,
> And every fair from fair sometime declines,
> By chance or nature's changing course untrimmed;
> But thy eternal summer shall not fade
> Nor lose possession of that fair thou ow'st,
> Nor shall death brag thou wander'st in his shade
> When in eternal lines to time thou grow'st.
> > So long as men can breathe or eyes can see,
> > So long lives this, and this gives life to thee.

Read the poem. Make a note of all of the uses of tropes or figurative language that you can find. Think about some of the following questions:

❏ Can the figures be divided into groups?
❏ Are any of these images familiar from other poems?
❏ Are some of them now clichés?
❏ Where do these images come from? Are they the invention of the writer, a 'true' description, or something else?
❏ What are the conventions that govern the writing of a sonnet?
❏ What is the argument of the poem? (Take it slowly, work line by line.)
❏ Does it provide an answer to the question with which it opens?

Try to write a description of the person being described based on the information given in the sonnet.

This is, as you may know, Shakespeare's Sonnet 18. The poem begins by asking about whether it is appropriate to make a comparison between a person and a summer's day. This is a proverbial comparison, where a summer's day is thought to be the best kind there is. But in asking the question, of course, the possibility of the comparison has already been put into the reader's mind. Is this, then, only a 'rhetorical' question, one that doesn't demand an answer?

The next few lines suggest that the poet has taken this rhetorical question very literally. While there are many things that could be said, let's just sketch an outline of the main argument. Aspects of summer such as its heat, winds, beauty and duration are held up for comparison, but they are found to contrast with the person described (see the 'But' in line 9). What we end up with is a sense that the comparison doesn't quite work, but the poem proposes in the final lines that the poem itself will preserve an image of the beloved person. So what is this image? What do the eyes that 'can see' see? And what do we make of the irony that the poem is concerned with light, the sun, and so on, which is what allows anything to be seen in the first place?

This brings us close to understanding how figurative language works. A trope or figure allows two senses to be conveyed at once. Sometimes this happens by the turn or swerve of the figure, which takes us away from the expected or usual sense in a memorable and surprising manner through the way that an idea is expressed. Or else the figure allows us to see something that it doesn't so much express as conjure up. This is one way of thinking about why the line 'Thou art more lovely and more temperate' manages to convey a meaning and a value for the image without giving us any description. The poem becomes an *allegory* in allowing us to see something that it doesn't show us (from the Greek *allos-agoreuein*, 'to speak something other', or 'to speak otherwise').

A later sonnet from the same sequence might help to illustrate this idea. Let's look at Sonnet 130:

> My mistress' eyes are nothing like the sun;
> Coral is far more red than her lips' red.
> If snow be white, why then her breasts are dun;
> If hairs be wires, black wires grow on her head.
> I have seen roses damasked, red and white,
> But no such roses see I in her cheeks;
> And in some perfumes is there more delight
> Than in the breath that from my mistress reeks.
> I love to hear her speak, yet well I know
> That music hath a far more pleasing sound.
> I grant I never saw a goddess go:
> My mistress when she walks treads on the ground.
>   And yet, by heaven, I think my love as rare
>   As any she belied with false compare.

Let's think again about where such images come from. Coral lips, white breasts, golden hair, rosy cheeks, perfumed breath, a voice like music and someone who walks as if floating on air are all the standard clichés of love poetry. Even 400 years ago, these were tired and unconvincing. But instead of minting new images (which stand a chance of becoming equally as worn and hollow), what Shakespeare does is to employ the old ones in a new way. The effect of this is to call into question the value of figurative comparison at all. The 'false compare' that he criticises makes us rethink more idealistic poems. In fact, this strengthens the impact of it as love poetry because it proposes that it takes a stronger love to accept someone who can be honestly seen and judged, than someone who exists as an ideal (or at least is idealised). Again, the true message only appears behind or between the lines, the poem is concerned with what we can't see, or what the person doesn't look like. And it conveys this through figures and tropes designed to give us images.

What these two poems suggest is that figurative language allows us to reflect on how language relates to the objects and ideas that it presents. Rather than simply being the expression of thoughts which could just as convincingly have been put in some other way, these poems show how the use of tropes and figures can shape thoughts, and how language can create ideas and images that it doesn't directly express. Language doesn't just tell us what someone has thought, it makes us think.

A9   **THE RECEPTION OF MEANING**

Language is generally regarded as having two primary aspects: it is the means of communicating content, and the medium of language itself has an aesthetic value. In face-to-face verbal interaction, content tends to be most prominent, unless the texture of the language is heavily emphasised such as in singing, chanting, shouting, whispering or verse recital, and so on. In speech, hearers can stop a speaker for clarification, and can take cues from the immediate context or from gestures and facial expressions.

Interpreting what a speaker means is straightforward, at least relative to inter-preting what a writer means. Writing introduces more complications: the writer is likely to be displaced either temporally or spatially from the reader. The writer might not have had this particular reader in mind when writing. The reader's historical, cultural or social context might differ so markedly from the point of writing that what the reader reads might bear little resemblance to what the writer meant to write. Furthermore, the visual and permanent characteristic of writing serves to make the texture of the language more visible, allowing the reader to return again and again to re-read, re-interpret and find patterns that were never put there consciously by the writer.

It is clear that language (especially writing) underdetermines meaning: a text or utterance carries only part of what a writer might have in mind; and the number of readings possible of even the simplest text suggests that readers bring additional material to the bare bones of the linguistic object. The easiest way of thinking about this process is as a sort of telepathy: utterers encode their thoughts in a piece of language, which is then sent as a text into the mind of a receiver, where it is decoded for meaning. The problem, even with this very simple model, is that it leaves a question for the language analyst of where to look for meaningfulness.

Meaningfulness could simply reside in the producer's intentions, of course (see strand 5 for a discussion of intentionality). This view leaves the uttered language as scraps for readers to pore over. Since intentionality is difficult to *see* – even for the person doing the intending, perhaps – the view that places meaningfulness wholly as intended meaning does not leave much for the language analyst to analyse.

The most obvious thing to analyse is the uttered text. But we have already said that text underdetermines meaning, and linguists have sidestepped this problem by separating out text from the various possible contexts which contribute to a text's meaning. Textual analysis can then proceed as a final arbiter of evidence for any contextual interpretation. This is rather unsatisfactory, since it rests on the artifical distinction of text and context and it does not offer a principled way of understanding how meaning is generated.

The third place to look for meaningfulness is in the receiver, and this seems at first more promising. We can follow E.D. Hirsch's (1976) distinction between *meaning* (which belongs to authorial intention) and *significances* (which belong to various readers and readings), even if we do not have to go along with the absolutely stable sense of authoritative 'meaning' that Hirsch seems to have intended. So, to choose a controversial example, when Jesus at the last supper broke bread and produced the utterance 'This is my body', he evidently had a meaning in mind, but the text has been given a whole host of different significances over the centuries that have resulted in doctrinal schism, clerical debates, executions, political intrigue and wars. The religious allusion is apt here too, in that Hirsch's view seems to regard meaning as fixed, authoritative and 'god-like', whereas we might prefer to see meaning-construction as a process with more indeterminate outcomes.

There is no doubt, though, that texts contain *indeterminacies* – gaps in denoted meaning which tend to be bridged by readerly inferencing, by cultural knowledge, or by leaps in interpretative understanding. There is readerly work to be done across the following two sentences, for example – 'We went to the restaurant. The waiter brought the bill with the tip included' – that explains the three definite articles in the second sentence. We need to know about restaurants to read these two sentences meaningfully. Similarly, the response 'I've got a car' is a reasonable and relevant answer to 'The party is on the other side of the city', even though strictly semantically it shouldn't make any sense. And similarly, imagining a conversation with a character from a Thomas Hardy novel is only one step further on from 'filling out' that character as a psychologised entity from what are, after all, only underdetermined marks on the page of *Jude the Obscure*.

Wolfgang Iser (1974, 1978), following the phenomenologist Roman Ingarden (1973), calls this 'filling out' the process of *concretization*. In a literary work (though the principle applies to all language events), the physical text itself serves only as an occasion for interpretation. There is an idealised meaning which the text embodies, but it is not in fact humanly attainable: what are attainable are the myriad different concretisations brought by different readers filling out different parts of the text with different bridging and inferencing patterns. Receivers draw on their *schematic* sets of idealised cultural knowledge to fix the text. Iser's view is a *reception theory*, which regards all texts as having an *implied reader*, a sort of idealised addressee who is sufficiently knowledgeable to fill out the work's indeterminacies. Linguists refer to this feature of textuality as *recipient design*, though Iser's view goes further in regarding the reading of a literary text as generating a reader who is open-minded and willing to be transformed by the experience.

Part of the difficulty of this view for language study is that it seems to place a reading subjectivity in isolation from any social, ideological or even idiosyncratic context. In other words, what if the actual receiver of an utterance is not the designed recipient, is not ideal or implied, or perhaps actively takes issue with the text or deliberately resists its message? What of the awkward reader, or the politically committed reader, or even the lazy reader? In principle, their readings should be equally valid, but in the reception theory framework, the idealised reading of the text somehow still constrains possible or allowable interpretations. For both Iser and Ingarden, the text's indeterminacies must be concretised to 'complete' the work – and there is a sense that this completion amounts to a limited range of correct readings. Pointedly, Iser sometimes refers to the concretisation process as 'normalizing'.

Writers within this tradition of reception or 'reader-response' theory vary in their commitment to allowing a range of readings. Some, like Iser, see the text as a tight constraint on possible readings. Others, like Roland Barthes, see any playful reading as an unlimited expression of the joy of the text. Treading a middle path between these views is Stanley Fish (1980), who blends individual reception with socially shared cultural knowledge in his notion of the *interpretative community*. Receivers of language, in this view, are neither simply individuals nor simply a blank canvas for the text to work on. Rather, groups of readers with similar cultural backgrounds can be said to share similar interpretative strategies, which are likely to produce interpretations that are consensual within their community.

There is a tricky circularity in defining the community by its interpretative strategies while then claiming that those ways of reading exist because of the shared community. Fish recognises this and allows it to persuade him that, ultimately, texts cannot be said to exist in an un-interpreted state: readings are always readings of other readings. Even if an analyst points to linguistic features in the text as evidence for a subsequent reading, it seems true that those features have been selected by the analyst (and thus have already been interpreted) for the contextual purpose at hand.

To get us off these various hooks, we might consider a useful distinction between *interpretation* and *reading*, that derives from the phenomenological hermeneutics of Hans-Georg Gadamer (1989). 'Reading' is the conscious process of rationalising meaning after a text or utterance has been received. Readings, however, for Gadamer, are always already conditioned by 'interpretation'. What he means is that a receiver of language has a set of expectations and resolutions ready to run against any incoming strings of language. Simply noticing certain utterances involves an elective act of interpretation. Who you are, what you believe, why you are where you are, your economic circumstances and the ideological views that you share or dispute with others are all the determinants of the interpretative line that you will have ready on each encounter with language.

This distinction also allows us to delineate different analytical procedures in language study and linguistics. Gerard Steen (1992, 1994) distinguishes interpretative and empirical approaches to language and text. The former concern themselves with readings addressing the significance and value of the message: they are hermeneutic, literary critical or reader-response criticism in the Anglo-Franco-American tradition. By contrast, empirical approaches to language concern themselves more with investigating the processes of reading: they are psychological, cognitive, and stylistic in orientation, and originate largely in the Germanic tradition of reception theory. Put simply, one is the study of interpretation, and the other is the study of reading.

Section B

DEVELOPMENT:
FURTHER ISSUES IN THEORY

B1   **WRITING GENDER**

The first unit (A1) on gendered language leaned towards a social and cultural understanding of gender. However, the psychological dimension is also an important factor
in the construction, perception and performance of gender. Although many writers
have been careful to draw distinctions between sex and gender, this position does
not deny the existence of biological *dimorphism*. However, the argument that gender
is a socio-psychological construct should also be seen as a reminder to notice that
the importance we attach to sexual difference is a matter of culture: think of all the
other possible 'natural' ways of differentiating people (hair colour, blood group,
number of freckles on the arms, and so on), and then think about why hormone
production and the primary and secondary sexual characteristics are so significant.

Nevertheless, the bipolar nature of sex has strongly influenced the perception of
gender as being similarly binary. Male and female have thus been overlaid onto
various binaries, such as:

masculine	feminine
active	passive
rational	irrational
logical	hysterical
possessing	possessed
dominant	submissive
culture	nature
authority	subjectivity
norm	other
unmarked	marked
writing	speech
speaking	listening
thinking	emotion
worker	carer
work	play
serious	trivial
adult	childlike
systematic	chaotic
public	domestic

and many others. Notice how the pattern here is not consistent: it is not possible
to assign one side as positive and the other always as negative qualities, and some
binaries clash with others, depending on the contextual focus. For example, writing,
also associated with culture, is set against the more chaotic patterns of natural
speaking, except for public speaking and speech-making, which are masculine because
of their systematic, rational and powerful aspects.

It is clear that we can easily think of such relative binaries, and assign them to
masculine and feminine social factors. It is part of the standard (heterosexual)
ideology of our world that masculine and feminine are paired and attractive to each
other, in a way that social class, age, culture and ethnic variations, for example, are

not. This makes gender a different sort of discourse practice that seems natural and easy. This easiness has been seen by some as evidence to suggest that gender is a mode of thinking which is deeply ingrained. In fact, it could be so much a part of our psyches as to make impossible any sort of imaginative projection from one gender to (the/an) other. In other words, it could be impossible for a man naturally to read as a woman, and impossible for a woman to write, without self-conscious artificiality, as a man.

This view means that there are constraints and limits if women are to intervene in the public life of the world. If women simply adopt the language of men, then there is something crucial that is being lost in the expression. If women want to reappropriate these forms of expression, they must rewrite the ideologies and histories of the world, challenging the underlying binary assumptions set out above. Alternatively, women can develop their own natural form of written expression, known from French philosophy as an *écriture féminine.*

This continental philosophical perspective draws heavily on the psychoanalytical tradition rather than the directly ideological and sociolinguistic. Differences which claim to be traceable to childhood psychosexual development are treated as meta-phorical symbols and abstracted onto linguistic practices. For example, the physical characteristics of male sexuality are seen as objective-oriented and lead to a psyche which is objectifying and aimed at desiring closure. This is contrasted with the more cumulative and process-oriented sexuality of women, metaphorically extended to the desire for openness, endlessness and the blurring of closure and other boundaries.

In practice, this means that 'écriture féminine' must be a style of writing charac-terised by fluidity of form in, for example, syntactic organisation. It must allow for ambiguity and polysemy of word choices, and must be open to readerly participation in a shared and potentially endless process of meaning-construction. It must also raise the enjoyment of linguistic texture to at least an equal level as the denotational recovery of constructed meaning.

One of the main proponents of this view, Hélène Cixous (who coined the term), further argues that 'écriture féminine' is a form of writing that takes its features from and correlates with the physiological basis of femininity. (An example of Cixous' writing is reproduced in C1, and see Cixous and Clément 1986.) This women's writing takes the feminine side of the binaries listed at the beginning of this section, and celebrates their position as playful counters to the masculine fixed polarities of the other list. Further, Cixous argues not only that the writing itself embodies a counter to masculinism, but also that thinking about the language must resist models of categorisation, analysis and decoding that would also be seen as part of the masculine polarity. In other words, women's writing must evade the analytical pro-cedure, must not be pinned down by the imposition of a rule system, and must question or transgress any attempts at binding it into a restricted category.

The psychoanalytical source material for many of these ideas becomes further apparent in the use of terms originally developed by both Freud and especially Lacan. The surface 'order' (in the sense both of rational symbolised propositions and of a systematic sequence) is identified with the conscious and socially regulated sphere;

while the freeplay of meaning, pre-rational intuitions and emotions are regarded as being in the realm of the unconscious, the latter reserved as being prominent in 'écriture féminine'.

There are problems in all of this, of course. Notice, first, how prescriptive is the notion of 'écriture féminine' – in the previous three paragraphs, it seemed to us entirely natural to use 'must' in describing the style of writing – though it could be countered that we are writing as men and this textbook is itself an example of authoritarian discourse. We might then answer in turn that we cannot imagine being able to produce a book like this in a feminine 'écriture', and might then again be answered that this is entirely the point: men should not be able to tell women what to do or how to think. Is the fact that we can write this paragraph dialogically an example of feminine writing that proves our point, or is the fact that we have unthinkingly presented the feminine counter-argument in a passive syntactic form a proof against us? If we did it 'unthinkingly', are we then participating in the feminine unconscious? By analysing the question, are we raising it to conscious (and thus controlled) awareness? What about our desire in this paragraph to have the last word?

Other arguments come from feminists who point to the essentialism, again, in the notion of a women's writing. It seems as if the realm of the non-rational, emotional and unanalytical unconscious is being made the woman's world, leaving the exercise of power, reason and public speech as the territory of men. How is this much different from sexist history down the ages? Furthermore, women's experience of sexuality and biology is again being seen as unitary, and then mapped rather simplistically onto linguistic texture. And it also collapses the distinction between sex and gender on which much progress has been based. These are points that have force-fully been made from within *queer theory*, where the heterosexual and other normative assumptions of a feminine 'écriture' have been questioned.

Queer theory draws attention again to the multiplicity of cultures which consti-tute femininity (and masculinity), and in fact serve to collapse the binary distinctions altogether. Ethnicities, languages, races and communities of all kinds tend to blend into each other at the edges and form continua, which are then packaged into nor-mative and discrete categories by the dominant ideological discourse. Sexuality and sexual practice are exemplified as determining one of these groups (in fact, as a 'com-munity of practice', to use a sociolinguistic term from A1). Queer theory largely emerges from gay and lesbian thinkers' dissatisfaction with binary 'identity categories' in the heterosexual account of gender: identity is something that is created and con-structed, fluidly and constantly renewed through linguistic practice. It has a built-in dynamic sense that incorporates the inescapable dimension of language change.

Activity   Think of more binaries that can be assigned as either masculine and feminine, and think of some real examples of them in action. How does this practical 'operationalising' of the theory alter your understanding?

Do you think it is possible to have a 'feminist linguistics'? What about a Catholic, Muslim or Jewish linguistics? A socialist or Marxist or liberal linguistics? What is the relationship between language study and the political or ideological stance adopted by the linguist?

Much of the discussion of women's language within sociolinguistics has focused on speech, while the focus within the philosophical tradition has tended to be on writing. What do you think each approach has to say to the other?

A consequence of anti-essentialism is that it is easy to take the next small step and say that certain minority, ethnic and racial groups do not 'really' exist. How might you argue your way out of this (politically undesirable) position, without embracing an essentialist view of the world?

While it can be argued (as above) that écriture féminine leaves a masculine arena of discourse, feminist thinkers like Cixous would point to the public nature of écriture féminine itself, and argue that what is traditionally defined as 'analytical' has been partial. What do you think of these two positions?

What do you think of our decision as textbook writers to attach queer theory to this strand on gender?

WRITING 'RACE'

In the first unit (A2) on language and 'race', we focused on the ways in which language expresses differences between different nations or groups within nations. We began to think about the fact that one of the most obvious ways in which language becomes entangled with the histories of encounters between nations is in the experience of colonialism and its aftermath.

When people discuss language in terms of a colonial or postcolonial experience, they tend to talk about the difference between their own language and the 'foreign' language that they have encountered. This is true of both the colonised and the coloniser. These encounters take place either because the colonisers meet an indigenous tongue or because the colonised have the foreign language imposed upon them, often through education or through a language becoming the 'official' language of a colonial government. This could be seen, for example, in the history of the British Raj in India in the nineteenth century. In describing such encounters between languages, emphasis is often placed on the differences between a new, foreign tongue and someone's own language.

What does it mean, though, to talk about having your 'own' language? One way of thinking about language is to see it as something to which human beings have a natural connection, just as fish might see water as their natural element. This sense of a natural, rather than cultural, relationship to language gives rise to ideas like having a 'mother tongue'. Just as children ideally have an intimate, natural feeling of connection to their mother, so a person may feel that there is a similarly close link between their sense of their own identities and the language that they inhabit. But what are the consequences of such a view?

One line of argument would suggest that the idea of possessing a language is a positive thing. Anyone who has tried to speak a foreign language on holiday will quickly realise how comfortable they feel in their 'own' language. Equally, even within a language, there are certain colloquial or dialect words and phrases that have to be 'translated' into Standard English, and there is always a sense that something is lost in the process, that there is no true equivalent. Even within their legal systems, many countries place a strong emphasis on requiring a witness to say something 'in your own words'. This view would privilege spoken language over written forms, and would privilege the familial, local or communal over any kind of universalising impulse.

If we transfer this argument into thinking about colonialism, we might want to adopt the position taken by a writer such Ngũgĩ wa Thiong'o. Ngũgĩ has written in English, but since 1980 he has chosen to write only in his native tongue, Gĩkũyũ. For Ngũgĩ, there is a direct connection between language and the memory of a culture. The only way to preserve this culture is to preserve the language. Ngũgĩ (1986) has therefore called on other African writers to abandon the use of English.

An alternative to this kind of argument would propose that people take on a colonial language and turn it around, using it against the authority from which they have acquired it. In Shakespeare's Caliban, one of the central characters in *The Tempest*, we find a figure who has often been seen as a figure for this type of colonial subject. Caliban has been taught a Western language, but he claims that what he has learnt from this education is how to curse. Similarly, in a process that is often described within postcolonial studies as 'writing back', many writers from countries that were subject to colonialism take on (in both senses) the European culture to which they have been exposed.

Rather than rejecting the language and texts of the coloniser, these writers use that material for their own purposes. Thus they create something that is *in* the language and culture of the coloniser but not *of* it. Famous examples of this would include Derek Walcott's epic poem, *Omeros* (a rewriting of Homer), J.M. Coetzee's *Foe* (a response to Daniel Defoe's *Robinson Crusoe*) or Jean Rhys's *Wide Sargasso Sea* (which takes up the story of Rochester's first wife, Bertha, from *Jane Eyre*). Rewriting the texts of the colonial power, writers such as Walcott also transform the language itself, introducing different vocabulary, rhythms, sounds and speech patterns. Rather than abandoning English, as Ngũgĩ has proposed, such writers try to make the English language (and its literatures) into something they can call their own.

Yet, whether one sees English as irretrievably tainted by the experience of colonialism, or whether one instead recognises the opportunities that the colonial encounter provides, there seems to be a shared sense of a connection between language and identity. We might wish, however, to call into question the whole idea that a language may be possessed, as if it were a kind of property that could be owned.

If the colonial experience makes clear that the relationship to language can appear to be an alien as well as a natural one, then this perhaps makes us reconsider all language. Do any of us feel that we possess language?

Try this exercise. Write down a brief definition of the following words:

- ❑ pencil
- ❑ train
- ❑ rose
- ❑ mountain
- ❑ braces

(You might want to discuss your definitions with a friend.) Chances are, these are all words with which you are familiar. You may have had to think about one or two of these words: is train a noun or a verb, for example? North American readers may have a different answer to British readers for the word 'braces'. Even so, finding a definition is not too hard in these cases. Now try these:

- ❑ paronomasia
- ❑ threnody
- ❑ trochaic
- ❑ acephalous
- ❑ clerihew

(You'll be relieved to know you can use a dictionary if you like.) Again, some of these words you might already know. But they aren't part of a familiar, everyday vocabulary. They have a distinct set of technical meanings (taken from poetics), but most people will feel a little uncomfortable if asked to define them. This discomfort is, however, quickly resolved by looking the words up. There doesn't seem to be much at stake in the definitions, since these are probably words about which we don't feel especially strongly. They aren't expressive of personal experience.

Now a final set. Try to be precise, imagining that you're describing the word for someone who has never encountered either it or the object or sensation it points to:

- ❑ blue
- ❑ warm
- ❑ alone
- ❑ safe
- ❑ joy

These are much harder. We use words like these every day, in the most ordinary circumstances, but if we were asked to define exactly what we meant or felt or imagined when we used them, most of us would have great difficulty. The problem here isn't a lack of familiarity with the words (as in the case of 'trochaic'), it is instead something to do with the words themselves.

Colour presents special difficulties. Ludwig Wittgenstein, the philosopher, asks:

> What am I to say about the word 'red'? – that it means something 'confronting us all' and that everyone should really have another word, besides this one, to mean his *own* sensation of red? Or is it like this: the word 'red' means something known to everyone; and in addition, for each person, it means something known only to him? (Or perhaps rather: it *refers* to something known only to him.)
>
> (Wittgenstein 2001: §273)

Language is often thought of as a system, and there have been many attempts to treat language scientifically. Words like 'blue' or 'red', though, show the problems with trying to be too precise in accounting for how language relates to people's experience. It is precisely a degree of imprecision at the heart of language, its approximation to what we mean or feel rather than its full rendering of what we mean to say, that marks our failure to coincide exactly with language.

What the problem of 'race' can lead us to is the revelation that all language evades our possession of it. There is perhaps no such thing as my 'own' language. So replacing English with another, more original, language will do little to solve the problems presented by all language use. This does not mean, however, that we are equally distanced from the language. Historically and culturally, English can appear to be far from neutral in the values that it encodes, and these values will have a different resonance for every person who encounters English, and who English encounters.

Activity   Once we begin to think about the connections between language and 'race', we are confronted by a series of questions. First of all, we have to remember that the relationship to the English language differs from country to country and region to region. It can also differ according to the 'community' within a country or region. Here are just a few of the other questions that we might want to consider:

Why do people in a particular country speak English? (What about your own country?)

Where and when did they acquire this language? (What is the 'history' of this acquisition?)

Are other languages spoken in the country? (Where do they come from?)

If so, what is the relationship between English and the other language(s)?

What functions does English serve in this country? (Is it an elite language, an official language, and so on?)

LANGUAGE, SOCIETY AND HISTORY

In the first unit of this strand (A3), we began to look at the relationships between language and what, for the sake of economy, we called 'society'. Society stood in for various institutions, and the approach that we took was to address the question of ideology.

Much of the impetus for the discussion of ideology comes from the work of Karl Marx. In 1869 Marx famously proposed that what was needed was not the interpretation of the world but instead the effort to change it, but he did not believe that this could happen through an act of will alone. In one of his most well-known statements of the problem, he explicitly draws an analogy with language:

> Men make their own history, but not of their own free will; not under circumstances they themselves have chosen but under the given and inherited circumstances with which they are directly confronted. The tradition of the dead generations weighs like a nightmare on the minds of the living. And, just when they appear to be engaged in the revolutionary transformation of themselves and their material surroundings, in the creation of something which does not yet exist, precisely in such epochs of revolutionary crisis they timidly conjure up the spirits of the past to help them; they borrow their names, slogans and costumes so as to stage the new world-historical scene in this venerable disguise and borrowed language . . . In the same way, the beginner who has learned a new language always retranslates it into his mother tongue: he can only be said to have appropriated the spirit of the new language and to be able to express himself in it freely when he can manipulate it without reference to the old, and when he forgets his original language while using the new one.
>
> (Karl Marx 1992: 146–7)

How does this analogy work? In Unit A3 we noted Aristotle's idea of man as a political animal, and also Althusser's rewriting of this so that man became instead an ideological animal. What both of these ideas suggest is that there is a fundamental connection between the human capacity for language and politics. So Marx similarly relates language and politics, thinking explicitly in terms of history. 'Borrowed language' brings with it borrowed ideas and attitudes – if one wishes to think new thoughts, one must not only learn a new language, one must free oneself from one's 'original' language.

This does not necessarily mean, however, that we must forget history. Just as thinking about the relationship of language to gender or 'race' involves considering both language-use and representation, so this must also be thought about in looking at language and society. One of the obvious things to do is to examine the ways in which particular social groups are portrayed and presented. But if we accept the idea that politics is in part based on the idea of having speech (as in Aristotle), then we also need to consider whether the voices of these social groups are ever heard.

This focus on the question of representation has led to interest in working-class writing and popular or 'genre' fiction (such as detective fiction, romance, horror, science fiction and so on). This has allowed for a broader sense not only of the kind of texts that are produced by a culture, but also of those that are read by it. Similarly, in the study of history, there was a movement in the twentieth century from a historiography that focused on kings, nobles, great events, wars and government ('history from above') towards a social history (or 'history from below') that took into account the everyday lives of so-called ordinary people.

What is the role of the critic or historian if the experience of these social groups has not been preserved? Walter Benjamin writes in a letter of his desire 'to read the history that has never been written'. Obviously, gaps in the available material create problems for any attempt to offer a positivist description of, say, working-class 'voices'. Benjamin's work offers one way of thinking beyond this, however. In a famous statement he proposes that 'There is no document of civilization which is not at the same time a document of barbarism' (Benjamin 1992: 248). This is because any text, including a work of art, is the product both of the individual who makes it (for example, the artist) and also of the anonymous workers who are also part of that society. Benjamin proposes a *historical materialism* that would be capable of recognising the anonymous members of a society as well as the notable individuals.

One of the reasons why this idea of representation has taken on such importance is because Western democracy is itself predicated on the notion of representation. Theoretically, every person deemed fit has a vote, and is thus said to have a 'voice' or to 'have their say'. Equally, with a few exceptions, any political idea can be presented to the electorate, and during elections even 'extreme' views are allowed to be aired. Thus, in Britain, the far right British National Party (much to many people's disgust) is given space for television broadcasts.

It is this connection between democracy and the ability for anything to be said that leads Jacques Derrida to suggest that there is a link between democracy and literature. Both depend on the right to say everything. It is for this reason that there is so much emphasis in democratic societies on notions such as the freedom of the press, or freedom of speech, and so on. Thus, Derrida proposes: 'No democracy without literature; no literature without democracy' (Derrida 1995: 28). As soon as literature is censured, he adds, democracy is endangered. It could be argued from this that the history of censorship allows us to see what it was possible to say in a given society. The history of censorship, then, is the history of the democratic ideal.

Another way of thinking about this is to note the link between representation as a political concept and representation in and by language. For if we are confronted by the fact of ideology (even if we believe that ideology is a 'distortion' of the facts), then it could never be a case of simply stepping outside it through texts which have themselves been produced from within this ideological formation. As Paul de Man (1986: 11) puts it:

> What we call ideology is precisely the confusion of linguistic with natural real-
> ity, of reference with phenomenalism [the objects themselves as phenomena].

So, if what we call ideology involves the confusion of a linguistic appearance – let's say,
for ease, text – with objects as they really are (or the world as it really is), then the same
confusion is involved in saying that a piece of 'working class' writing shows the *real*
state of things. Again we face the question, how would we know? De Man immediately
continues, however:

> It follows that, more than any other mode of inquiry, including economics,
> the linguistics of literariness is a powerful and indispensable tool in the
> unmasking of ideological aberrations, as well as a determining factor in
> accounting for their occurrence. Those who reproach literary theory for
> being oblivious to social and historical (that is to say ideological) reality are
> merely stating their fear at having their own ideological mystifications
> exposed by the tool they are trying to discredit. They are, in short, very poor
> readers of Marx's *German Ideology*.
>
> (de Man 1986: 11)

Since what we call ideology is a confusion that involves language, it is through an
analysis of language (and in particular the 'linguistics of literariness') that ideological
'aberrations' and the means by which they occur can be recognised. We must be
careful here. In using the word aberration, de Man is implying a kind of wandering
or straying from the right path, but he is probably also thinking about a specific sense
of the word which relates to the faculty of reason itself (see the *OED*, sense 4).

What he is clearly saying is that those who believe that behind or beneath
ideology we can touch a pure, unmediated reality are themselves prey to the workings of ideology. What such a view relies upon is the confusion of linguistic with
phenomenal or natural reality. De Man doesn't suggest that either of these things
don't exist (he doesn't propose either that there is *only* language, nor that language
is separated from reality), simply that we should be wary about believing that we are
capable of finding one (nature or phenomena) through the other (language).

Are there any political ideas that you believe should not be publicly aired?   **Activity**

Think of a case of censorship. What exactly is it that is being censored? What does
this tell us about the values of the censors?

In his essay on 'Ideology and Ideological State Apparatuses', Althusser proposes the
following as ISAs:

❑   the religious ISA (the system of the different Churches)
❑   the educational ISA (the system of the different public and private 'schools')

❏   the family ISA
❏   the legal ISA
❏   the political ISA (the political system, including the different parties)
❏   the trade union ISA
❏   the communications ISA (press, radio and television, etc.)
❏   the cultural ISA (literature, the arts, sports, etc.).

Think of specific examples of how these different ISAs might be seen to work from a linguistic perspective. What is it that makes these things ISAs? Can you think of any other ISAs? How might we recognise the operations of ideology in the texture of language? (This is the field of Critical Discourse Analysis: see, for example, Fairclough 1989 and 1995. Fairclough (1992), in particular, engages with the work of Althusser.)

LANGUAGE PERFORMS

In Unit A4 we began to think about the ways in which language acts in and on the world, considering in particular speech act theory, performatives and promises. Here, we will extend this thinking and demonstrate some of the strengths and pitfalls of performatives. We promise. Here and now.

Austin's work on speech acts hinged on the central distinction between performatives and constatives. Performatives tend to take place in the present tense, and to be spoken in the first person: 'I bet', 'I declare war', I promise', and so on. Austin proposes that an easy way of recognising a performative is to see if you could insert the word 'hereby' into the utterance: 'I (hereby) bet', 'I (hereby) declare war'. The emphasis is thus placed on the here and now. Every performative contains a silent affirmation: 'At this very moment, in this place, here I am and I bet/promise/. . . .'

It is important, then, that we are able to say with some assurance that constatives don't work in this way. Constatives are, as we saw previously, statements of fact. But as several commentators have pointed out, even statements of fact can be thought of as 'implicit performatives'. Let's take an example. If we say to you 'That car is blue', then that would seem to be a constative utterance, a description. You could look at the car and decide whether what we had said was true or false. But there is an implicit performative lurking here. We could rephrase 'That car is blue' as 'We hereby affirm that in our opinion that car is blue'. This second utterance contains the word 'hereby', it is in the present tense and in the form of an affirmation, and as an affirmation it is a performative. From this perspective, constative utterances are not opposed to performative utterances; constatives are a kind of performative.

This may be illustrated by recalling de Man's playful rewriting of Martin Heidegger. Heidegger (1971: 190) famously stated: '*Die Sprache spricht*' – 'Language speaks', not man. This becomes, in de Man's text, '*Die Sprache verspricht (sich)*' – 'Language promises (itself)' (de Man 1979: 277). On one level, this is playful, utilising the proximity in German between *spricht* and *verspricht*. But there is something else going on here that is best understood in terms of performativity. What de Man seems to be asserting is something like 'Language promises that there may be language'. In other words, he is suggesting that reference, that meaning, may be possible. As Jacques Derrida suggests in his discussion of de Man's essay:

> This is another way of saying that the essence of speech is the promise, that there is no speaking that does not promise, which at the same time means a commitment toward the future through what we too hastily call a 'speech act' and a commitment to keep the memory of the said act, to keep the acts of this act.
>
> (Derrida 1989: 97)

The promise here is read not as one linguistic expression among others but rather as the essence of speech. This is because alongside every linguistic utterance there is an implicit performative, silently stating: 'In saying this I am promising that this utterance is language, that it will be possible for this to mean something.'

The example that we used a moment ago can also lead us to think about performativity in another way. What happened when we said to you 'That car is blue'? Perhaps you pictured a blue car. (If the blue car doesn't work for you, what about: 'Is this a dagger which I see before me?') Now, this isn't an actual car, it isn't a car that exists in what some would hastily call the real world. Where, then, is it? One answer would be to say that you only imagined a blue car, and that therefore the car only exists in your imagination (wherever that is). Are we sure that the imagination can be separated off from the real world? Alternatively, you may have remembered a blue car that you have actually seen. The car is then 'in' memory, but does this make it real or fictional? Our statement concerning the blue car was not descriptive but instead acted to conjure up a car, to make one.

This raises again the question of the serious or non-serious use of language. A standard distinction that is made is between fiction and reality. Let's think for a moment about what is going on here. Right now. This is a textbook. It makes a promise, signalled by the fact that it's labelled 'A resource book for students'. (Austin (1976) makes a similar promise in naming his book *How To Do Things With Words*.) It is explicitly written with the intention of making you, the reader, think. Now we can't control what you think: you might be thinking 'I'd never thought about promises in that way before', or perhaps 'I don't believe that at all'. In either case, something has happened, to you, as a result of this book. If you have followed some of the exercises (or if, in reading Unit A4, you did actually say out loud 'I name this ship the *Anonymous*'), then something has happened in the world. All texts are potentially performative, from a textbook that makes you name imaginary ships to a joke that makes you laugh. And there's nothing more serious than a decent joke.

For performatives are a serious business. While what Austin outlines is fundamentally concerned with the individual, ordinary speech acts by which social interactions occur, the theory of performativity has led in directions that Austin could not have predicted. This is, of course, part of the point of the performative – its effects are never entirely programmable. Probably the most forceful use of the concept of performativity has been offered by Judith Butler (see D4).

In her work on gender and queer theory, Butler uses the concept of the performative to address the repetitive processes by which individuals assert and reassert a gendered identity. Put crudely, what we believe to be a 'girl' is a cultural construction that persists because people repeatedly play the part of a 'girl'. These identities are not fixed or given, but are instead confirmed and reconfigured through repeated acts of identification. While these acts of confirming and conforming are in response to processes of *subjectivation*, they do not entirely coincide with these roles (see Butler 1990 and 1993). There is a gap between the role offered and the role performed.

This may seem a long way from Austin, but Butler's extension of performativity into a more general political and cultural notion of the act may be traced back to speech acts. Crucial to Butler's elaboration of the performative is the idea of repetition. It is also on the question of repetition that Jacques Derrida focuses in his engagement with Austin's work.

Austin's exclusion of the non-serious speech act (including literature, stage performances and so on) prompts Derrida to question the distinction made between the serious and the non-serious (see Derrida 1982: 309–30). How can we tell the difference? Part of the problem, Derrida insists, is that for any utterance to be an utterance it must be possible for it to be repeated. And this repeatability opens it up to the possibility of being 'grafted' into a new and non-serious context. Since this context is, as Austin has himself admitted, part of what gives the utterance its meaning or force, a change in context must entail a change in that meaning or force. Derrida calls the structural possibility for this repetition in different contexts *iterability*. A repetition is never a pure repetition (the same thing happening over and over again), it is always a repetition plus difference (the difference between the 'first' time and the fact that it isn't the first time, for example).

The easiest way to understand this is to think about citation. When we cite or quote a statement, we take it out of its original context and place it in a new one. Put simply, we always quote, by definition, 'out of context'. And we can go on quoting a statement, any statement, in a variety of contexts, more or less indefinitely. If we can't do this, then the statement doesn't strictly belong to language, since all language requires that a word or sentence be repeatable if it is to be intelligible. Thus all linguistic acts are open to unpredictable repetitions in unforeseeable contexts.

As Derrida points out, this creates problems for any attempt to make an original declaration, or to make one which would be unequivocally serious. This is as true of documents of historical importance as it is of the everyday expressions analysed by Austin. It is also this difference that intervenes, as in Butler's work, in the attempts to coincide with a social role, even something as apparently simple as being 'me'.

Activity

The question of what it is permissible to say in a given society or context has long been debated. Famous examples include prohibiting the shouting of 'Fire!' in a crowded theatre. Should free speech be protected? Should we be protected from free speech? What notions of linguistic performance would you have to rely upon in order to justify either of these positions?

In classic definitions of speech act theory, there is rarely a concern with the political or moral consequences of the acts described. Does this constitute a weakness in the theory? Think in particular about the notion of context with which speech act theory works.

DISLOCATING INTENTION

B5

In Unit A5, we began to address the question of intention by thinking about where meaning is generated. By asking who creates meaning, where, and when this happens, we could start to unpack some of the basic assumptions about the origins of meaning. Of course, what we found was that these assumptions, and the arguments around them, are far from basic. The overlapping and competing relationships between speaker–writer, hearer–reader and language itself mean that meaning is always a matter of negotiation.

Irrespective of the complexity of these relationships, there are, of course, several reasons to be cautious in speaking too quickly of intention at all, particularly in the case of written texts. Let's think again about some of the questions that were posed in Unit A5.

One of the possible locations for the generation of meaning was the speaker or author. Even within this conception of the origin of meaning, there are cases that complicate matters. For example, if we wish to locate the origin of meaning in a thought in the mind of the speaker or author, then what do we do with collaborative work? One of the most explicit examples of the problem is posed by dramatic scripts. Theatrical texts, in particular, are always to some extent the product of collaboration. The meaning of any performance is produced by a process that involves at least one author, the director, actors, and designer. We should also begin to think about the role of the audience, of conventions of staging, of movement, of spatial organisation and of a host of other contextual factors.

But theatrical scripts are only an explicit example of problems faced by any attempt to account for the origin of meaning. What about this book? It names two authors on the cover. Which of them is responsible for the sentence that you are now reading? Since all collaboration of this kind involves one writer editing and being edited by the other (even if we ignore the roles of editors at the publisher, and so on), in whose mind do the thoughts contained in this book originate? As the References section at the end of the book indicates, many of the ideas are not 'ours' in any strong sense at all. Equally, even in the case of a text produced by a single writer, editing and revision complicate any attempt to locate the time of origination. Unless we see language as merely an inert container for thoughts, then changing the language changes the thought. Which draft of a text contains the original of the thought that we read?

These attempts to locate meaning in thought to some extent depend upon the idea that language is a form of expression, and thus that there is something to be expressed (a thought) which exists prior to and independently of its utterance (for another attempt to deal with this question, see Unit A8). Ludwig Wittgenstein proposes:

> We speak of understanding a sentence in the sense in which it can be replaced by another which says the same; but also in the sense in which it cannot be replaced by any other. (Any more than one musical theme can be replaced by another.)
>
> In the one case the thought in the sentence is something common to different sentences; in the other, something that is expressed only by these words in these positions. (Understanding a poem.)
>
> (Wittgenstein 2001: §531)

What Wittgenstein is referring to is a certain philosophical assumption that it should be possible to paraphrase any thought or argument; in other words, that the thought could be expressed in another way without being changed for either better or worse. As such, each sentence or utterance is susceptible to substitution. But this is not the case, Wittgenstein suggests, with all sentences, and the most obvious example is a poem. There is always the risk that putting a poem 'in other words' might lose everything that gave it value as a poem in the first place.

What this might lead us to think about is the question of translation. Is it possible to say 'the same thing' in two different languages? Or even, is it possible to say the same thing in the same language, but using two different sets of words? Texts are translated all the time, but what exactly is it that passes from one language to another? Anyone who has ever tried to make a literal translation will recognise the difficulties that arise, and this is especially evident in computer programs that offer to translate. Famous examples of the problem include a translation of the title of the film *The Grapes of Wrath* which became (in the other language) *The Angry Raisin*.

'Automatic' translations by computer are frequently misleading. The Google website (www.google.com) offers an automated translation service. The effects are easy to demonstrate. Here is one we tried:

1   Type: 'The cat sat on the mat.'
2   Use the program to translate from English into French.
3   This gives you: 'Le chat s'est reposé sur la natte.'
4   Use the program to translate this sentence from French into English.
5   You get: 'The cat rested on the plait.'

Let's try a more complicated one. This is a common sentence in British English, used as a tongue-twister. It is supposed to be difficult to say because of the repetition or alliteration of the 'p' and 'k' sounds. A peck in this context is a measurement of quantity:

1   Type: 'Peter picked a peck of pickled pepper.'
2   Translate it into Italian.
3   This gives you: 'Peter ha selezionato un peck di pepe marinato.'
4   [As you can see, the word 'peck' has not been translated.]
5   Translate back into English.
6   You get: 'Peter has selected a peck of marinato pepper.'

This time the word 'marinato' has been left in Italian. But one of the effects of this is to have lost something crucial about the original. This sentence isn't used because of what it means, but instead for how it sounds. And the substitution of 'selected' for 'picked' and 'marinato' for 'pickled' loses that alliteration.

Now there isn't much at stake in these examples. But again, if we think about literary works, where the meaning and the rhythms and sounds of the words themselves are all equally important, we can see the problems in a stark fashion.

In the case of a work of art, what are we trying to translate? On the one hand we could aim to transmit a meaning. But what of the tone, the rhythm, the emotion that the work is attempting to convey, the effect that it has on a reader? Even a word which apparently means the same thing in another language (and which we might think adequate for use in conversation or in a technical manual), can carry with it connotations that lead a text to say something that is not present in the original. The difficulties facing translators led Walter Benjamin to propose that 'no translation would be possible if in its ultimate essence it strove for likeness to the original' (1992: 73).

So-called free translations must also be the product of a series of choices. Is the aim for the translated text to sound as if the work had been written in the target language (so it would sound as if Flaubert had written *Madame Bovary* in English) or is it instead to bring something of the foreignness of the text into English? *Madame Bovary* would thus remain a 'French' text, even for its English readers. Similarly, we might also think about how it would be possible to render historical difference in translation. How would you choose to translate a text such as *Don Quixote* or Dante's *Inferno*? Would you aim to make them sound like texts written in the same period in English, or would you use modern Standard English?

One way of thinking about the series of questions that we have raised regarding meaning is to consider whether you believe that language conveys meaning or whether it is always an attempt to indicate a meaning that remains beyond it. Samuel Beckett once commented on the difference between his own attitude to language and that of James Joyce:

> I realised that Joyce had gone as far as one could in the direction of knowing more, [being] in control of one's material. He was always adding to it; you only have to look at his proofs to see that. I realised that my own way was in impoverishment, in lack of knowledge and in taking away, in subtracting rather than adding.
>
> (Knowlson 1996: 352)

This doesn't mean, of course, that his works are meaningless, but that they are instead a simultaneous recognition of both the limits and the potential of language. He isn't suggesting that we should give up on language. It isn't as if we had anything else to hand. The point is to fail better, as one of his characters says.

Summing up a view that takes into account questions of authorial intention, the text as object, the context (in a broad sense), and the role of the reader, Jonathan Culler suggests:

> The meaning of a work is not what the author had in mind at some point, nor is it simply a property of the text or the experience of a reader. Meaning is an inescapable notion because it is not something simple or simply determined. It is simultaneously an experience of a subject and a property of a text. It is both what we understand and what *in* the text we *try* to understand.
>
> (Culler 1997: 67)

From this, Culler proposes that ultimately we must favour context, including in that term linguistic rules as well as historical circumstance or the situation of an utterance. But, Culler stresses, this is only appropriate so long as we also accept the fact that context is ultimately boundless.

Activity Try to think of examples of cultural investment in the idea of the author. To get you started, think about where we encounter authors in modern life (bookshops, interviews, publicity, biographies, photographs on the back covers of books, and so on). Why are people interested in authors?

Adam Phillips has suggested: 'We are never misunderstood, we are just sometimes understood in ways we don't like' (1996: 120). Even if you agree with this statement, try to think of some possible objections to it. Upon what notions of intention would your objections rely?

Can we be held responsible for the things that we say and write? Should we be? Think about cases such as pornography, racist material, sexist ideas, or warmongering. Now also think about freedom of speech, political satire, attempts to criticise institutions for racism, sexism, and so on. Are there other examples? Where do you draw the line between the need to protect certain groups within society and the desire to preserve people's right to express their opinion?

How would you approach an anonymous text or statement from the perspective of intention?

What does censorship assume about intention?

MIND READING   B6

Much theorising about language over the course of the last century has been based on a fundamental distinction between different levels of the mind. In A6, we discussed different ways of understanding consciousness and the unconscious mind, and much modern linguistics has also based its models on a similar dualism. Modern linguistics, for example, starts (after Ferdinand de Saussure) by distinguishing *langue* (the system of signs that constitutes the abstract sense of the language) from *parole* (the actual physical sounds or marks of language that are performed in the world). This distinction allows linguists to separate out the messy business of material language, with its social distortions and nuances, its idiosyncrasies, errors and noisy creativity, from the clear and idealised system of rules which underlies each language and indeed all languages. Such idealisation was seen as a necessary first step in formulating general linguistic principles.

This placement of linguistic rules deep in the abstract mind results in a view that sees language as prior to conscious thought. Edward Sapir, for example, writing in 1921, asserts:

> From the point of view of language, thought may be defined as the highest latent or potential content of speech . . . At best language can but be the outward facet of thought on the highest, most generalized, level of symbolic expression. To put our viewpoint somewhat differently, language is primarily a pre-rational function. It humbly works up to the thought that is latent in, that may eventually be read into, its classifications and its forms; it is not, as is generally but naively assumed, the final label put upon the finished thought.

> Most people, asked if they can think without speech, would probably
> answer, 'Yes, but it is not easy for me to do so. Still I know it can be done.'
> Language is but a garment! But what if language is not so much a garment
> as a prepared road or groove?
>
> (Sapir 1921: 14–15)

Here, language is necessary for thought to emerge, so that what he later calls 'language
and our thought-grooves' (p. 217) can be regarded as identical. Crudely, this view
states that having a word for something is what allows you to perceive it. So communities in Canada and Greenland have many words for different types of what in English
is designated generally as 'snow'. You might start to think about problems with this
position, firstly by recalling how many English words there are in fact for 'slush',
'rime', 'hail', 'black ice', 'powdery snow', 'snowball snow', 'drifting snow' and so on,
and then by considering how new concepts might be created and lexicalised, consistent with this view.

The notion of a deep level and a surface level, however, has persisted in modern
linguistics, especially in the work of Noam Chomsky (1957, 1964, 1965). Beginning
with the observation that children seem to know more language than they are exposed
to, Chomsky set out an *innateness hypothesis* which asserted that human brains
are 'hard-wired' for language at a deep structural level. This deep structure (often
labelled simply 'S') represents the linguistic *competence* of a language user, which
is transformed by the particular rules of their own local language into the surface
structure of English, French, Cantonese, Shona or whatever. This material surface
language is merely the *performance* level generated by the deep structure, and is of
little interest to 'generativist' linguists except as a means of checking the validity
of their hypotheses.

S is rewritten into actual surface language by a series of *transformations* which
can be expressed as rules. So, for example, most languages initially transform S into
a noun phrase (NP) and a verb phrase (VP) constituent, still at a deep level of logical
representation. This can be formulated as: S → NP + VP (S rewrites as a noun phrase
and a verb phrase). NPs and VPs can be further structured into constituent elements
to produce nouns with modifiers and qualifiers, verbs with NPs as direct objects,
prepositional phrases and all the elements of English syntax. Other transformations
apply further down the structure, so that S can be realised as a passivisation, as having
a dummy subject (by a rule called 'There-insertion') or even as a new S subordinated
to the main clause (by a rule called 'Raising'). There are many other such rules,
often drawn as tree diagrams linking the surface sentence with the deep structure S.
The principle of recursion allowed by subordinating another S within the phrase-
structure allows the model to account for every possible *well-formed* grammatical
sentence that has ever been or will ever be performed in the language.

The innateness hypothesis presupposes a sort of language module in the brain,
which has evolved a *universal grammar* common to all existing and possible human
languages. Transformational generative (TG) linguists set out to formulate the rules
for this grammar by working out the syntactic principles of the world's languages.

As we suggested above, the project depends on disregarding the messy social reality of surface utterances: Chomsky distinguishes *externalised language* from *internalised language*, and Jerry Fodor (1979) even proposes that the latter is a form of 'mentalese' – a representation system that is *the* language of the mind.

Non-generative forms of linguistics have criticised this deliberate bracketing-off of the sociolinguistic and material aspects of discourse. For Chomsky, empirical evidence from speech or writing cannot tell you anything directly about the internalised language system: this can only be theorised by appeal to a native speaker's introspective sense of well-formed sentences. Almost all of the examples of language offered by generativists are invented for the purpose of illustration. Features such as accent and dialect variation, historical change, ideological representation, metaphor and euphemism, in this view, are matters for social scientists but are of no concern for the theoretical linguist.

However, out of an interest in the interpretative and meaning-carrying aspects of linguistic theory, some students and colleagues of Chomsky developed an alternative branch of TG known as *generative semantics*. In the standard theory, the deep structure is a matter purely of syntax: transformations are meaning-neutral, and semantic meaning is simply a matter of reading at the surface level. Denying the centrality of the notion of deep structure, the generative semanticists insisted on a set of semantic primitives (such as *do, cause, want*) that can be combined in the phrase-structure to produce meaningful sentences. This innovation collapses the strict distinction between syntax and semantics, and led to a heated debate within generativism (see Chomsky 1981, 1988, 1992, and Huck and Goldsmith 1995). Traditionalists saw the innovation as an unprincipled confusion of the two levels of competence and performance that were regarded as necessary for the maintenance of a pure theoretical linguistics.

The generativist approach remains a major paradigm in linguistics, though challenged by forms of applied and empirical language study such as sociolinguistics, computer corpus linguistics, psycholinguistics and critical discourse analysis. Some of those involved in generative semantics, such as George Lakoff (1987), went on to move even further away from generativism, and challenge the very notion of dualities such as competence and performance, deep and surface structure, and even the mentalism that separated mind, body and world. This tradition has come to be known as *cognitive linguistics*.

Cognitive linguistics redraws the distinctions between language, mind and the material world again. The main dimensions of the approach rest on metaphor, categorisation and schematisation. First, cognitive linguistics sets itself against the notion of a separate 'language module' in the brain, seeing the processes of language and thought as part of an embodied mind: that is, Cartesian dualism is again rejected in favour of a view which emphasises the materiality of experience. Events which are experienced either by individuals or as collective cultural events are abstracted, generalised and idealised into *cognitive models*, schemas which represent a memory tool that can be used to negotiate similar situations as they arise in the future. Basic level categories – those which are most commonly experienced and lexicalised – tend to be embodied in the sense that they are understood on a human scale and in relation to remembered experience. Cognitive linguistics asserts that the 'objectivism' of traditional linguistics is a myth, which should be replaced by an 'experientialist' myth as a better way of understanding that both the world and the unconscious mind can only be understood through cognitive processes (see Lakoff 1987).

The traditional linguistic understanding of classification into fixed categories is also challenged by cognitive linguistics. A much more fluid principle of categorisation is proposed, where elements are seen as central or peripheral examples of a category, and decisions on whether concepts fit together or not in language are taken on the basis of contextual purpose. Categories are 'soft-assembled' as they are needed (see Gibbs 2003, Turner 1987, Lakoff and Turner 1989). For example, a knife is usually regarded as a prototypical piece of cutlery but a rather bad example of, say, a mechanic's toolkit. However, if you have ever found yourself lacking a screwdriver and have been forced to use the point of a knife, you will have found yourself re-categorising the knife as a good example of a tool for the situation at hand. This fluid edge to categorisation is what allows you to see that a potato is a better example of a fruit than a pencil, even though both are rather poor examples compared with an apple. The peculiar circumstances of the last sentence have encouraged you, temporarily, to redraw the boundaries of your 'fruity' cognitive model.

This everyday creativity finds its basis in our faculty for mapping one cognitive model onto another, in order to understand new concepts in terms of familiar ones. Cognitive linguistics has discovered many such *conceptual metaphors* which act as very strong cultural determiners; widespread ones such as LIFE IS A JOURNEY, GOOD IS UP, ANGER IS HOT LIQUID IN A CONTAINER, LOVE IS WAR, THEORIES ARE BUILDINGS, DEATH IS DEPARTURE, LIFE IS A STAGEPLAY and COMMUNICATION IS SENDING generate many everyday metaphors by which we conceptualise the world and ourselves. The project to delineate conceptual metaphors which seem to occur universally in the languages of the world suggests that some cognitive linguists retain the generativist urge towards universal grammar and a structure that underlies the surface of linguistic expression.

Activity   How would you answer the question, 'What is the mind?' Consider the implications of your answer for your theory of language.

What can we say about the truth-values of fictional worlds (see A6)? Can you measure the differences between different sorts of possible worlds, on the basis of how close to our actual world they are? When you think about your past, your future, or imagine yourself in a different situation, how are statements you make about these possible worlds different from propositions you make about the here-and-now?

The comedian and film director Woody Allen once declared that 'the problem with psychoanalysis is that it is untesticle'. Do you think psychoanalysis can be tested as conventional scientific theories can, or is it a rhetorically suggestive view of the mind? Is this an advantage or a flaw in the approach?

How might you produce language evidence against Sapir's linguistic relativism view?

According to the principle of the scientific method, a theory only counts as a theory if it is falsifiable and available for replication by others. How could you falsify Chomsky's theory of deep structure without simply appealing to an intuitive sense of well-formedness?

Linguistic relativists suggest that thought is an emergent property of language. Generativists claim that material language is an emergent property of structures of thought. Cognitivists assert that both language and thought are emergent properties of consciousness. You might follow up some of the reading in these areas to try to determine your own thinking.

CREATING WORLDS

B7

Creativity, creation, originality, invention, imagination, inspiration, genius, craft and construction all seem to lean towards the *production* of language rather than its reception. However, most approaches to language and meaning adopt a version of a sort of co-operative contract that is assumed to operate between language users. That is, an assumption is made that speakers and writers intend to communicate something, and receivers intend to gain something; furthermore, receivers act as if their interlocutors intend to communicate, even when the speaker or writer is being deliberately obscure, absurd or difficult. When speakers or writers appear not to want to communicate clearly, this 'meta-message' in itself is taken as the intended communication, following the co-operative assumption.

Several theories of communication explicitly assume a co-operative principle in this way: speech act theory in the hands of Austin and Grice (see A4 and B4 and H.P. Grice, 1975); or the relevance theory of Sperber and Wilson (see B9), for example. Such theories are sometimes criticised for offering a cosy, consensual view of society, in which every-one wants to communicate clearly and without conflict or ideological distortion. However, the 'rules' of such theories are presented rather as normative maxims that are more often deliberately transgressed than followed rigidly. In this way, the framework assumption of a co-operative principle is part of the theoretical mechanism rather than a commitment to consensualism. One important dimension of such pragmatic approaches is that they draw attention to the creative role of the receiver in communication.

It has long been recognised that reading is creative. Words on a page are not simply decoded: each word carries cultural associations and personal resonances. Any non-literal language is mapped against readerly knowledge and experience. Readers even tend to notice and remember certain parts of a text more readily than others, so that the *texture* of the text is a matter of creative reading as well as the material textuality of the language.

How readers build up a sense of the discursive space generated by a reading has been the ground of a 'worlds'-based approach to creativity. Originating with the seventeenth century German rationalist Gottfried Leibniz, the notion of a *possible world* was taken up by philosophers of language in the twentieth century as a means of accounting for the truth-values of propositions expressed in ordinary language sentences. Simply, a sentence expressing a proposition is true or false not in any absolute sense, nor even merely judged against intuition, experience or empirical evidence, but on the basis of whether it describes a state of affairs in relation to a possible world. That possible world might or might not be our actual world – our actual possible world is only one of many possible worlds available for determining truth, falsity and modal logic (see Putnam 1990, Ryan 1991, Ronen 1994).

For example, 'This book was written by Peter and Mark' is true in our actual possible world. 'This book was written by Miffy and Edouard' is false in our actual possible world, but could be true in a different possible world. In the actual possible world, Miffy and Edouard refer to stuffed toy characters in Peter's daughter Ada's cot: one is a Dutch rabbit and the other a French duck. It would be possible for these same referents to participate in the proposition, 'This book was written by Miffy and Edouard', but that sentence would only be true in a possible world very different from our own – one in which children's cartoon characters have an interest in language theory and are able to write. It is possible to imagine this paragraph in that world, in which Miffy speculates on a strange but possible world in which 'Peter' and 'Mark' have written this book.

Possible worlds have internal logic, of course, so it cannot be simultaneously true that Miffy and Edouard wrote this book and also did not write this book. Apart from this non-contradiction, there also has to be consistency: there cannot be a third possibility between the two propositions just set out. Any world containing contradiction or a prohibited middle-ground is by definition an *impossible world*.

Possible worlds can be measured on a scale of accessibility, on the basis of whether they share the same set of objects, history, natural laws, ethics and language. The book in your hands still exists in the Miffy and Edouard world, which you might be imagining as roughly similar to our actual possible world, with the stated exception that stuffed toys have consciousness. The fact that you can imagine this quite easily explains why possible world theory (an epistemic model) has been taken up as the basis of readerly world construction (as a metaphysical or at least psychological model). Readers tend to build rich worlds from textual linguistic input, rather than the simple sets of states-of-affairs used in possible worlds theories. In the Miffy and Edouard world, you too might be a stuffed toy; your children might have small cartoon humans to play with; and you could easily imagine an ongoing narrative of the rest of your day involving shopping for new stuffing or a more shiny plastic eye, perhaps. We have, of course, moved into the realm of the fictional, but our ability to run the logic of this sort of possibility is the consequence of creative world-construction.

Of course, readers go even further than this. Readerly creativity does not simply involve the mental engineering of textual space into a rich world; it also involves the creative interaction of the thing that is read with the experiential world of the reader. Since using the Miffy and Edouard analogy above, I have been making further connections between the real and the cartoon authors of this book. 'In what way is Mark like Edouard the French duck?' has been running through my head. Mark certainly has an interest in French philosophy. Edouard wears a soft flat cap that makes him look somewhat like the critical theorist Terry Eagleton, so there seems to be a generic commonality there too. These rather whimsical creations go far beyond the original intention of the example, but illustrate how readerly world-construction can take on a life of its own.

In his *Text World* approach, Paul Werth (1999) addresses the question of how receivers of language build up rich worlds in encountering text, and use that mental representation to manage further discourse. Werth argues that the limits of the text world are determined by the text, not in the restricted sense that only semantic denotations create referents but in the broader sense that a reader's choice of relevant knowledge is 'text-driven'. That is, readers run their inferencing, associative and contextual senses on strings of language in order to build up not only a world in which the sentence is coherent, but also a world which has a texture and consistency sufficient to go beyond the immediate denotations of the text in hand.

Any piece of language sets up *world-builders* (the inventory of objects and characters in their spatio-temporal locations) and *function-advancers* (the relations and processes by which the represented world is dynamic). The text world is constructed by the discourse participants, typically a speaker and a hearer, placing concepts into the common ground of the immediate text world. This looks again like a co-operative principle at work, but Werth emphasises the receptive creativity inherent in the process.

The elegance of text world theory is the fractal structure of the model: just as the imagined text world is a working version of an actual discourse world, so the text world can itself contain many sub-worlds, all operating on the same principles of cognition. Sub-worlds allow language users to keep track of embedded spaces, such as remembering what a fictional character is thinking at a particular point, or what a character in a gossip narrative believes, or what another person wants to happen in a story recounted before it happens. Unrealised possibilities, hypotheses, plans, second-hand reports, flashbacks and anticipations are all examples of sub-worlds with their world-building elements and function-advancing propositions that allow readers to keep track and make sense of discourse.

Thinking about the work required for readerly creativity in this way should make us think again about what creativity is. We could see it as the essence of communication, rather than as the inspired moment of production. We could notice the creativities of the world around us, as well as the specially valued creativity of prestigious verbal icons in literature. We could re-examine our notions of imagination, originality and authenticity, and think about how these notions have changed through time.

Activity ✪   Is the impossible unimaginable?

Are some objects more 'creative' than others? Is writing a poem more creative than designing a scientific experiment? Is a scientific theory more creative than testing it out? Is this textbook – partly collated from a variety of sources, partly the product of new thinking – a creative object? In other words, do you have a qualitative scale of creativity? Could it be measured quantitatively?

Creation and creativity are prototypically regarded as active processes. Can creativity be contemplative and interior? Does imagination have to be verbalised to count as creativity? Does this make language an essential element in creativity?

Consider the different connotations of 'crafted' and 'created', or the origins of the word 'inspiration', or 'genius', or 'originality'. What do these etymologies tell you about how these terms have developed in their usage?

Do you have a responsibility to the text, or to communicativeness in principle? What are the consequences of different views on this?

Do you think creativity implies newness? Is there any creativity in imitation, impersonation or plagiarism? What are the issues at stake in these concepts?

The Activities scattered throughout this book are designed to encourage creative thinking. Would we be more responsible authors if we provided more guidance or some 'answers' to the questions we raise? How is a textbook different from other sorts of writing? In other words, who is most responsible for your reading of this book?

B8   FIGURATION

Classical rhetoric delineates many tropes or 'figures of speech', of which *metaphor* is merely one among dozens. Others include *simile, metonymy, synecdoche, litotes, hyperbole* and many others which you can look up in a dictionary if you like. What you might find as a result of your search is that many of these tropes can be understood as involving a basic conceptual process of understanding one idea by using a word or phrase that is commonly used for quite another referent entirely. 'Let me give you a hand', by which I mean I will devote my entire body to helping you, rather than the product of a quick amputation. 'I've told you a million times about exaggerating', by which I jokingly mean to emphasise that I really have told you a lot of times. 'I read that book in a flash', meaning rather quickly indeed.

In other words, all of these tropes involve a sort of conceptual metaphorical process, whatever their surface form of expression. A simile ('quick as a flash') can be seen as a weaker form of metaphor ('quickflash'). This causes us terminological problems, since it means that the word 'metaphor' exists for a particular surface form as well as being the name for the general underlying process – we really need to call the latter something else, but *conceptual metaphor* is the best we can do. It is the process of creating figures of speech and drawing attention to them: *figuration*.

Using metaphor can be seen as a sort of mental mapping between two domains: a target (the new element that is being focused upon) and a source (which is being used to reconfigure our understanding of the target). In the most famous example from Shakespeare, 'Juliet is the sun' – where the new target 'Juliet' is understood by reference to the familiar source 'the sun'. Here we have a visible metaphor, since both target and domain elements are explicitly mentioned on the surface of the text. The previous line in the play, 'But soft, what light through yonder window breaks?' is invisible, since 'light' is being used to stand metaphorically for 'Juliet', but she does not appear in that sentence. In fact, the metaphor only becomes visible when Romeo says next: 'It is the east, and Juliet is the sun.'

The form in which a conceptual metaphor is expressed matters enormously to the ways in which it could be interpreted. 'Juliet is the sun' (a copula-based metaphor) is more intense than 'sunny Juliet' (a premodifier metaphor). It should even be noted that conceptual metaphors are readerly features: all that exists is deviant language, which a reader might resolve by interpreting the deviance metaphorically. In a text-level metaphor such as an allegory or fable, which makes sense in its own right as well as having a metaphorical dimension, the conceptual metaphor involved is invisible and it is up to the reader to realise there could be a metaphorical interpretation. The expression of metaphor can thus be used as a rhetorical function for political and ideological purposes, prompting readers to make subliminal or subversive connections and implicating themselves in the creative process.

Of course, a key question in the cognitive linguistic understanding of metaphor as a mapping between domains is: how do we know which features of the source domain are mapped onto the target? Juliet is warm, beautiful, life-giving and glorious; but is not 93 million miles away, the product of atomic fusion, with a deadly stream of charged particles emanating from her. Why not? It is obvious that certain cultural competencies are being drawn on that predispose the audience of the play to read this metaphor appropriately in context: part of their sense that the discourse of love is relevant, rather than the discourse of astronomy. The context of the world in the play and the theatrical experience set up the audience for a particular metaphorical resolution.

In other circumstances, different interpretative resolutions might be appropriate. Imagine you are an astronomer who has just discovered a large gas giant planet around a distant star, previously catalogued as M731-X. You decide to assign a more imaginative designation, so you call the planet 'Romeo' and the star 'Juliet'. Explaining to a party of visiting schoolchildren that the distant star system is just like our own local solar system, you say, 'The gas giant is "Romeo", and "Juliet" is the sun'. There is still a metaphor involved here, but in this case it is explanatory rather than poetic, and it relies on the analogy between the distant star system and our own solar space. The distant star is like our own sun. Analogies and similes are also conceptual metaphors, but they tend to serve a more explanatory purpose (see Stockwell 2000, 2002).

The problem for a theory of language in all this is that, pressed hard enough, all expressions turn out to be fundamentally metaphorical. In fact, just examine that sentence: 'the problem . . . in all this' assumes that problems are objects and that sets of ideas are containers ('in'). The container is material enough to be 'pressed', and the idea can be 'turned out'. 'Fundamentally' relies on a notion that reality is at the bottom (the 'fundament'), leaving the top for surface, cosmetic things. Notice how even this explanation cannot evade a metaphorical usage – and neither can this sentence! Indeed, a quick visit to a good etymological dictionary will reveal that most words consist of older meanings that have been adapted by metaphorical change, or borrowed from other languages. Even the prepositions we use (*in, through, between, from*, and so on) tend to express spatially, and thus metaphorically, the nouns they connect.

We could simply cast our hands up in the face of this and throw in the philosophical towel. If even the fabric of thought, expressible only through language, is inescapably metaphorical, then literal thinking is impossible and our prospects for self-reflection look rather bleak. Alternatively, we can accept that metaphor is the basis of the language game, and we should study how our conceptual systems work through it. This might create a philosophy of language that is explicitly based on artificial frameworks, that privileges rhetoric in argument rather than any solid material logic, but we could argue that at least this is a more responsible way of thinking.

For example, certain conceptual metaphors (see also B6) – while still undeniably metaphorical – have become so ingrained and naturalised in everyday discourse as to have become perceived as stable 'truisms'. LIFE IS A JOURNEY, GOOD IS UP, IDEAS ARE OBJECTS AND PHILOSOPHIES ARE CONTAINERS, A NATION IS A FAMILY, NATIONS ARE PEOPLE, WAR IS A FAIRY TALE, and many others. The first few of these conceptual metaphors are widespread across many languages and cultures: the *idealised cognitive models* of a JOURNEY or of CONTAINERS are more or less universal, even if, for example, the prototypical image of a container might vary across cultures and over time. Extended conceptual metaphors like these come to underlie the forms of thinking, speaking and writing of a society.

The last few examples mentioned above are more contentious. Where LIFE IS A JOURNEY is a conceptual metaphor common to American English, Arabic and Chinese, for example, A NATION IS A FAMILY, or WAR IS A FAIRY TALE are more particularly ideologically focused. Sending 'our sons' out to fight for the country, or projecting national economic planning like a household account, or configuring the public as children and the government as parents are all ways in which the NATION IS A FAMILY metaphor has been used in the United States. Expressions that manifest this metaphor are found consistently in politicians' discourse and are echoed in the press and broadcast media, making the metaphoric basis of the presentation invisible and conventionalised, so that it becomes the 'natural' and 'common-sense' way of understanding the issues. Similarly, mapping WAR as a FAIRY TALE involves the child-like assignment of good and evil, justifies the use of force, treats foreign populations as homogenous and monstrous, and excuses enemy deaths as part of the struggle for the greater good. This conceptual metaphor has been popular in the West from the two great European wars (1914–45), through the Cold War (1945–89) and the Gulf and Iraq Wars (1990–2003).

Where certain conceptual metaphors are seen as explanatory or poetic, there also seems to be a very strong sense in which the repeated use of a conceptual metaphor becomes *constitutive* of reality. Arguing against the dominant view of the NATION as A FAMILY is difficult without questioning the very basis of the contemporary popular perception of the nation-state. The power of this rhetoric also relies not only on the naturalisation of the metaphor but also on the cultural shape of the idealised cognitive model in the first place. The FAMILY, in the American use, is a rather conservative and stereotypical sort of family, with the father as head, a mother who bakes, and two or three children. Consider how the conceptual metaphor would run if the FAMILY model were based on a single-parent context, or a homosexual partnership, or culturally diversified into an Asian Indian model of the extended family, or the Chinese model of single offspring.

The point is that all our understanding and all our means of expressing that thought rely unavoidably on metaphorical processes (see Ungerer and Schmid 1996). Those processes are partly historically accumulated, partly culturally determined; they are part of the way that society has come to be structured, and they are subject to political and ideological manipulation; they are determined partly by the biological facts of our human shape, and partly by the way our individual experiences have shaped our mental models of the world.

In A8 and B8 we have presented a view of metaphor and the process of figuration as being central to meaningfulness and understanding. However, would you prefer to return to Aristotle's position from which metaphor was judged as 'an ornament to the sense'? How would you defend the Aristotelian view against modern perceptions?

 Activity

Since every word in English is either borrowed from another language or has been created by compounding existing words, or both, and has then been subject to historical change, it is true that the etymological origins of words seem to indicate that every word is basically metaphorical. (This is without considering that the process of reference itself is also a metaphorical process where a word stands for a thing.) However, is it fair to maintain a distinction between living, novel, creative, poetic or noticeable metaphors, and 'dead' metaphors? How would you maintain this useful distinction in a principled way?

Consider the ways in which we have expressed philosophical ideas throughout this book. What are the main conceptual metaphors we have used? What are the main conceptual metaphors that underlie your own ideas about the world and language?

CONSTRUCTING INTERPRETATIONS

Given that meanings result from a combination of textuality and contextual input, how can we understand how text and context function together? In other words, faced with even a simple sentence such as 'The cat sat on the mat', how do we know which information held encyclopedically either in mind or in some abstract idealised sense is pulled down and deployed to read this sentence? Can we even say that knowing the denotations of each of the words is a linguistic and textual, not a contextual matter? The likely context that this sentence brings to mind for native English speakers is probably the memory of a children's book, possibly a book to learn reading. Is this contextual information *necessary* to read the sentence?

In fact, it is probable that none of us ever actually had a children's book with that sentence in – it has become a sort of stereotypical children's book sentence that might not ever have been actually encountered by any of us. Can we then say we are using a sort of communal group memory of context? And if so, what can this possibly mean? Clearly, every sentence involves using some background knowledge. The key question for all linguistic approaches to meaning is: what are the principles by which background information is relevant, necessary and used in interpreting a sentence? The opposite of the question might help us: of all the millions of things we know, how do we decide, when confronted by a new sentence to interpret, which of those items are not needed on this occasion?

Traditional structuralist linguistics focused exclusively on the material features of the language utterance itself, but even this absolute formalism involves implicit readerly input. For example, discussing the semantic denotation of words involves an individual vocabulary, a mental inventory of items that activate references in the receiver's mind. You need to know what a 'cat' and a 'mat' are. You need to know what 'sat' means. And you also need to know how the two 'the's specify particular definite cats and mats, and you even need to know what 'on' means as the end-point of a process that begins with being 'off'.

One model for understanding the salience of certain bits of background knowledge is provided by *schema theory*. Originating loosely with Kant, and developed by Nietzsche in the 1870s but adapted as a psychological model a century later by artificial intelligence researchers, the theory suggests that certain commonly encountered scenarios are held in background memory like scripts (see Cook 1994, Semino 1997, Cockcroft 2002). These are 'schemas' (or 'schemata' if you want to be pedantic), and they provide ready-made interpretative tools which we can pull down every time we find ourselves in a similar situation. So, for example, in the two sentences – 'We went to the restaurant. The waiter brought the bill with the tip included' (see A9) – there are two elements in the first sentence that act as 'headers' which trigger our 'restaurant schema': the motion verb and the location. Most people's restaurant schema would include object elements such as waiters, bills, tables, cutlery, food, and so on, as well as processes such as ordering, eating and tipping. Your restaurant schema will also include the knowledge that there is a whole process of sitting down, ordering and eating which must have happened between the two sentences. The fact that your restaurant schema is likely to be running is what allows the definite articles to be used coherently in 'the waiter', 'the bill' and 'the tip'.

Schema theory neatly encompasses the fact that communities of people often act in similar ways, as well as the fact that individuals often also do things differently. It might be apparent to you that the writer of those two sentences above is British, using the UK 'bill' rather than, say, the American 'check'. Your own sense of the norms of a restaurant schema might lead you to interpret the two sentences together as being a complaint that the tip was automatically included rather than being optional. All these are factors that arise from your own experience, the accumulation of which serves to configure your own personal restaurant schema.

This neat model is not without its problems, of course. The 'script' notion in schema theory explains how you know what to do and say, but does not explain very well how other people interact appropriately with you. For communication to work perfectly, they must possess the same schema, but then they would have to have had exactly your experiences too. In other words, schema theory is rather overly consensual and asocial in its approach; it does not account for situations where there is a conflict in goals, or disagreement over which schema is in operation. Furthermore, at the theoretical level it is not clear what schemas are in psychological terms: is my restaurant schema just a track through my eating schema, or my transaction schema; or in fact do I have specific schemas for different sorts of restaurant, or even a schema for every restaurant I've ever been in? The determination of the boundaries and level of the schema seems rather random and unprincipled.

An alternative approach to the problem of identifying appropriate background knowledge is offered by *relevance theory*. Developed by anthropologist Dan Sperber and linguist Deirdre Wilson (1986), relevance theory is based on the pragmatic speech act approach of Grice and Austin (see strand 4). Assuming that a co-operative principle (CP) is operating, speakers take utterances as a signal that communication is intended. The meaning of any utterance is then determined by its maximal relevance to the context. Most utterances display strong relevance and are easy to process. Relevance theory includes the assumption that the brain operates for optimal efficiency, so that once a relevant and satisfactory interpretation is arrived at, processing usually stops.

Other sorts of utterances might be indirect and require greater processing. For example, someone might say 'The party is on the other side of the city', and you reply 'I've got a car'. This is not immediately relevant; however, the other person is likely to work out the weaker inferential proposition that you are offering a lift to the party. This inference is worked out by drawing down the knowledge that, say, at that time of night there are no buses and a taxi would be expensive, and that you are implying you would be willing to drive both of you to the party. You might also draw down other cultural knowledge such as the laws and ethics against drinking alcohol and driving, so that a third utterance 'So you don't want to drink?' makes relevant sense in this context. In this way, relevance theory delineates which parts of background knowledge are likely to be drawn down to allow successful interpretation.

A theoretical problem with both schema theory and relevance theory is that they both seem to offer explanations only after the fact. It would be nice if they could predict likely interpretations in advance of the linguistic exchange happening. One reason why this is probably impossible is the practical fact that the permutations of utterance and context are unimaginably numerous. Even restricting analysis just to three strings of language as above allows for hundreds of interfering variables: aside from intonation and gesture, the specific relationship between the interlocutors, the time of day, the place and history, what each thinks of the other, and many other factors all could be relevant. Then, of course, the immediately preceding discourse is also a determinant, as is any exchange which might follow this one.

Even setting all these practical problems aside, there is a big theoretical assumption behind schema theory, relevance theory and, in fact, most existing linguistic theories of meaning: for the sake of analytical convenience, all separate language from its context. In other words, a distinction is made between the utterance itself (with its phonological and morphological properties, and its semantic denotation) and all the possible connotations and associations, the personal resonances and social significances of which the utterance might be only one part. That is, the boundaries of 'language' – in most linguistic theories – have been set by analytical convenience rather narrowly compared with the encompassing possibilities of 'communication'.

Much modern theorising about language rests on the original distinction between *langue* and *parole*, between the view of language as an idealised system and the material actuality of language performed and in use. In B6, we said:

This distinction allows linguists to separate out the messy business of material language, with its social distortions and nuances, its idiosyncrasies, errors and noisy creativity, from the clear and idealised system of rules which underlies each language and indeed all languages. Such idealisation was seen as a necessary first step in formulating general linguistic principles.

However, we might now ask whether this has been a mistake.

The separation of text from context, or the distinction between the abstract system and the actual usage, has been branded 'segregationist' linguistics by *integrationist* linguists. Writers such as Roy Harris (1998) and Michael Toolan (1996) argue that bracketing off context in order to examine the language itself results in the object of investigation ceasing to be language at all. There can be no repetition of language, because every repeat of the string of words includes as part of its meaning the recognition that those words have been used previously. Equally, there can be no absolute synonymy of linguistic meaning for the same reason: it isn't that the context must be different to render the utterance-meaning different; it is that the new utterance involves those new circumstances as an inherent and indivisible part of itself. That paragraph from B6 that we quoted just above, for example, has a holistically and radically different meaning here than it did when you read it there.

Integrationists argue that most linguistic theories of meaning are based on what they scornfully call 'telementation' – the code model of language by which complete meaning is almost telepathically regarded as being passed by a determinate message from speaker to hearer. Instead, they argue, meanings are constructed freshly by receivers out of a holistic sense of the entire communicative situation, including what we arbitrarily categorise as the utterance, the gesture, the immediate situation, the hearer's knowledge of the circumstances and the speaker's assumptions.

In this view, there is no such thing as 'a' language; there are only instances of communication. A language cannot be described by formulating and listing its rules, since no rules could ever encompass every instance of use, and integrationists in any case doubt the psychological status (the 'mentalism') of such rules. Linguistic and interpretative communities cannot be defined as having members who all use the same language, and no notion of 'ideal' speakers, hearers or readers can apply; only actual groups of people can be investigated to see how they communicate. There is no distinction between language as system and language as performance for integrationists, and there can be no segregation of speech and writing, since speech always depends on visible signs such as gesture and situation, and literate cultures always implicate speech in their writing alongside all other aspects of communicativeness.

When do you think reading begins? And when does it end?   Activity

What role do you think the utterer's intention has in the meaningfulness of an utterance? If, for example, a writer says that he never meant his novel to be an attack on Muslims, are readings by Muslims which take it as such invalid? Can it be acceptable to say that an utterance means whatever readers think it means?

What are the problems with the notion of an interpretative community (see A9)?

Try to define *meaning* (without using the word itself, of course). In sketching out a definition, work out what you have left out that other people might think should be included.

What comes first, reading or interpretation?

Once you have done some more reading about schema theory, how would you defend the approach against some of the deficiences outlined above? Could you imagine a schema theory that was inter-subjective?

What do you think of the integrationist critique of linguistics? How would you actually *do* integrationism?

Section C
EXPLORATION:
INVESTIGATING
LANGUAGE IN THEORY

C1   **READING GENDER**

In this unit we present three passages for your consideration. The first is an example of 'écriture féminine', and the second is an example of a woman's writing in an instructional context. As well as considering the questions we pose, you should think about these two texts in relation to each other. What else do they signify beyond what we suggest here? The third piece provides an opportunity for thinking about the way we categorise sex and gender.

Écriture féminine

The following are extracts from the beginning of the essay 'Sorties: Out and Out: Attacks/Ways Out/Forays', in which Hélène Cixous writes 'écriture féminine':

> We see that 'victory' always comes down to the same thing: things get hierarchical. Organisation by hierarchy makes all conceptual organisation subject to man. Male privilege, shown in the opposition between *activity* and *passivity*, which he uses to sustain himself. Traditionally, the question of sexual difference is treated by coupling it with the opposition: activity/passivity.
>
> [. . .] [W]oman is always associated with passivity in philosophy. Whenever it is a question of woman, when one examines kinship structures, when a family model is brought into play. In fact, as soon as the question of ontology raises its head, as soon as one asks oneself 'what is it?,' as soon as there is intended meaning. Intention: desire, authority – examine them and you are led right back . . . to the father. It is even possible not to notice that there is no place whatsoever for woman in the calculations. Ultimately the world of 'being' can function while precluding the mother. No need for a mother, as long as there is some motherliness: and it is the father, then, who acts the part, who is the mother. Either woman is passive or she does not exist. What is left of her is unthinkable, unthought.
>
> [. . .] There is an intrinsic connection between the philosophical and the literary (to the extent that it conveys meaning, literature is under the command of the philosophical) and the phallocentric. Philosophy is constructed on the premise of woman's abasement. Subordination of the feminine to the masculine order, which gives the appearance of being the condition for the machinery's functioning.
>
> Now it has become rather urgent to question this solidarity between logocentrism and phallocentrism – bringing to light the fate dealt to woman, her burial – to threaten the stability of the masculine structure that passed itself off as eternal-natural, by conjuring up from femininity the reflections and hypotheses that are necessarily ruinous for the stronghold still in possession of authority. What would happen to logocentrism, to the great philosophical systems, to the order of the world in general if the rock upon which they founded this church should crumble?

If some fine day it suddenly came out that the logocentric plan had always, inadmissibly, been to create a foundation for (to found and fund) phallocentrism, to guarantee the masculine order a rationale equal to history itself.

So all the history, all the stories would be there to retell differently; the future would be incalculable; the historic forces would and will change hands and change body – another thought which is yet unthinkable – will transform the functioning of all society. We are living in an age where the conceptual foundation of an ancient culture is in the process of being undermined by millions of a species of mole (Topoi, ground mines) never known before.

When they wake up from among the dead, from among words, from among laws.

Once upon a time.

(Cixous in Cixous and Clément 1986: 64–5)

❑ Consider the style in which this passage is written. Is the style gendered? Is your reading of it gendered? Compare your reactions and thinking on this issue with someone not of your gender.

❑ Écriture féminine is intended to resist logical and analytical examination, where the discursive practices of 'analysis' through the ages have been determined by masculine norms. Does this excerpt resist this sort of analysis? What do you think it says? Do you think the passage could be 'translated' into a more masculine style, and if so do you think anything would be lost?

❑ Even bearing in mind that the original here is in French, what do you think of the use of the generic 'woman'? What relations does the excerpt draw between men, women, masculinity, femininity, literature, philosophy and language?

Crème Brûlée

The following passage is extracted from a recipe written by cookery writer Nigella Lawson. Consider it as an example of women's writing.

❑ A recipe is an interesting case for considering language and gender, of course, because it is an instructional, authoritative form of writing that has to involve little room for ambiguity. Yet it is also a discourse associated with the traditionally feminine sphere of the domestic, and here is a woman writing a recipe for a classic of French cuisine, often thought to be difficult, for a modern readership. Consider these gender issues in relation to the linguistic performance of role. Note especially the demarcation of addresser and addressee, and the conversational style.

❑ There is, in this author's style, a relish and tactile enjoyment of food and its preparation that draws heavily on sensuous and sexual connotation, allusion and imagery. What do you make of this? Is this woman's writing a form of 'écriture féminine', or does it conform to masculine expectations? If you were to 'translate' the imagery into male-oriented terms, how would the passage be different, and what conclusions could you then draw about language and gender?

Crème Brûlée

The first thing you should know about crème brûlée is that it's not hard to make. And few puddings are as voluptuously, seductively easy to eat. [. . .] There is something so welcoming about a big bowlful, the rich, smooth, eggy cream waiting to ooze out on the spoon that breaks through the tortoiseshell disc on top.

You don't need me to tell you about the blowtorch bit; this has been rehearsed enough. But it isn't a gimmick or a gratuitous act of showmanship: just the best way of burning the sprinkled-over sugar to instant, brittle compactness. You can get a blowtorch now from more or less any kitchen shop; and there's something curiously satisfying about wielding it.

600ml double cream	**3 tablespoons caster sugar**
1 vanilla pod	**approx. 6 tablespoons demerera sugar**
8 egg yolks	

Put a pie dish of about 20cm diameter in the freezer for at least 20 minutes. Half-fill the sink with cold water. This is just a precaution in case the custard looks as if it's about to split, in which case you should plunge the pan into the water and whisk the custard. I'm not saying it will – with so many egg yolks in the rich cream, it thickens quickly and easily enough – but I always feel better if I've done this.

Put the cream and vanilla pod into a saucepan and bring to boiling point, but do not let boil. Beat the eggs and caster sugar together in a bowl, and, still beating, pour the flavoured cream over it, pod and all. Rinse and dry the pan and pour the custard mix back in. Cook over medium heat (or low, if you're scared) until the custard thickens: about 10 minutes should do it. You do want this to be a good, voluptuous crème, so don't err on the side of runny caution. Remember, you've got your sinkful of cold water to plunge the pan into should it really look as if it's about to split.

[. . .]

Put back in the fridge if you want, but remember to take it out a good 20 minutes before serving. At which stage, put the bowl on the table and, with a large spoon and unchecked greed, crack through the sugary carapace and delve into the satin-velvet, vanilla-speckled cream beneath. No more talking: just eat.

(from *Nigella Bites* (Lawson 2001: 192))

Sex, gender and sexuality

In the following excerpt, Eve Kosofsky Sedgwick ponders the relationships and disjunctions between these commonly interchanged terms.

Sex, gender, sexuality: three terms whose usage relations and analytical relations are almost irremediably slippery. The charting of a space between something called 'sex' and something called 'gender' has been one of the most influential and successful undertakings of feminist thought. For the purposes of that undertaking, 'sex' has had the meaning of a certain group of Homo sapiens who have XX and those who have XY chromosomes. These include (or are ordinarily thought to include) more or less marked dimorphisms of genital formation, hair growth (in populations that have body hair), fat distribution, hormonal function, and reproductive capacity. 'Sex' in this sense – what I'll demarcate as 'chromosomal sex' – is seen as the relatively minimal raw material on which is then based the social construction of *gender*. Gender, then, is the far more elaborated, more fully and rigidly dichotomized social production of male and female identities and behaviours – of male and female *persons* – in a cultural system for which 'male/female' functions as a primary and perhaps model binarism affecting the structure and meaning of many, many other binarisms whose apparent connection to chromosomal sex will often be exiguous [extremely small] or nonexistent. Compared to chromosomal sex, which is seen (by these definitions) as tending to be immutable, immanent in the individual, and biologically based, the meaning of gender is seen as culturally mutable and variable, highly relational (in the sense that each of the binarized genders is defined primarily by its relation to the other), and inextricable from a history of power differentials between genders. [. . .]

'Sex' is, however, a term that extends indefinitely beyond chromosomal sex. That its history of usage often overlaps with what might, now, more properly be called 'gender' is only one problem. [. . .] Beyond chromosomes, however, the association of 'sex', precisely through the physical body, with reproduction and genital activity and sensation keeps offering new challenges to the conceptual clarity or even possibility of sex/gender differentiation. [. . .]

For meanwhile the whole realm of what modern culture refers to as 'sexuality' and *also* calls 'sex' – the array of acts, expectations, narratives, pleasures, identity-formations, and knowledges, in both women and men, that tends to cluster most densely around certain genital sensations but is not adequately defined by them – that realm is virtually impossible to situate on a map delimited by the feminist-defined sex/gender distinction.

(Sedgwick in Leitch 2001: 2438–9)

❑ In order to investigate how the three terms are used, you might search for them using a computer concordancing program (these are widely available on the internet). Or you could explore how they are used differently when comparing an academic context and a more populist context such as a magazine or Sunday newspaper supplement.

❑ There is a terminology clash particularly in linguistics, where 'gender' has been traditionally used also as a grammatical category for noun-types (masculine, feminine, and also neuter, in some languages). First-learners of such languages are often warned that 'natural' sex and gender do not correspond (French has the feminine 'la barbe' for 'beard', for example) – however, can you discover whether in fact the grammatical gender distinctions also carry loose associations of sex-gender for speakers of these languages? You might interview native speakers to gain an insight into their thinking.

❏ Consider the ways in which gender and sexuality are projected and performed. As a fieldwork experiment, you might take one small shopping street in your local town or city centre, and walk along it, noting down every feature in the street that relates to gender or sex in any way. What sorts of gendered messages are being enacted, and how are they being used?

READING 'RACE'

This unit first offers three examples of writing related to the topics discussed in Units A2 and B2. All three take up the question of the perception of racial difference, and how this is reflected in language use. Each extract also contains some form of response to those perceptions. When reading the passages from Said, Morrison and Ellison, try to think about how this dual perception (by perceiver and perceived) is working. While you are reading and comparing the passages, you might like to consider the following issues:

❏ Are there any terms used by these writers that seem to imply a judgement, or to ascribe a value to the person?
❏ Are there terms that seem to be neutral?
❏ What is the 'point of view' of each passage? Is there only one?
❏ Is this viewpoint how the person or culture would see her-, him- or itself?
❏ Would you like to be described in these ways? If not, which particular aspects of the description do you dislike? If you like these descriptions, what does that tell you about your own values?
❏ Does it matter who has written each text?
❏ Does it matter whether the description is fiction or non-fiction?
❏ Try to compare the passages. Are there significant similarities or differences?

The Oriental and the Orientalist
The extract from Edward Said's *Orientalism* gives both an example of what Said sees as Orientalist discourse and an example of his commentary.

The Oriental is given as fixed, stable, in need of investigation, in need even of knowledge about himself. No dialectic is either desired or allowed. There is a source of information (the Oriental) and a source of knowledge (the Orientalist), in short, a writer and a subject matter otherwise inert. The relationship between the two is radically a matter of power, for which there are numerous images. Here is an instance taken from Raphael Patai's *Golden River to Golden Road*:

> In order properly to evaluate what Middle Eastern culture will *willingly accept* from the embarrassingly rich storehouses of Western civilization, a better and sounder understanding of Middle Eastern culture *must first be acquired*. The same prerequisite is necessary in order *to gauge* the probable effects *of newly introduced traits* on the cultural context of tradition directed peoples. Also, the ways and means *in which new cultural offerings can be made palatable* must be studied much more thoroughly than was hitherto the case. In brief, the only way in which *the Gordian knot of resistance* to Westernization in the Middle East *can be unraveled* is that of studying the Middle East, *of obtaining a fuller picture* of its traditional culture, a better understanding of *the processes of change taking place* in it at present, and *a deeper insight* into the psychology of human groups brought up in Middle Eastern culture. *The task is taxing, but the prize, harmony between the West* and a neighboring world area of crucial importance, is well worth it.
>
> (Patai 1969: 406)

The metaphorical figures propping up this passage (I have indicated them by italics) come from a variety of human activities, some commercial, some horticultural, some religious, some veterinary, some historical. Yet in each case the relation between the Middle East and the West is really defined as sexual: as I said earlier in discussing Flaubert, the association between the Orient and sex is remarkably persistent. The Middle East is resistant, as any virgin would be, but the male scholar wins the prize by bursting open, penetrating through the Gordian knot despite 'the taxing task'. 'Harmony' is the result of the conquest of maidenly coyness; it is not by any means the coexistence of equals. The underlying power relation between scholar and subject matter is never once altered: it is uniformly favourable to the Orientalist. Study, understanding, knowledge, evaluation, masked as blandishments to 'harmony', are instruments of conquest.

(Said 2003: 308–9)

Undecipherable language

This passage is an extract from Toni Morrison's 1987 novel *Beloved*:

The day Stamp Paid saw the two backs through the window and then hurried down the steps, he believed the undecipherable language clamoring around the house was the mumbling of the black and angry dead. Very few had died in bed, like Baby Suggs, and none that he knew of, including Baby, had lived a livable life. Even the educated colored: the long-school people, the doctors, the teachers, the paper-writers and businessmen had a hard row to hoe. In addition to having to use their heads to get ahead, they had the weight of the whole race sitting there. You needed two heads for that. Whitepeople believed that whatever the manners, under every dark skin was a jungle. Swift unnavigable waters, swinging screaming baboons, sleeping snakes, red gums ready for their sweet white blood. In a way, he thought, they were right. The more coloredpeople spent their strength trying to convince them how gentle they were, how clever and loving, how human, the more they used themselves up to persuade whites of something Negroes believed could not be questioned, the deeper and more tangled the jungle grew inside. But it wasn't the jungle blacks brought with them to this place from the other (livable) place. It was the jungle whitefolks planted in them. And it grew. It spread. In, through and after life, it spread, until it invaded the whites who had made it. Touched them every one. Changed and altered them. Made them bloody, silly, worse than even they wanted to be, so scared were they of the jungle they had made. The screaming baboon lived under their own white skin; the red gums were their own.

(Morrison 1988: 198–9)

Voicing invisibility

This is the opening to Ralph Ellison's 1952 novel *Invisible Man*:

I am an invisible man. No, I am not a spook like those who haunted Edgar Allan Poe; nor am I one of your Hollywood-movie ectoplasms. I am a man of substance, of flesh and bone, fibre and liquids – and I might even be said to possess a mind. I am invisible, understand, simply because people refuse to see me. Like the bodiless heads you see sometimes in circus side-shows, it is as though I have been surrounded by mirrors of hard, distorting glass. When they approach me they see only my surroundings, themselves, or figments of their imagination – indeed, everything and anything except me.

Nor is my invisibility exactly a matter of bio-chemical accident to my epidermis. That invisibility to which I refer occurs because of a peculiar disposition of the eyes of those with whom I come in contact. A matter of the construction of their *inner* eyes, those eyes with which they look through their physical eyes upon reality. I am not complaining, nor am I protesting either. It is sometimes advantageous to be unseen, although it is most often rather wearing on the nerves. Then too, you're constantly being bumped against by those of poor vision. Or again, you often doubt if you really exist. You wonder whether you aren't simply a phantom in other people's minds.

Say, a figure in a nightmare which the sleeper tries with all his strength to destroy. It's when you feel like this that, out of resentment, you begin to bump people back. And, let me confess, you feel that way most of the time. You ache with the need to convince yourself that you do exist in the real world, that you're a part of the sound and anguish, and you strike out with your fists, you curse and you swear to make them recognise you. And, alas, it's seldom successful.

(Ellison 1965: 7)

Language and race

❑ Does writing in a colonial language reinforce that colonial inheritance, or might it offer a form of resistance? And what do you think is the role of language education in this context – liberation or imposition? Think of real examples from around the world.

❑ Is there such a thing as 'black writing'? If so, how can it be recognised? Try to produce an example of it (or another sort of 'racialised' or 'ethnicised' writing).

❑ How do abstractions such as 'nation' or 'fatherland' interact with ideas about a 'mother tongue'? Might there be reasons to be suspicious of such terms?

❑ It has been proposed by Gayatri Spivak that black women are subject to a 'double colonisation'. Think about the relationships of gender to 'race' and ethnicity.

❑ What are the difficulties presented to attempts to legislate for racial equality by the idea that 'races' do not exist? Should equality be the aim, and what does equality actually mean? How might this desire for equality be marked in language use?

❑ If language expresses a particular kind of experience, what problems does this present for translation?

❑ Are there certain words that should never be used? Try to justify your decision in terms of the view of language it entails.

❑ Finally, you might consider these issues again after reading the following excerpt from Frantz Fanon.

I ascribe a basic importance to the phenomenon of language. That is why I find it necessary to begin with this subject, which should provide us with one of the elements in the coloured man's comprehension of the dimension of *the other*. For it is implicit that to speak is to exist absolutely for the other.

The black man has two dimensions. One with his fellows, the other with the white man. A Negro behaves differently with a white man and with another Negro. That this self-division is a direct result of colonialist subjugation is beyond question. . . . No one would dream of doubting that its major artery is fed from the heart of those various theories that have tried to prove that the Negro is a stage in the slow evolution of monkey into man. Here is objective evidence that expresses reality.

[. . .]

To speak means to be in a position to use a certain syntax, to grasp the morphology of this or that language, but it means above all to assume a culture, to support the weight of a civilization. Since the situation is not one-way only, the statement of it should reflect the fact. Here the reader is asked to concede certain points that, however unacceptable they may seem in the beginning, will find the measure of their validity in their facts.

The problem that we confront [. . .] is this: The Negro of the Antilles will be proportionately whiter – that is, he will come closer to being a real human being – in direct ratio to his mastery of the French language. [. . .]

Every colonized people – in other words, every people in whose soul an inferiority complex has been created by the death and burial of its local cultural originality – finds itself face to face with the language of the civilizing nation; that is, with the culture of the mother country. The colonized is elevated above his jungle status in proportion to his adoption of the mother country's cultural standards. He becomes whiter as he renounces his blackness, his jungle. In the French colonial army, and particularly in the Senegalese regiments, the black officers serve first of all as interpreters. They are used to convey the master's orders to their fellows, and they too enjoy a certain position of honour.

(Fanon 1986: 17–18)

C3 READING THE POLITICAL

The extracts offered here follow on from the ideas raised in Units A3 and B3. The first two passages, from John Berger and D.H. Lawrence, are examples of how working people have been seen and represented. The third, from George Orwell, looks at the political consequences of language use, focusing in particular on vocabulary. The unit ends with an excerpt from Raymond Williams.

For each of these three passages:

❑ Pay close attention to the lexical choices made by the authors and to the use of figures and tropes (see Units A8 and B8).

❑ What are the people described compared to, and how does this reflect a sense of value?

❑ What is the point of view and empathy expressed in the passages? Do the writers identify with those they describe? Are they inside or outside that world?

❏   What kind of reactions are these writers trying to encourage in the reader? How, linguistically, do they set about producing this reaction?
❏   Do you identify with the people described?
❏   Are there aspects of your own use of language that you can recognise in these passages?

Seeing the political

The following is a passage from a work by John Berger, the art critic, poet, essayist and Booker Prize winning novelist. Berger's work is never easy to categorise, and in this piece he is describing a photograph that he does not reproduce (for reasons he explains below).

The photograph which lies on the table in front of me has become incriminating. Better not to print it – even thousands of miles away from Turkey. It shows six men standing in a line, in a wooden-panelled room somewhere on the outskirts of Ankara. The photo was taken after a political committee meeting, two years ago. Five of the men are workers. The eldest is in his fifties, the youngest in his late twenties.

Each one is as unmistakably himself as he would be in the eyes of his own mother. One is bald, one has curly hair, two are thin and wiry, one is broad-shouldered and well-covered. All are wearing skimpy, cheap trousers and jackets. These clothes bear the same relation to the suits of the bourgeois as the capital's shantytowns, where the five live, bear to the villas with French furniture where the bosses and merchants live.

Yet, with their clothes taken off, in a public bath, a police or army officer would have little difficulty in identifying them as workers. Even if the five half-closed their eyes so as to mask their expressions, so as to pretend to a commendable indifference, their social class would still be evident. [. . .]

It is as if a court, at the moments of their conception, had sentenced them all to have their heads severed from their necks at the age of fifteen. When the time came, they resisted, as all workers resist, and their heads remained on their shoulders. But the tension and obstinacy of that resistance has remained, and still remains, visible – there between the nape of the neck and the shoulder blades. Most workers in the world carry the same physical stigma: a sign of how the labour power of their bodies has been wrenched away from their heads, where their thoughts and imaginings continue, but deprived now of the possession of their own days and working energy.

For the five in the wood-panelled room, resistance is more than a reflex, more than the muscles' primitive refusal of what the body knows to be an injustice – because what its effort is continually creating is immediately and irredeemably taken out of its hands. Their resistance has mounted, and entered their thoughts, their hopes, their explanations of the world.

The five heads, whose eyes pierce me, have declared their bodies, not only resistant, but militant.

(Berger 1984: 16–17)

The politics of seeing

Here is a passage from *Women in Love*, a novel by D.H. Lawrence first published in 1920.

They were passing between blocks of miners' dwellings. In the back yards of several dwellings, a miner could be seen washing himself in the open on this hot evening, naked down to the loins, his great trousers of moleskin slipping almost away. Miners already cleaned were sitting on their heels, with their backs near the walls, talking and silent in pure physical well-being, tired, and taking physical rest. Their voices sounded out with strong intonation, and the broad dialect was curiously caressing to the blood. It seemed to envelop Gudrun in a labourer's caress, there was in the whole atmosphere a resonance of physical men, a glamorous thickness of labour and maleness, surcharged in the air. But it was universal in the district, and therefore unnoticed by the inhabitants.

To Gudrun, however, it was potent and half-repulsive. She could never tell why Beldover was so utterly different from London and the south, why one's whole feelings were different, why one seemed to live in another sphere. Now she realised that this was the world of powerful, underworld men who spent most of their time in the darkness. In their voices she could hear the voluptuous resonance of darkness, the strong, dangerous under-world, mindless, inhuman. They sounded also like strange machines, heavy, oiled. The voluptuousness was like that of machinery, cold and iron.

[...]

There came over her a nostalgia for the place. She hated it, she knew how utterly cut off it was, how hideous and how sickeningly mindless. Sometimes she beat her wings like a new Daphne, turning not into a tree but a machine. And yet, she was overcome by the nostalgia. She struggled to get more and more into accord with the atmosphere of the place, she craved to get her satisfaction of it.

She felt herself drawn out at evening into the main street of the town, that was uncreated and ugly, and yet surcharged with this same potent atmosphere of intense, dark callousness. There were always miners about. They moved with their strange, distorted dignity, a certain beauty, and unnatural stillness in their bearing, a look of abstraction and half resigna-tion in their pale, often gaunt faces. They belonged to another world, they had a strange glamour, their voices were full of an intolerable deep resonance, like a machine's burring, a music more maddening than the siren's long ago.

(Lawrence 1998: 118–19)

C

The politics of language

This is an extract from George Orwell's famous essay of 1946/7, 'Politics and the English Language'. Orwell is primarily concerned in this essay with questions of style. Try to identify modern equivalents to the kinds of language use, such as euphemism, vagueness, and so on, that Orwell notes. You might also compare Orwell's views here with his fictionalised view of language presented in C6.

In our time it is broadly true that political writing is bad writing. Where it is not true, it will generally be found that the writer is some kind of rebel, expressing his private opinions, and not a 'party line'. Orthodoxy, of whatever colour, seems to demand a lifeless, imitative style. The political dialects to be found in pamphlets, leading articles, manifestos, White Papers and the speeches of Under-Secretaries [senior civil servants] do, of course, vary from party to party, but they are all alike in that one almost never finds in them a fresh, vivid, home-made turn of speech. When one watches some tired hack on the platform mechanically repeating the familiar phrases – *bestial atrocities, iron heel, blood-stained tyranny, free peoples of the world, stand shoulder to shoulder* – one often has a curious feeling that one is not watching a live human being but some kind of dummy: a feeling which suddenly becomes stronger at moments when the light catches the speaker's spectacles and turns them into blank discs which seem to have no eyes behind them. And this is not altogether fanciful. A speaker who uses that kind of phraseology has gone some distance towards turning himself into a machine. The appropriate noises are coming out of his larynx, but his brain is not involved as it would be if he were choosing his words for himself. If the speech he is making is one that he is accustomed to make over and over again, he may be almost unconscious of what he is saying, as one is when one utters the responses in church. And this reduced state of consciousness, if not indispensable, is at any rate favourable to political conformity.

In our time, political speech and writing are largely the defence of the indefensible. [. . .] Thus political language has to consist largely of euphemism, question-begging and sheer cloudy vagueness. [. . .] The great enemy of clear language is insincerity. When there is a gap between one's real and one's declared aims, one turns as it were instinctively to long words and exhausted idioms, like a cuttlefish squirting out ink. In our age there is no such thing as 'keeping out of politics'. All issues are political issues, and politics itself is a mass of lies, evasions, folly, hatred and schizophrenia. When the general atmosphere is bad, language must suffer.

(Orwell 2000: 2468–9)

Language change and social change

In this extract, Raymond Williams begins by noting the first of several theoretical problems:

It is common practice to speak of the 'proper' or 'strict' meaning of a word by reference to its origins. One of the effects of one kind of classical education, especially in conjunction with one version of the defining functions of dictionaries, is to produce what can best be called a sacral attitude to words, and corresponding complaints of vulgar contemporary misunderstanding and misuse. The original meanings of words are always interesting. But what is often most interesting is the subsequent variation. The complaints that get into the newspapers, about vulgar misuse, are invariably about very recent developments. Almost any random selection of actual developments of meaning will show that what is now taken as 'correct' English, often including many of the words in which such complaints are made, is the product of just such kinds of change. [. . .]

The other theoretical problems are very much more difficult. There are quite basic and very complex problems in any analysis of the processes of meaning. Some of these can be usefully isolated as general problems of signification: the difficult relations between words and concepts; or the general processes of sense and reference; and beyond these the more general rules, in social norms and in the system of language itself, which both enable sense and reference to be generated and in some large degree to control them. In linguistic philosophy and in theoretical linguistics these problems have been repeatedly and usefully explored, and there can be no doubt that as fundamental problems they bear real weight on every particular analysis.

Yet just because 'meaning', in any active sense, is more than the general process of 'signification', and because 'norms' and 'rules' are more than the properties of any abstract process or system, other kinds of analysis remain necessary. The emphasis of my own analyses is deliberately social and historical. In the matters of reference and applicability, which analytically underlie any particular use, it is necessary to insist that the most active problems of meaning are always primarily embedded in actual relationships, and that both the meanings and the relationships are typically diverse and variable, within the structures of particular social orders and the processes of social and historical change.

(Williams 1983: 20–2)

❏ Williams does go on to say that language doesn't simply reflect society and history, some changes do occur within language, but the general direction of his argument is that linguistic study is (or should be) inseparable from an understanding of the social and political circumstances of discourse. The argument is similar to that of Bakhtin (see C7). What do you think of this position? Is there no place or opportunity at all for a decontextualised and purely linguistic analysis?

❏ You might explore the possibilities Williams opens up here by taking a text in which the author argues for a prescriptivist approach to language, for example, by insisting on standard conservative grammatical usage, railing against apostrophe misuse, modernised spellings, or Americanisms. Do you think that there should be attempts made in Anglophone countries, as there have been in France, to 'protect' the language from outside influence? Try to set the arguments about language being proffered into your evaluation of the political and ideological position of the writer.

LANGUAGE'S PERFORMANCES

In order to consider issues of performativity and action in language, we provide three items which are all concerned with how particular performatives are recognised.

Identifying performativity

J.L. Austin's work on performativity and speech act theory might be seen to rely on a particular notion of the subject. In the following passage, we see the grammatical necessity of this, along with Austin's attempt to think beyond this tendency. Try to think of the possible problems surrounding Austin's key terms, including 'origin', 'signature' and 'reference'. What distinctions must hold securely for Austin's theory to work?

> We said that the idea of a performative utterance was that it was to be (or to be included as part of) the performance of an action. Actions can only be performed by persons, and obviously in our cases the utterer must be the performer: hence our justifiable feeling – which we wrongly cast into purely grammatical mould – in favour of the 'first person', who must come in, being mentioned or referred to; moreover, if in uttering one is acting, one must be doing something – hence our perhaps ill-expressed favouring of the grammatical present and grammatical active of the verb. There is something which is *at the moment of uttering being done by the person uttering.*
>
> Where there is *not*, in the verbal formula of the utterance, a reference to the person doing the uttering, and so the acting, by means of the pronoun

'I' (or by his personal name), then in fact he will be 'referred to' in one of two ways:

(a) In verbal utterances, *by his being the person who does* the uttering – what we may call the utterance-*origin* which is used generally in any system of verbal reference-co-ordinates.

(b) In written utterances (or 'inscriptions'), *by his appending his signature* (this has to be done because, of course, written utterances are not tethered to their origin in the way spoken ones are).

The 'I' who is doing the action does thus come essentially into the picture. An advantage of the original first person singular present indicative active form – or likewise of the second and third and impersonal passive forms with signature appended – is that this implicit feature of the speech-situation is made *explicit*. Moreover, the verbs which seem, on grounds of vocabulary, to be specially performative verbs serve the special purpose of *making explicit* (which is not the same as stating or describing) what precise action it is that is being performed by the issuing of the utterance: other words which seem to have a special performative function (and indeed *have* it), such as 'guilty', 'off-side', &c., do so because, in so far as and when they are linked in 'origin' with these special explicit performative verbs like 'promise', 'pronounce', find', &c.

(Austin 1976: 60–1)

Speaking the unspoken

Austin, as we have seen, notes certain forms of performative that include a hidden or unspoken sense of what it is that is being performed. The implicit act (which he refers to as a 'hereby' or 'Thus I declare that . . .') raises the question of how we know what a performative is doing. Below you will find two lists. One is a list of things that performatives can do. The other is a list of sentences or locutions that might be performatives. Try to match up the locutions with the possible performances. Some will offer more than one possibility, some may not seem to fit any. At what point does a performative cross over into being a constative again (of the form 'I state that . . .')?

Possible performances

- ❏ Bet
- ❏ Promise
- ❏ Threaten
- ❏ Warn
- ❏ Name
- ❏ Declare
- ❏ Swear
- ❏ Challenge
- ❏ Congratulate
- ❏ Appoint

- ❏ Advise
- ❏ Estimate
- ❏ Protest
- ❏ Welcome
- ❏ Toast
- ❏ Thank
- ❏ Apologise
- ❏ Vow
- ❏ Guarantee
- ❏ Order

Locutions

❏ Not in here.	❏ It's better than it sounds.
❏ Uncle Colin.	❏ Tiger.
❏ Done.	❏ Guilty.
❏ Well done.	❏ Rarely with a banjo.
❏ Fifty pounds.	❏ I wouldn't if I were you.
❏ Sir Francis Bacon.	❏ Stop.
❏ At least five hundred.	❏ Don't stop.
❏ Never on a Tuesday.	❏ I'll be there.
❏ It was my fault.	❏ Fire.
❏ You can't do that.	❏ Without a doubt.
❏ You're dead.	

You could also try deliberately to mismatch some of these to see what the effect would be. Consider why the following utterances are most likely not to be the performative that they apparently claim to be:

❏ I'll smash your teeth in, and that's a promise.
❏ Losing his wallet and his car in the same day – I bet he's happy about that.
❏ I don't mean to be rude but you're an ugly useless moron.
❏ Welcome to the mad house.
❏ She said, 'I apologise'.

Declarations

In an essay on the American Declaration of Independence, in which the United States founds itself as an independent state in the name of the people, Jacques Derrida asks the following question: 'who signs, and with what so-called proper name, the declarative act that founds an institution?' (Derrida 2002: 47). In attempting to answer this question, Derrida engages with some of the central suppositions of speech act theory.

> Such an act does not come back to a constative or descriptive discourse. It performs, it accomplishes, it does what it says it does: this at least would be its intentional structure. Such an act does not have the same relation to its presumed signer – to whatever subject (individual or collective) engages itself in producing it – as a text of the 'constative' type, if in all rigor there are any 'constative' texts and if one could come across them in 'science', in 'philosophy', or in 'literature'. The declaration that founds an institution, a constitution, or a state, requires that a signer engage him- or herself. The signature maintains a link with the instituting act, as an act of language and an act of writing, a link that has absolutely nothing of the empirical accident about it. [. . .]

Here, then, are the 'good people' who engage themselves and engage only themselves in signing, in having their own declaration signed. The 'we' of the Declaration speaks 'in the name of the people'.

But these people do not exist. They do *not* exist as an entity, the entity does *not* exist *before* this declaration, not *as such*. If it gives birth to itself, as free and independent subject, as possible signer, this can hold only in the act of signature. The signature invents the signer. This signer can only authorize him- or herself to sign once he or she has come to the end – if one can say this of his or her own signature in a sort of fabulous retroactivity. That first signature authorizes him or her to sign. This happens every day, but it is fabulous [. . .]

(Derrida 2002: 47, 49–50)

❏ What is a signature, in this sense, and how does it relate to Austin's notion of a present subject?
❏ Think back to the Austin passage about signatures. What does Derrida's analysis tell us about the performative action of signing?
❏ How does Derrida seem to view the distinction between constative and performative utterances? What are the consequences for speech act theory?

Pretending to perform

❏ What are the implications of performativity for theories of authorial intention? What happens when there is a mismatch between what a speaker means to say and what a hearer thinks they meant to say? Or can we instead argue that performativity is in fact a readerly notion: the speech act performed is whatever the audience takes it to mean. Consider the practical consequences that would follow this view.
❏ How do felicity conditions realign thinking on gendered, racial or class-based language use? In other words, do you have to *be* a woman (or white, or working class) to speak felicitously *as* a woman (or as a white person, or as a working-class person)?
❏ If language is seen as the performance of a pre-existing and socially agreed set of speech acts, where does this leave any notion of innovation or creativity? In other words, what does the notion of iterability do to a notion of language as expressive?
❏ Must we be held responsible for the performative dimensions of our speech? For example, is it possible to be racist without intending to be racist? Is it alright to tell Jewish or Irish jokes if the comedian is Jewish or Irish? Sometimes people dismiss the offence they cause to others with the accusation that they lack a sense of humour or irony: do the speech acts of 'being humorous' or 'being ironic' then have a superordinate power over all other performatives?

❏   In the final passage in this unit, Etienne Balibar and Pierre Macherey suggest
    that the relationship between reality and representation, as performed by literary
    fiction or imagination, is the reverse of the traditionally held view. How far does
    the performative view of language as action compromise the view of language
    as representation? How can the same piece of language simultaneously enact and
    represent?

All 'fiction', it seems, has a reference point, whether to 'reality' or to 'truth',
and takes its meaning from that. To define literature as fiction means taking
an old philosophical position, which since Plato has been linked with the
establishing of a theory of knowledge, and confronting the fictional discourse
with a reality, whether in nature or history, so that the text is a transposi-
tion, a reproduction, adequate or not, and valued accordingly and in relation
to standards of verisimilitude and artistic licence.
        [. . .]
    Literature is not fiction, a fictive image of the real, because it cannot
define itself simply as a figuration, an appearance of reality. Literature is the
production, by a complex process, of a certain reality – not indeed (one
cannot over-emphasise this) an autonomous reality, but a material reality –
and of a certain social effect [. . .] Literature is not therefore fiction, but the
production of fictions: or better still, the production of fiction-effects (and
in the first place the provider of the material means for the production of
fiction-effects).
    Similarly, as the 'reflection of the life of a given society', historically
given (Mao), literature is still not providing a 'realist' reproduction of it,
even and least of all when it proclaims itself to be such, because even then
it cannot be reduced to a straight mirroring. But it is true that the text
does produce a reality-effect. More precisely it produces simultaneously
a reality-effect and a fiction-effect, emphasising first one and then the
other, interpreting each by each in turn but always on the basis of their
dualism.
    So, it comes to this once more: fiction and realism are not the concepts
for the production of literature but, on the contrary, notions produced by
literature. But this leads to remarkable consequences, for it means that the
model, the real referent 'outside' the discourse which both fiction and
realism presuppose, has no function here as a non-literary non-discursive
anchoring point predating the text. (We know by now that this anchorage,
the primacy of the real, is different from and more complex than a 'representation'). But it does function as an effect of the discourse. So, the literary
discourse itself institutes and projects the presence of the 'real' in the manner
of an hallucination.
                                (Balibar and Macherey in Mulhern 1992: 46–7)

C5   DESIRING INTENTION

Following on from the discussion in Units A5 and B5, the four passages included in this unit take up the relationship between language, authors, biography and interpretation. In asking what we want of authors the extracts lead us from a concern with intention towards reading. Both Freud and Barthes discuss the desire that is always part of reading, critical or otherwise, and the poem from John Donne raises the problems surrounding how seriously we take another's desire. The unit ends with an excerpt from the ideas of Jürgen Habermas.

The desire for biography

On winning the Goethe Prize in 1930, Sigmund Freud prepared an address, supposed to be delivered in the Goethe House in Frankfurt. Due to illness Freud was unable to deliver it himself. The idea of the speech was that it addressed the prize recipient's relationship to Goethe, and so Freud raised the bigger question of what we want from authors, and what shapes the nature of our attitudes towards them.

We all, who revere Goethe, put up, without too much protest, with the efforts of his biographers, who try to recreate his life from existing accounts and indications. But what can these biographies achieve for us? Even the best and fullest of them could not answer the two questions which alone seem worth knowing about. It would not throw any light on the riddle of the miraculous gift that makes an artist, and it could not help us to comprehend any better the value and the effect of his works. And yet there is no doubt that such a biography does satisfy a powerful need in us. We feel this very distinctly if the legacy of history unkindly refuses the satisfaction of this need – for example in the case of Shakespeare. It is undeniably painful to all of us that even now we do not know who was the author of the comedies, tragedies and sonnets of Shakespeare, whether it was in fact the untutored son of the provincial citizen of Stratford, who attained a modest position as an actor in London, or whether it was, rather, the nobly-born and highly cultivated, passionately wayward, to some extent *déclassé* aristocrat, Edward de Vere, seventeenth Earl of Oxford, hereditary Lord Great Chamberlain of England. But how can we justify a need of this kind to obtain knowledge of the circumstances of a man's life when his works have become so full of importance to us? People generally say that it is our desire to bring ourselves nearer to such a man in a human way as well. Let us grant this; it is, then, the need to acquire affective relations with such men, to add them to the fathers, teachers, exemplars whom we have known or whose influence we have already experienced, in the expectation that their personalities will be just as fine and admirable as those works of art of theirs which we possess.

(Freud 1990: 470–1)

The death of the author

In a brief and journalistic essay which still arouses considerable critical (and much uncritical) ire, Roland Barthes ushered in a whole new phase of concern in critical theory. While the *author* has always been of some consequence for criticism, it was Barthes' 1968 essay 'The death of the author' that pushed the question of the author into the forefront of literary debate. Barthes quotes from Balzac's (1830) novel *Sarrasine*: 'She was Woman, with her sudden fears, her inexplicable whims, her instinctive fears, her meaningless bravado, her defiance, and her delicious delicacy of feeling.'

Who speaks in this way? Is it the hero of the tale, who would prefer not to recognize the castrato hidden beneath the 'woman'? Is it Balzac the man, whose personal experience has provided him with a philosophy of Woman? Is it Balzac the author, professing certain 'literary' ideas about femininity? Is it universal wisdom? Romantic psychology? We can never know, for the good reason that writing is the destruction of every voice, every origin. Writing is that neuter, that composite, that obliquity into which our subject flees, the black-and-white where all identity is lost, beginning with the very identity of the body that writes.

[. . .]

We know now that a text consists not of a line of words, releasing a single 'theological' meaning (the 'message' of the Author-God), but of a multi-dimensional space in which are married and contested several writings, none of which is original: the text is a fabric of quotations, resulting from a thousand sources of culture.

[. . .]

In multiple writing, in effect, everything is to be *disentangled*, but nothing *deciphered*, structure can be followed, 'threaded' (as we say of a run in a stocking) in all its reprises, all its stages, but there is no end to it, no bottom; the space of writing is to be traversed, not pierced; writing constantly posits meaning, but always in order to evaporate it: writing seeks a systematic exemption of meaning. [. . .]

Here we discern the total being of writing: a text consists of multiple writings, proceeding from several cultures and entering into dialogue, into parody, into contestation; but there is a site where this multiplicity is collected, and this site is not the author, as has hitherto been claimed, but the reader: the reader is the very space in which are inscribed, without any of them being lost, all the citations out of which a writing is made; the unity of a text is not in its origin but in its destination, but this destination can no longer be personal: the reader is a man without history, without biography, without psychology; he is only that *someone* who holds collected into one and the same field all of the traces from which writing is constituted.

(Barthes 1989: 49–55)

Reading irony

The following piece in this unit is a poem by John Donne. 'The Canonization' is one of his most famous poems, but it has been read in very different ways. For some it is a love poem, extolling the glories of the erotic life over the everyday concerns of the world. But there are those who see it as saying precisely the opposite, drawing on knowledge of Donne's marriage, which had a disastrous effect on his worldly ambitions. For these readers, the tone of the poem is fundamentally ironic, and it is argued that readers familiar with Donne's life would have known this and read it appropriately. What do you think? Try to reconstruct the evidence from the poem that such diverse readings might use. How can you choose between these two readings in the absence (as Paul de Man once noted) of any diacritical mark to denote irony?

(If you want to read more on this poem, see Brooks 1947, Marotti 1986 and Culler 1983.)

The Canonization

For God's sake hold your tongue, and let me love,
    Or chide my palsy, or my gout,
My five grey hairs, or ruined fortune flout,
      With wealth your state, your mind with arts improve,
        Take you a course, get you a place,
        Observe his Honour, or his Grace,
Or the King's real, or his stamped face
    Contemplate; what you will, approve,
    So you will let me love.

Alas, alas, who's injured by my love?
    What merchant's ships have my sighs drowned?
Who says my tears have overflowed his ground?
    When did my colds a forward spring remove?
      When did the heats which my veins fill
      Add one more to the plaguy bill?
Soldiers find wars, and lawyers find out still
    Litigious men, which quarrels move,
    Though she and I do love.

Call us what you will, we are made such by love;
    Call her one, me another fly,
We are tapers too, and at our own cost die,
    And we in us find the eagle and the dove,
      The phoenix riddle hath more wit
      By us; we two being one, are it.
So to one neutral thing both sexes fit
    We die and rise the same, and prove
    Mysterious by this love.

We can die by it, if not live by love,
    And if unfit for tombs and hearse
Our legend be, it will be fit for verse;
    And if no piece of chronicle we prove,
        We'll build in sonnets pretty rooms;
        As well a well-wrought urn becomes
The greatest ashes, as half-acre tombs,
    And by these hymns, all shall approve
    Us canonized for love:

And thus invoke us; 'You whom reverend love
    Made one another's hermitage;
You, to whom love was peace, that now is rage;
    Who did the whole world's soul contract, and drove
        Into the glasses of your eyes
        (So made such mirrors, and such spies,
That they did all to you epitomize,)
    Countries, towns, courts: beg from above
    A pattern of your love!'

Intentions, reflections and projections

The final passage is taken from the work of Jürgen Habermas. He is describing, in philosophical terms, the experience of linguistic deixis – the means by which language users keep track of the different referents for 'I/you', 'here/there' and 'then/now', as well as other social relationships.

Fundamental to the paradigm of mutual understanding is [. . .] the performative attitude of participants in interaction, who coordinate their plans for action by coming to an understanding about something in the world. When ego carries out a speech act and alter takes up a position with regard to it, the two parties enter into an interpersonal relationship. The latter is structured by the system of reciprocally interlocked perspectives among speakers, hearers, and non-participants who happen to be present at the time. On the level of grammar, this corresponds to the system of personal pronouns. Whoever has been trained in this system has learned how, in the performative attitude, to take up and to transform into one another the perspectives of the first, second, and third persons.

    Now this attitude of participants in linguistically mediated interaction makes possible a *different* relationship of the subject to itself from the sort of objectifying attitude that an observer assumes towards entities in the external world. The transcendental-empirical doubling of the relation to self is only unavoidable so long as there is no alternative to this observer-perspective; only then does the subject have to view itself as the dominating counterpart to the world as a whole or as an entity appearing within it. No mediation is possible between the extramundane [outside the world] stance of the transcendental I and the intramundane [inside the world] stance of the empirical I. As soon as linguistically generated intersubjectivity gains primacy, this alternative no longer applies. Then ego stands within an inter-personal relationship that allows him to relate to himself as a participant in an interaction from the perspective of alter. And indeed this reflection undertaken from the perspective of the participant escapes the kind of objectification inevitable from the reflexively applied perspective of the observer. Everything gets frozen into an object under the gaze of the third person, whether directly inwardly or outwardly. The first person, who turns back upon himself in a performative attitude from the angle of vision of the second person, can *recapitulate* the acts it just carried out. In place of reflectively objectified knowledge – the knowledge proper to self-consciousness – we have a recapitulating reconstruction of knowledge already employed.

(Habermas 1998: 296–7)

Consider the following questions in the light of this passage and the preceding extracts in this unit:

❑ How far is intentionality recoverable?
❑ Can we speak of apparent or even readerly intentionality?
❑ In pragmatics (see strand 4), a co-operative principle is often thought to operate, such that interlocutors assume the other is intending to communicate some-thing. How does your thinking on intentionality square with the co-operative principle?
❑ Is something more or less 'true' because it is said by a particular person or from a particular position?
❑ Think about the choices made when one text is translated into another. What can translation tell us about the problems of intention?

C6　　LANGUAGE AND MIND

The key question for this thread is: *what is the relationship of language to knowledge?* Of course, to even begin to answer this, you have to decide what is the scope of your definition of *language*, and what kinds of *knowledge* are involved. In this unit, we present three extracts for you to use to think about the question.

The principles of Newspeak

George Orwell's 1948 novel *Nineteen Eighty-Four* is set in a repressive future society dominated by a Stalinist regime, IngSoc, and its leader known only as Big Brother. The English language of this dystopia is being revised, and the following passage is taken from the Appendix to the novel, in which Orwell sets out 'The Principles of Newspeak'.

> The purpose of Newspeak was not only to provide a medium of expression for the world-view and mental habits proper to the devotees of IngSoc, but to make all other modes of thought impossible. It was intended that when Newspeak had been adopted once and for all and Oldspeak forgotten, a heretical thought – that is, a thought diverging from the principles of IngSoc – should be literally unthinkable, at least so far as thought is dependent on words. Its vocabulary was so constructed as to give exact and often very subtle expression to every meaning that a Party member could properly wish to express, while excluding all other meanings and also the possibility of arriving at them by indirect methods. This was done partly by the invention of new words, but chiefly by eliminating undesirable words and by stripping such words as remained of unorthodox meanings, and so far as possible of all secondary meanings whatever. To give a single example. The word *free* still existed in Newspeak, but it could only be used in such statements as 'This dog is free from lice' or 'This field is free from weeds'. It could not be used in its old sense of 'politically free' or 'intellectually free' since political and intellectual freedom no longer existed even as concepts, and were therefore of necessity nameless. Quite apart from the suppression of definitely heretical words, reduction of vocabulary was regarded as an end in itself, and no word that could be dispensed with was allowed to survive. Newspeak was designed not to extend but to *diminish* the range of thought, and this purpose was indirectly assisted by cutting the choice of words down to a minimum.
>
> (Orwell 1948: Appendix 1)

❑   What assumptions does Orwell make about the relationship between language and thought?

❑   Using your knowledge of linguistics (especially historical change and linguistic creativity), how might you demonstrate that Newspeak could never happen?

Like the country ('Airstrip One') contained in *Nineteen Eighty-Four*, the novel presents Britain and tendencies in English usage as an extreme caricature for fictional and political purposes. However, similar patterns have been identified in the language of current politicians and their media representations. In particular, the metaphors and euphemisms used by the media are often exposed by critical discourse analysts to reveal the 'distortions' present in their worldviews. Euphemisms for war, invasion, racism and genocide are particularly important. Think of the associations involved in the phrases 'ethnic cleansing', 'peacekeeper missile', 'neighbourhood pacification' and many others. Or think of how international disputes are framed as households, as schoolyard bullying, or as a case of the 'goodies' and 'baddies' of children's fiction.

The assumption is that prolonged exposure to a particular rhetorical pattern will make it seem natural and will thus reconfigure the thinking of the reading public. What do you think of the relationship between rhetorical pattern and cognitive impact being assumed here? Does talking about a political issue in certain terms restrict your thinking about the issue? Is political argument simply the clash of rhetorics rather than the evaluation of material issues? Even if you reject the strong position that certain representations can 'corrupt' the reader/viewer, does exposure to particular forms of language *encourage* thinking along one ideological line rather than another? Think about these questions with a newspaper page in front of you.

The origins of grammar

In the following passage, cognitive linguist Mark Turner takes issue with the innateness hypothesis – the idea that humans are 'hard-wired' to speak language. His notion of *parable* consists of a sense of a story-structure matched with the human capacity for mapping one sort of knowledge onto another set of knowledge. This basic metaphorical skill is what, according to Turner, allowed language to exist, emerging from existing psychological and neurological structures.

> The dominant contemporary theory of the origin of language proposes that genetic change produced genetic instructions for building a special module for grammar in the human brain. Before genetic specialization for grammar, people had no grammar at all: no grammatical speech, no parsing of grammar, no concept of grammar. To be sure, they communicated (birds and bees communicate), but their communication was totally ungrammatical. It was not language. This grammar module was autonomous: it borrowed no structure or processes from any other capacities like vision [. . .]. Adherents of this theory – who form a large group of distinguished scholars that includes Noam Chomsky, Steven Pinker, and Paul Bloom – disagree only about which evolutionary mechanisms were responsible for the genetic specialization for grammar.
>
> Naturally, it is a corollary of this theory that the development of language in any modern human child comes entirely from the autonomous grammar module in the child's brain, which is built entirely from the special instructions in its genes. The language the child hears prompts it to shut down the parts of the language module it does not need.
>
> I think this theory of the historical origin of language is wrong. A carefully adjusted version of it might not in principle be absolutely impossible, but at best it offers a hypothesis of last resort: since we cannot discover a straightforward way in which language might have arisen, let us postulate

the mysterious origin of a special, autonomous black box that mysteriously
does everything we need to explain language, including everything we don't
yet know we need.

If we reject the hypothesis that genetic specialization for grammar was
the origin of language, what can we propose instead? Let us consider the
possibility that parable was the origin of language, that parable preceded
grammar.

[...]

Stories have structure that human vocal sound – as sound, not language
– does not have. Stories have objects and events, actors and movements,
viewpoint and focus, image schemas and force dynamics, and so on.
Roughly, parable takes structure from story and gives it to voice [...].
Parable creates structure for voice by projecting structure from story. The
structure it creates is grammar. Grammar results from the projection of story
structure. Sentences come from stories by way of parable.

[...]

Grammar arose in a community that already had parable. The members
of that community used parable to project structure from story to create
rudimentary grammatical structure for vocal sound.

(Turner 1996: 140–1)

❏   What do you think of Turner's argument here? How could the innateness
    hypothesis be defended against this position?
❏   Examine Turner's rhetorical style. How does he make logical connections and
    how far does his argument rest on certain metaphors? What different conceptual
    metaphors does the innateness hypothesis rest on?

Knowledge about language

In the following passage, the critical theorist Paul de Man sets rhetoric against the
other classical practices of logic and grammar. He insists that the rhetorical dimension of language (such as self-consciously literary or creative discourse) serves
constantly to undercut the desire to fix meaning. In this extract, he attacks the 'resistance to theory' typically presented by those who would see an easy or direct
relationship between language and the world.

The resistance to theory is a resistance to the use of language about language.
It is therefore a resistance to language itself or to the possibility that
language contains factors or functions that cannot be reduced to intuition.
But we seem to assume all too readily that, when we refer to something
called 'language', we know what it is we are talking about, although there
is probably no word to be found in the language that is as overdetermined,
self-evasive, disfigured and disfiguring as 'language'. Even if we choose to

consider it at a safe remove from any theoretical model, in the pragmatic history of 'language', not as a concept, but as a didactic assignment that no human being can bypass, we soon find ourselves confronted by theoretical enigmas.

[...]

Logic and grammar seem to have a natural enough affinity for each other and, in the tradition of Cartesian linguistics, the grammarians [...] experienced little difficulty at being logicians as well. [...] Grammar is an isotope of logic.

It follows that, as long as it remains grounded in grammar, any theory of language, including a literary one, does not threaten what we hold to be the underlying principle of all cognitive and aesthetic linguistic systems. Grammar stands in the service of logic which, in turn, allows for the passage to the knowledge of the world. [...] Difficulties occur only when it is no longer possible to ignore the epistemological thrust of the rhetorical dimension of discourse, that is, when it is no longer possible to keep it in its place as a mere adjunct, a mere ornament within the semantic function.

(de Man 1986, reprinted from *Yale French Studies* 63 (1982))

❏ Do you agree with de Man's rejection of what cognitive linguists would call 'objectivism'? Do you agree that the only knowledge language can securely offer is about itself?

❏ There are two possible strategies that could arise from de Man's arguments. First, you could recognise that meanings are not stable but are dependent on rhetoric, which in turn is dependent on political force – so arguments about meaning are really arguments about politics. Alternatively, you could decide that rhetoric can also be studied systematically as a fully contextualised (see Culler in B5) exploration of style in its social and psychological environment – a socially situated cognitive linguistics. Which of these possibilities appeals to you most? Do you think they are mutually exclusive?

C7   FORMS OF CREATIVITY

Creativity as an intentional act or as a coincidental act is the theme of this unit. We set out several examples of unintended creativity that call into question the status of originality and invention in the creative process.

Finding creativity

The US Secretary of State for Defence, Donald Rumsfeld, often mangled his press briefings during the Gulf and Iraq wars (2002–3). Some of his statements, recorded by the press and listed on the Pentagon website, were subsequently published, set to music and even sung by a soprano. Here is Rumsfeld's most famous statement, which was set in this poetic form and posted anonymously across the internet by email:

The Unknown

As we know,
There are known knowns.
There are things we know we know.
We also know
There are known unknowns.
That is to say
We know there are some things
We do not know.
But there are also unknown unknowns,
The ones we don't know
We don't know.

(US Department of Defence news briefing,
12 February 2002)

❏ In what sense is this creative? Who is responsible for its creativity? Consider what assumptions you are making about creativity in deciding on your answer. What does Rumsfeld mean? Is this different from what the text means?

❏ The poem counts in a tradition of *found poetry* – invented by the Dadaists and developed by the Surrealists in the 1920s as a means of removing the authority of the author, 'found poetry' became popular as a democratising statement in the 1960s and is now much used in second language teaching. You can easily create your own 'found poem' by writing down the first ten pieces of language you see and hear when looking around the room you are in now. Alternatively you can pick sentences at random by flicking through this book; or by walking down the road and writing down any text on signs and posters that you see. Give your poem a title and invite others to interpret it. What does the experience show you about creativity and interpretation?

Everyday creations

What is the function of the following everyday examples of creative language use? Are they all creative in the same way, or can you delineate different sorts of creativity here?

- ❏ Emerald Oil (name of an Irish petrol company)
- ❏ So I went into the takeaway and said, Do you deliver, and he says No, we do beef, we do pork, we do chicken (comedian Peter Kay)
- ❏ Pukka people pick a pot of Patak's (advertising slogan for a spicy food manufacturer)
- ❏ Art Angels (name of a greetings card company)
- ❏ I'm shivering like a shiteing dog (on entering a snowed-in working men's club in Yorkshire)
- ❏ Bloke for sale, immaculate condition, 35, attrac model, intellig, fit & straightforward, good runner, also climbs, dives and cooks. Sensible offers considered from quirky, feisty F. N. Yorks/Co. Durham. Call 0905 555 5555 (*Guardian* newspaper classified ads)
- ❏ Tanfastique (solarium in Middlesbrough)
- ❏ Last Quango in Powys (UK Channel 4 TV news headline about the abolition of a Welsh economic development agency)
- ❏ You've tried the cowboys, now try the indians (slogan on a van belonging to the Patel Brothers, builders and decorators)
- ❏ I wouldn't say she was an unattractive woman, but she had legs like bottled porridge (comedian Les Dawson)
- ❏ Public Hair (former name of a hairdressers in Nottingham)
- ❏ To be honest, 0–0 flatters both teams (TV football reporter Ivan Gaskell)
- ❏ You need a Tac flap (said to Japanese colleague Takamori ('Tak') who had just locked himself out of his flat)
- ❏ Cool House; Shagtag; Playboy Mansion; Inferno; High Voltage; Love Zoo; BlowPop; Godskitchen; Escape; Time Flies, The Mothership Convention; Roar; The Gallery; FabricLive; Eat Your Own Ears; Stretch; Ultraphunk; Naughty But Nices; Lush; Death Disco; I-Candy; Dedbeat 4; Trash; THIS!; Klub Sub; Sunrise; Warm/Sonar Kollektiv; Raucous; Scream; Promise; Miss Moneypenny's; Fabric; NYC Deep; The Boutique; Frantic Presents Timeless (names of clubs and club-nights in the UK Midlands in April 2004)

How do these examples differ from more 'literary' or artistic forms of creativity?

Creative howlers
The following are all examples of what teachers call 'howlers' produced in public examinations by British 16-year-olds, collected from a variety of sources. What is their status as creative objects, and how has their status changed by being reproduced here? How much creative work do you have to do as a reader for each one? Where does the humour come from: the author, the text, you or somewhere else?

1 Ancient Egypt was inhabited by mummies and they all wrote in hydraulics. They lived in the Sarah Dessert and traveled by Camelot. The climate of the Sarah is such that the inhabitants have to live elsewhere.

2 Moses led the Hebrew slaves to the Red Sea, where they made unleavened bread which is bread made without any ingredients. Moses went up on Mount Cyanide to get the ten commandments. He died before he ever reached Canada.

3 Actually, Homer was not written by Homer but by another man of that name.

4 Joan of Arc was burnt to a steak and was cannonized by Bernard Shaw. Finally Magna Carta provided that no man should be hanged twice for the same offence.

5 In midevil times most people were alliterate. The greatest writer of the futile ages was Chaucer, who wrote many poems and verses and also wrote literature.

6 Another story was William Tell, who shot an arrow through an apple while standing on his son's head.

7 Queen Elizabeth was the 'Virgin Queen.' As a queen she was a success. When she exposed herself before her troops they all shouted 'hurrah.'

8 It was an age of great inventions and discoveries. Gutenberg invented removable type and the Bible. Another important invention was the circulation of blood. Sir Walter Raleigh is a historical figure because he invented cigarettes and started smoking. And Sir Francis Drake circumcised the world with a 100 foot clipper.

9 One of the causes of the Revolutionary War was the English put tacks in their tea. Also, the colonists would send their parcels through the post without stamps. Finally the colonists won the War and no longer had to pay for taxis. Delegates from the original 13 states formed the Contented Congress. Thomas Jefferson, a Virgin, and Benjamin Franklin were two singers of the Declaration of Independence. Franklin discovered electricity by rubbing two cats backwards and declared, 'A horse divided against itself cannot stand.' Franklin died in 1790 and is still dead.

10 *Give an example of a sentence with a direct and indirect object.* 'She was a cat and a dog.'

Creativity and singularity

Derek Attridge defines *singularity* (see also A7) as follows:

The singularity of a cultural object consists in its difference from all other such objects, not simply as a particular manifestation of general rules but as a peculiar nexus within the culture that is perceived as resisting or exceeding all pre-existing general determinations. Singularity, that is to say, is generated not by a core of irreducible materiality or vein of sheer contingency to which the cultural frameworks we use cannot penetrate but by a configuration of general properties that, in constituting the entity (as it exists in a particular time and place), go beyond the possibilities pre-programmed by a culture's norms, the norms with which its members are familiar and through which most cultural products are understood. Singularity is not *pure*: it is constitutively impure, always open to contamination, grafting, accidents, reinterpretation, and recontextualization. Nor is it inimitable: on the contrary, it is eminently imitable, and may give rise to a host of imitations.

Strictly speaking, therefore, singularity, like alterity and inventiveness, is not a property but an event, the event of singularizing which takes place in reception: it does not occur outside the responses of those who encounter and thereby constitute it. It is produced, not given in advance; and its emergence is also the beginning of its erosion, as it brings about the cultural changes necessary to accommodate it.

(Attridge 2004: 63–4)

❏ How does Attridge's notion of singularity relate to older concepts such as uniqueness, deviance, defamiliarisation, intertextuality, the evolution of genre and canonisation?
❏ What do you think are the degrees of individuality and communality in the concept of creativity?
❏ What are the limits of improvisation or play? Are they set by the genre, by the function, by institutions or simply by the desires of the speaker?
❏ Consider the role of creativity not just in the construction and maintenance of objects but also of our public and private selves.

Creativity and linguistic study

In the following passage, the Marxist thinker Mikhail Bakhtin – writing as 'V.N. Vološinov' – considers the social process of creation and subsequent systematisation. Writing in the 1920s, he queries the power of linguistics as a formal systematic study to be able to account for the 'dialogic' and polyvalent richness of viewpoints and ideologies in language.

True creators – the initiators of new ideological trends – are never formalistic systematizers. Systematization comes upon the scene during an age which feels itself in command of a ready-made and handed-down body of authoritative thought. A creative age must first have passed; then and only then does the business of formalistic systematizing begin – an undertaking typical of heirs and epigones [successors who do not live up to their illustrious forebears] who feel themselves in possession of someone else's, now voiceless word. Orientation in the dynamic flow of generative process can never be of the formal, systematizing kind. Therefore, formal, systematizing grammatical thought could have developed to its full scope and power only on the material of an alien, dead language, and only could have done so provided that that language had already, to a significant degree, lost its affective potency – its sacrosanct and authoritative character. With respect to living language, systematic, grammatical thought must inevitably adopt a conservative position, i.e., it must interpret living language as if it were already perfected and ready-made and thus must look upon any sort of innovation in language with hostility. Formal, systematic thought about language is incompatible with living, historical understanding of language. From the system's point of view, history always seems merely a series of accidental transgressions.

Linguistics [. . .] is oriented toward the isolated, monologic utterance. Linguistic monuments comprise the material for study, and the passively understanding mind of the philologist is brought to bear on that material. Thus all the work goes on within the bounds of some given utterance. As for the boundaries that demarcate the utterance as a whole entity, they are perceived faintly or sometimes not at all. Research is wholly taken up in study of immanent connections on the inside territory of the utterance. [. . .] The structure of a complex sentence (a period) – that is the furthest limit of linguistic reach. The structure of a whole utterance is something linguistics leaves to the competence of other disciplines – to rhetoric and poetics. [. . .] When we relegate a literary work to the history of language as a system, when we regard it only as a document of language, we lose access to its forms as the forms of a literary whole. There is a world of difference between referring a work to the system of language and refer-ring a work to the concrete unity of literary life, and that difference is insurmountable on the grounds of abstract objectivism.

(Vološinov 1996: 78–9)

❏ Can you think of historical examples of the sort of process Bakhtin invokes at the beginning of this piece: creative innovation followed by an attempt to system-atise and regularise the novel concept or usage?

❏ Do you agree that grammatical description is always and necessarily conserva-tive? What do you think of Bakhtin's later characterisation of linguistics? The linguistics of his time was bounded by the sentence: how do later innovations in linguistics force us to revise his arguments, or do they still retain their validity? Consider the impact of developments such as pragmatics (see strand 4), schema theory (B9) or cognitive linguistics (strand 8).

❏ You might compare Bakhtin's thinking here with the later position adopted by integrationism (see B9 and D9). Bakhtin's sense of the social fabric in which language resides is informed by a Marxist perception of ideology and power relationships. You could read more extensively in integrationism to discover whether the modern argument is a development or a refutation of Bakhtin's thinking.

C8   **MAKING METAPHORS**

Metaphor can be seen as a readerly strategy for resolving deviant language, as well as a textual pattern. In this unit, we present material that allows you to consider the effect of the form of metaphor, the status of unintentional metaphor, and two uncompromising views of the metaphoricity of all language and thought.

Metaphorical forms

A conceptual metaphor, such as LANGUAGE IS AN OBJECT, can be realised in a range of stylistic forms:

Simile, analogy and *extended metaphor*	'Your argument is like a parcel. It gets passed around, becoming more and more tatty and degraded, until eventually it's as if it just falls apart from over-use'
Copula constructions	'In the beginning was the word'
Apposition and other *parallelisms*	'Language, the loaded weapon'
Partitive and *genitive expressions*	'Words are the currency of the world' 'The word on the street'
Premodification and *compounds*	'Wordsmith' 'Newspeak'
Grammatical metaphor	'He didn't keep his word' 'I give you my word'
Sentence metaphor (including *negation*)	'Do you get my meaning?' 'The pen is mightier than the sword' 'Sticks and stones may break my bones but words can never harm you' 'Chop the sentence up'
Fiction and *allegory*	*The Phantom Tollbooth* by Norton Juster, in which words are real objects and characters, or allegories such as *Everyman, Piers Plowman,* or *Pilgrim's Progress* where words such as 'Patience' are characters.

Taking other common conceptual metaphors (see B6 and B8), try to express each one in all of these different stylistic realisations. How does the form of a metaphoric expression alter or give a shading to its meaning? How does this experiment affect your view of the nature of metaphor?

Misfiring metaphors

The following are all real utterances collected from a variety of sources (literary texts, students' essays, television commentary, and stand-up comedy). For each, something has clearly misfired: can you determine why each example of deviant language or simple oddity is unlikely to be resolved with a straightforward metaphorical reading? What else is going on with these examples of language use? How do they exploit the natural process of human figuration?

1   The little boat gently drifted across the pond exactly the way a bowling ball wouldn't.
2   And the crowd are literally glued to their seats.
3   Her eyes were like two brown circles with big black dots in the centre.
4   Her vocabulary was as bad as, like, whatever.
5   He was as tall as a six-foot-three-inch tree.
6   The hailstones leaped from the pavement, just like maggots when you fry them in hot grease.
7   Long separated by cruel fate, the star-crossed lovers raced across the grassy field toward each other like two freight trains, one having left York at 6:36 p.m. travelling at 55 mph, the other from Peterborough at 4:19 p.m. at a speed of 35 mph.
8   John and Mary had never met. They were like two hummingbirds who had also never met.
9   You can literally see history unfolding in front of you.
10 The thunder was ominous sounding, much like the sound of a thin sheet of metal being shaken backstage during the storm scene in a play.
11 The red brick wall was the colour of a brick-red crayon.
12 The young fighter had a hungry look, the kind you get from not eating for a while.
13 He was as lame as a duck. Not the metaphorical lame duck either, but a real duck that was actually lame. Maybe from stepping on a land mine or something.
14 I was busy as the blue-arsed proverbial.
15 It came down the stairs looking very much like something no one had ever seen before.
16 The sky was the colour of television tuned to a dead channel.
17 The ballerina rose gracefully *en pointe* and extended one slender leg behind her, like a dog at a lamppost.
18 The revelation that his marriage of 30 years had disintegrated because of his wife's infidelity came as a rude shock, like a surcharge at a formerly surcharge-free cashpoint.
19 The dandelion swayed in the gentle breeze like an oscillating electric fan set on medium.
20 It hurt the way your tongue hurts after you accidentally staple it to the wall.

Metaphor and truth

The diametric opposite of Aristotle's view of metaphor as merely an 'ornament to the sense' is to be found in Friedrich Nietzsche's essay 'On truth and lying in a non-moral sense'. He begins by asking, 'What is a word?', questioning the supposed relationship between the object the word is supposed to describe and a physical reaction to that object.

The 'thing-in-itself' (which would be, precisely, pure truth, truth without consequences) is impossible for even the creator of language to grasp [. . .]. He designates only the relations of things to human beings, and in order to express them he avails himself of the boldest metaphor! The image is then imitated by a sound: second metaphor! And each time there is a complete leap from one sphere into the heart of another, new sphere. [. . .] We believe that when we speak of trees, colours, snow, and flowers, we have knowledge of the things themselves, and yet we possess only metaphors of things which in no way correspond to the original entities. [. . .]

Let us consider in particular how concepts are formed; each word immediately becomes a concept, not by virtue of the fact that it is intended to serve as a memory (say) of the unique, utterly individualised, primary experience to which it owes its existence, but because at the same time it must fit countless other, more or less similar cases, i.e. cases which, strictly speaking, are never equivalent, and thus nothing other than non-equivalent cases. Every concept comes into being by making equivalent that which is non-equivalent. Just as it is certain that no leaf is ever exactly the same as any other leaf, it is equally certain that the concept 'leaf' is formed by dropping these individual differences arbitrarily, by forgetting those features which differentiate one thing from another, so that the concept then gives rise to the notion that something other than leaves exists in nature, something which would be 'leaf', a primal form, say, from which all leaves were woven, drawn, delineated, dyed, curled, painted – but by a clumsy pair of hands, so that no single example turned out to be a faithful, correct, and reliable copy of the primal form. [. . .]

What, then, is truth? A mobile army of metaphors, metonymies, anthropomorphisms, in short a sum of human relations which have been subjected to poetic and rhetorical intensification, translation, and decoration, and which, after they have been in use for a long time, strike a people as firmly established, canonical, and binding; truths are illusions of which we have forgotten that they are illusions, metaphors which have become worn by frequent use and have lost all sensuous vigour, coins which, having lost their stamp, are now regarded as metal and no longer as coins.

(Nietzsche 1999: 144–6)

❏ Nietzsche prefigures many of the concerns of modern linguistic theory here: schema theory, conceptual metaphor, referentiality, cognitive modelling and prototype theory. It would be instructive to follow up your reading in any of these areas while thinking back to Nietzsche's views. How do his ideas correspond with these more recent approaches?

❏ How do you interpret the metaphorical rhetoric of Nietzsche's own writing here? How would his argument appear different if you try to substitute some of his metaphors?

❏   If Aristotle and Nietzsche represent the opposite extremes of our understanding
    of metaphor, where do you stand in relation to this argument?

In the following passage, the phenomenologist Emmanuel Levinas draws
Nietzsche's view to its conclusion. He points out that the ubiquity of metaphor entails
a constant remaking of meaning on every occasion of use. You might compare this
with psychologist Ray Gibbs's (2003) notion of meanings being 'soft-assembled' as
and when they are needed (see B6). Or you might place Levinas's argument in relation
to the way in which a text-world is modelled in cognitive linguistics (see Werth 1999,
and B7).

> But a metaphor – the reference to an absence – can also be taken as an
> excellence that belongs to an order quite different from pure receptivity. The
> absence to which the metaphor leads would then not be another given
> but still to come or already past. The meaning would not be the consola-
> tion for a delusive perception but would only *make perception possible.* Pure
> receptivity, in the sense of a pure sensible without any meaning, would be
> only a myth or an abstraction. [. . .] There is no given already possessing
> identity; no given could enter thought simply through a shock against the
> wall of receptivity. To be given to consciousness, to sparkle for it, would
> require that the given first be placed in an illuminated horizon – like a word,
> which gets the gift of being understood from the context to which it refers.
> The meaning would be the very illumination of this horizon. But this
> horizon does not result from an addition of absent data, since each datum
> would already need a horizon so as to be able to be defined and given. This
> notion of horizon or *world*, conceived after the model of a context and
> ultimately after the model of a language and a culture – with everything
> that is historically adventitious and 'already happened' involved – will be
> the locus in which meaning would then be located.
>   Already words are seen not to have isolable meanings, such as those in
> dictionaries, which one might reduce to some content or given. They could
> not be congealed into a literal meaning. In fact there would be no literal
> meaning. Words do not refer to contents which they would designate, but
> first, laterally, to other words. Despite the mistrust Plato shows for written
> language (and even, in the seventh letter, for all language), he teaches in the
> *Cratylus* that even the names given to the gods – the proper names attached,
> conventionally, as signs, to individual beings – refer, through their ety-
> mology, to other words which are not proper names. In addition, language
> refers to the positions of the one that listens and the one that speaks, that
> is, to the contingency of their history. To try to inventory up all the contexts
> of language and of the positions in which the interlocutors can find them-
> selves would be a demented undertaking. Each word meaning is at the
> confluence of innumerable semantic rivers.
>   (Levinas 1996: 36–7)

Towards the end here, Levinas attacks the sort of language study which would try to attain predictive power by identifying and quantifying all the possible permutations of text, co-text and context involved in the utterances of interlocutors. The criticism applies to forms of historical linguistics, philology and pure descriptive linguistics, as well as to forms of historicism that seek to place the meanings of texts in a context that is presumed to be recoverable. Do you have a defence of such archaeological exploration of language that could be raised against Levinas's view? You might like to consider your own thinking before these ideas are developed in the next unit.

CREATING INTERPRETATIONS

Reading and interpretation have been the key issues in this strand so far. In this unit, you are invited to consider the limits and nature of interpretation by addressing different dimensions of the same problem. We start with a science fictional text, often a good place to start a theoretical discussion.

Therolinguistics

In Ursula Le Guin's 1974 short story, 'The Author of the Acacia Seeds and other Extracts from the *Journal of the Association of Therolinguistics*', she imagines a new branch of linguistics devoted to investigating the 'languages' of animals, insects, and even the 'non-communicative' languages of plants and rocks. The following is an extract from a scent-script left on emptied seed-pods in an ant colony. It accompanies various other apparently revolutionary messages:

> *Seeds 30–31*
>   Eat the eggs! Up with the Queen!
>   There has already been considerable dispute over the interpretation of the phrase on Seed 31. It is an important question, since all the preceding seeds can be fully understood only in the light cast by this ultimate exhortation. Dr Rosbone ingeniously argues that the author, a wingless neuter-female worker, yearns hopelessly to be a winged male, and to found a new colony, flying upward in the nuptial flight with a new Queen. Though the text certainly permits such a reading, our conviction is that nothing in the text *supports* it – least of all the text of the immediately preceding seed, No. 30: 'Eat the eggs!' This reading, though shocking, is beyond disputation.
>   We venture to suggest that the confusion over Seed 31 may result from an ethnocentric interpretation of the word 'up'. To us, 'up' is a 'good'

direction. Not so, or not necessarily so, to an ant. 'Up' is where the food comes from, to be sure; but 'down' is where security, peace, and home are to be found. 'Up' is the scorching sun; the freezing night; no shelter in the beloved tunnels; exile; death. Therefore we suggest that this strange author, in the solitude of her lonely tunnel, sought with what means she had to express the ultimate blasphemy conceivable to an ant, and that the correct reading of Seeds 30–31, in human terms, is:

Eat the eggs! Down with the Queen!

The desiccated body of a small worker was found beside Seed 31 when the manuscript was discovered. The head had been severed from the thorax, probably by the jaws of a soldier of the colony. The seeds, carefully arranged in a pattern resembling a musical stave, had not been disturbed. (Ants of the soldier caste are illiterate; thus the soldier was presumably not interested in the collection of useless seeds from which the edible germs had been removed.) No living ants were left in the colony, which was destroyed in a war with a neighbouring anthill at some time subsequent to the death of the Author of the Acacia Seeds.

(Le Guin 1974: 1–3)

Use this passage to discuss the following issues of how interpretation proceeds.

❏ Do you think a 'therolinguistics' (from the Greek 'theros' for animal?) would ever be possible? Or put another way, would you have to have experienced life embodied as an ant to be able to speak 'antese'?
❏ The language of the ant stands for the language of any other person who doesn't share the reader's culture. Can the communicativeness of language bridge these distances? How much difference would prevent communication: geographical distance, historical distance, political differences, gender differences, class differences, age differences, religious differences, species differences? Think of real examples.
❏ How do you read Le Guin's message here? For example, is it significant that the revolutionary ant is (sort of) female? What then is Le Guin's message in having the revolutionary individual destroyed by the colony, which is in turn destroyed by war? Whatever your interpretation, try to work out where it comes from.

The start of interpretation

Imagine you have just finished discussing Emily Brontë's novel *Wuthering Heights* with a group of friends. Now imagine you have just closed the last page. Now imagine you are reading the middle of the novel. Now imagine you are reading the first page. Now imagine you are looking at the cover. Now imagine you are flicking through the book in a bookshop just before buying it. Now imagine you are going into the bookshop with the sole intention of buying Emily Brontë's *Wuthering Heights*. Now imagine why you have decided to go and buy that novel. Now imagine the previous day. At which point did you start reading *Wuthering Heights*? At which point did you finish reading it? Where does your interpretation come from?

Misreadings

❏   Can there be such a thing as *misreading*? How might it be identified or measured? Take a text that is well known to you, and produce a deliberate misreading of it. You might create a reading that is as ludicrous as you can imagine, or one that is at least in touch with what the text is usually taken to mean. (For example, you could take Shakespeare's *Macbeth* as a tourist campaign for holidaying in Scotland, or the US Constitution as working rules for a farm, or even Hitler's *Mein Kampf* as a hilarious and ironic send-up of an anti-Semitic rant. The more passionately held views on your choice of text, the better.) Defend your reading against attack by other people.

❏   How do we get beyond notions of reading as information extraction? What is the role of the texture of a text or utterance, its aesthetic qualities, its rhetorical and stylistic patterning? Can message and texture be separated like this? You might try to take a text that you think has a prominent texture (like a song lyric, a favourite poem, lullaby or nursery rhyme, or a football chant) and deliberately destroy its texture by rewriting it. Feel free to alter any aspect of the language, or you might imagine the text performed in a completely unfamiliar circumstance: a football chant in a job interview; a lullaby on a railway station announcement system; or even a song lyric written down on a CD sleeve, for example. Does what you are left with convey the same message as the original?

Re-readings

Roy Harris writes:

> Within an integrational framework, the challenge of finding a solution to the Heraclitian problem of stepping into the same context twice is not difficult to meet. The context will be 'the same' when it is perceived by the participants as being 'the same' in communicationally relevant aspects. But that perception, clearly, may vary from one participant to another. Consider how a conversation between *A* and *B* might be affected by the arrival of *C*. Depending on the relationships between the three persons, on the topic of conversation, on the relevance of that topic to the continuance of the conversation, on whether *C* was expected, etc., *C*'s arrival might or might not be perceived as creating a new context. Or it might do so for *A* but not for *B*, depending on their respective willingness to say certain things in *C*'s presence, etc. All conversation involves an ongoing process of contextualization and recontextualization of discourse by the participants. A single remark may suffice to 'change the context' or to prompt a reassessment of everything that has been said hitherto. The 'same context' is a function of that continuous monitoring of discourse that participation in discourse itself

requires. All one can say in general is that certain changes in the bio-mechanical, macrosocial and circumstantial conditions might well be expected to provoke a recontextualization, and some almost certainly will.

(Harris 1998: 105)

❏   What do the inverted commas around 'the same' and the 'same context' mean? Is this statement a compromise on the integrationist denial of the text/context segregation or not? Can an integrationist use the notion of 'contextualization' – what does it mean? What sort of things might an integrationist investigator actually do?

❏   How is re-reading different from reading? Perhaps more importantly, how is reading for the third time different from the first re-reading? For example, in a crime fiction narrative, do you read for informational clues the first time before you discover the murderer, but read more for the 'texture' of the narrative the second time when there are no suprises? Are there no surprises on repeated readings? It may be that integrationalism is right to say there can be no repetition or synonymy in language, but the miniscule divergences in repeated meanings might mean that this conclusion is negligible. What do you think?

Reading and interpretation

We can distinguish several different sorts of 'reading', as follows:

R1:	Mechanical eye-movements	muscular and optical
R2:	Motivated eye-movements	optical and perceptual
R3:	Visual field texturing	perceptual and cognitive
R4:	Symbol recognition	cognitive and social
R5:	Sense realisation	social and cultural
R6:	Discourse processing	textual competence
R7:	World creation	the construction of coherence
R8:	World management	maintenance and manipulation
R9:	World texturing	the affective dimension
R10:	Significance assignment	primary local evaluation
R11:	Salience assignment	evaluation related to self
R12:	Value assignment	evaluation related to culture

Can you think of any other forms of reading? Which of these can be measured experimentally, and which directly? Would you want to bracket any of these levels together? Taken all together, do these levels of reading amount cumulatively to a rank-structure for *interpretation*? If not, why not?

Section D

EXTENSION:
READINGS OF
LANGUAGE IN THEORY

D1

Deborah Cameron

GENDER

The reading for this strand on issues of gender and language broadens the topic into the whole sphere of language, identity, and political intervention in language. In her book, *Verbal Hygiene*, Deborah Cameron (1995) places feminist intervention in language in the context of popular discourse about language. The term 'verbal hygiene' is used for all those discursive practices which aim to intervene in the system and practice of language, to 'tidy it up' or regulate it. She identifies the metaphorical equation of social order and linguistic order, to the extent that 'ordering' language is magically regarded as a means of making society more orderly.

On the state of the state of the language

Deborah Cameron (reprinted from *Verbal Hygiene*, London: Routledge, 1995: pp. 214–19).

Our commonplace narratives about language are themselves a kind of verbal hygiene: they are bits of discourse whose function is to tidy up the messiness of linguistic phenomena and package them neatly in forms that make sense; they do not have to be consistent with one another to fulfill this function. I do not doubt that we need stories about language, just as we need creation myths and botanic classification systems and theories about the dimensions of the universe or the causes of disease, to give us a better grasp of the world we inhabit. But I do think that in the case of language we are especially tenacious in clinging to stories that distort and mystify far more than they explain.

Against nature

Stories which represent language as solely or primarily a 'natural' phenomenon are problematic, whether they are written in the scientific jargon of experts or the vernacular of popular cliché. What they distort and mystify is our relationship to language and the extent of our responsibility for shaping it. Natural forces operate irrespective of what humans say, do or believe about them (the apple fell before Newton; the rain comes or doesn't come whether you take readings from a satellite or pray to the gods), but social practices, even at their most habitual and unreflective, do not work in the same mechanical way. Language-using is a social practice: what people think language is, or should be, makes a difference to the way they use it, and therefore to what it becomes.

We may pay lip-service to the idea of language as a 'living thing', impervious to our efforts to exert control over it, but [. . .] much of our behaviour belies this rhetoric. The notion of linguistic 'naturalness' is one people deploy strategically, to suit the needs of the moment. If they dislike a particular change, such as the loss of the apostrophe or the spread of the glottal stop, they will conveniently forget that change is meant to be 'natural', and demand that it be halted; conversely, if the object of disapproval is clearly not a 'natural' development – if it is, say, a feminist demand for 'non-sexist language' – its opponents will criticize it as unwarranted interference with nature.

Deborah
Cameron

The fact is that we are constantly intervening in language, whether in support of
what we perceive as the *status quo* or in pursuit of something different. We are con-
vinced that [. . .] 'some kinds of language really are more worthwhile than others', and
we regularly act on that conviction. We think and argue about the words we use; we
correct the speech and writing of our children (and our students); we look things up
in usage guides and dictionaries; some of us increase our word power with the *Reader's
Digest*, while others take courses in Elocution or Neurolinguistic Programming, or join
societies devoted to such linguistic causes as spelling reform, Esperanto and even
Klingon. Activities like these are difficult to square with an account according to which
language-using is as unreflective as digestion, and language change as natural as the
phases of the moon.

To the extent that we can identify a 'state of the language', therefore, we should
acknowledge that it is not simply a phenomenon of nature, at which we marvel from
a distance: our own actions have played a part in producing it, and they will also
play a part in maintaining or changing it. It must also be acknowledged, however,
that these actions do not only reflect our concerns and beliefs about *language*: other
motivations influence the things we do, or would like to do, with words.

The social functions of verbal hygiene

I argued [earlier] that verbal hygiene arises out of the normative character of language-
using as a human social activity. Our propensity to make reflexive critical judgements
on language use has an obvious utility in the process of communication – enabling
us, for instance, to judge when something is amiss in interaction and perform what
discourse analysts call 'repair', to recognize and interpret metaphor and irony, and
in general to make, in the phrase familiar to linguists, 'infinite use of finite means'.
At the same time it is evident that the practices I have focused on [. . .] deploy our
critical metalinguistic abilities for purposes that are not necessarily or primarily to do
with the workings of language.

One function of verbal hygiene is quite simply to entertain. Interest and delight
in language for its own sake is a common motivation, and in some cases the main
one. The Klingon phenomenon is an obvious case in point, one which belongs with
the weird and wonderful obsessions of the 'anoraks' described in the preface [to
Cameron's book]. *The Wall Street Journal* reporter Carrie Dolan (1994) notes the existence of 'Klingon newsletters, Klingon Internet conversation groups and audio
cassettes with titles like "Conversational Klingon" and "Power Klingon"', and quotes
a spokesman for the Klingon Language Foundation defending people's enthusiasm for
such things as 'no more bizarre than sports trivia, or knowing the details of engines
of cars that haven't been manufactured in 20 years'.

Even this strangest of instances, though, hints at additional and perhaps 'deeper'
motivations. If splitting into factions over a Klingon Bible looks as absurd on the face
of things as the dispute between the Big- and Little-endians in *Gulliver's Travels*, it
may nevertheless be observed that the actual point at issue in the argument – essentially a question about the commensurability of different world-views – is part of a
long-running debate which has non-trivial applications back on Planet Earth. It has
frequently been pointed out that space fictions like *Star Trek* are in part moral and

political allegories. The Klingon project, similarly, offers a way to explore contentious issues imaginatively and thus 'safely'.

There is an analogy here, perhaps, with the debates on grammar and 'political correctness' [. . .]: in both cases, arguments about language provided a symbolic way of addressing conflicts about race, class, culture and gender. It is true that this symbolic deployment of language tends to obscure the true sources of disagreement and discomfort. I am not defending it, but simply pointing out that one common function of arguments about language is to stand in for arguments on subjects people are reluctant to broach more directly.

The Klingon project has a further social function: if there is no Klingon speech community in the conventional sense, the proliferation of discourse on Klingon has nevertheless brought into existence another kind of community, one in which some people may find a supportive social network, or at least a sense of belonging to some collectivity. This creation of community is a function of many apparently pointless pastimes, with their social apparatus of newsletters, conventions, swap-meets, and so forth; and it is no small matter in societies where more traditional forms of community can be hard to sustain. Several of the verbal hygiene practices [I have] examined [. . .] are partly about creating communities and networks where individuals can bond together through their engagement in a shared project.

The notion of belonging to a community or collectivity has its obverse (not converse: they are two sides of one coin) in the notion of individual identity, and this is also important in understanding verbal hygiene. Take [the story of] the upper-class woman prisoner who complained about other prisoners 'mangling the English language'. She wanted her audience to believe that she had borne without complaint the loss of her liberty, the humiliation of being labelled a common criminal, the lack of privacy and of luxury, the separation from loved ones; but that having to bear the other women's glottal stops and split infinitives (her own illustrative examples, not mine) had driven her to distraction. What are we to make of such a claim?

The most obvious non-literal interpretation of the woman's remark is that the story is 'really' about social class. Prison inmates are overwhelmingly poor people (that is what made the story of the upper-class prisoner newsworthy in the first place): thus the tale of a gentlewoman distressed by bad grammar and sloppy diction is actu-ally about her distress at being forced to associate with her social inferiors, at being treated as if she were no different from them. It is possible that she really did appre-hend the loss of her class status as the ultimate humiliation (though it is also possible that she was deliberately playing to a stereotype of upper-class women as plucky eccentrics for the benefit of the press). Yet it is significant that the woman fastened on *language* as the mark of class distinction. Had she deplored the way her cellmates smelled instead of the way they talked, she would have appeared as no more than a crashing snob. But in this context there is more mileage to be had from verbal hygiene than from personal hygiene, because language is symbolically inflected with a rich set of meanings, and resists reduction to any one of them.

The woman's concern about glottal stops and split infinitives need not be read solely as a matter of class. It is also a concern about preserving the orderliness of the world and the integrity of the self against the forces of disorder and fragmentation.

Deborah Cameron

The woman's determination to keep up linguistic standards functions in this prison story much as a daily routine of exercising or bible study might function in the account of a different kind of prisoner; as something people do in extreme and adverse circumstances to recapture a semblance of the dignity and self-respect they valued in their previous, 'normal' lives. The discourse of verbal hygiene offered the upper-class woman a way to articulate contradictory responses: on one level she could use it to figure her real distress at the assault on her sense of self that imprisonment represented, while on another level it could signify her difference from the other inmates and her consequent ability to rise above the 'real' humiliations of prison life.

Verbal hygiene in the prison story signified the maintenance of order and meaning in one individual's life; but as we have seen, it can also address analogous concerns at the level of the wider society. Style rules, grammatical rules, conventions of 'politically correct' language and the norms of 'assertive' or 'effective' communication all function (among other things) to tidy up messy or troublesome realities. The rules affirm basic distinctions like true/false, good/bad, correct/incorrect, and they insist that those distinctions are categorical absolutes, not matters of opinion or arbitrary convention, and not contingent judgements that could vary with the context. Thus some expressions are neutral, others biased; some are correct and others incorrect. [. . .] If directness or transparency is a virtue in one context, then it must be a virtue in all contexts. Messiness, fuzziness, uncertainty and relativism may be part of life, but if we try we can banish them from the more tractable sphere of language. In the words of Professor Grammar, a tiresome character who addresses foreign learners of English on the BBC World Service, 'there's a rule for everything'. If there isn't, we can make one.

The most fundamental desire to which verbal hygiene appeals is this desire for order, and the most fundamental fear it is used to ward off is the corresponding fear of disorder. The rhetoric of pro-grammar conservatives [. . .] renders this conjunction of desire and fear in an astonishingly literal form: despairing of the lawlessness of working-class youth, the bewildered, frightened and vindictive people encountered by Marilyn Butler [earlier in Cameron's book] really had pinned their hopes on the discipline of grammar – on linguistic law and order as a surrogate for the real thing.

The desire for order and the fear of chaos are at their most spectacular in the grammar example, but are also discernable elsewhere: in hyper-standardization as practised by stylistic authorities, for instance, where orderliness takes the form of an endless quest to make the rules exhaustive and absolute, dotting every i and crossing every t (it is interesting that we use this metaphor, specifically an image of *writing*, to signify an obsession with order more generally). The fear of chaos is often manifested in resistance to certain kinds of language change, so-called 'politically correct' language being a notable case in point. In this case, what is feared in particular is the disintegration of shared norms for using language, which raises the spectre of communicative breakdown.

Taken literally, this is an unfounded fear. Humans have always managed to communicate to their mutual satisfaction for various purposes in the absence of a shared language, and the differences which provoke most anxiety on this score are in any case too trivial linguistically to pose any serious threat to meaningful interaction. But the underlying fear is not the literal fear of being unable to make yourself understood. It is the fear that the meanings which anchor your own view of the world are not, after all, shared by everyone; which in turn expresses a more general fear of difference, otherness, relativity.

Activity   **Issues to consider**

❑   The basic methodological premise of much academic practice is that it should primarily be descriptive (this is especially true of those disciplines that like to think of themselves as being scientific or analytical). This has often been taken to mean that the writer should not participate in the phenomenon being described. Much feminist thinking, of course, takes the opposite view: as language users, we have a political responsibility to intervene in language. What do you think?

❑   It might be argued that women have had to learn to write like men through the ages, and are thus 'biliterate'. Men have not had to learn the same skill. Do you think men can write as women? Is there such a thing as a masculine or feminine text? Try to distinguish their features, then try to find a real example of each, or you could try to write one yourself.

❑   Find out what you can about the apparent cognitive differences between male and female brains. Is there anything natural in the ways men and women think and perceive their worlds, or are these actually discursive practices which are acquired and performed?

❑   Think about the extent to which language constitutes reality. Do particular forms of expression close off alternative patterns of thinking; or do they reinforce certain patterns by habituation; or do other non-linguistic factors have to be set alongside the patterns of language? You might think about examples of 'politically correct' language to help you.

D2   **RACE**

The reading for this strand on language and 'race' tackles the problem of whether it is possible to 'possess' language. As such, it calls into question some of our standard ideas about how language has been used (either by the colonisers or the colonised) in a colonial context. The extract from Jacques Derrida's *Monolingualism of the Other* (1998) draws upon Derrida's 'autobiographical' recollections of his childhood as a Jewish boy in Algeria, then under French rule and thus subject to the Vichy regime that collaborated with the German occupation of France during the Second World War. Derrida remarks on the fact that he has always thought of French, the official language of his Algerian childhood, as 'his' language. But, like all Jews, under the Vichy government, he was stripped of his French citizenship, and thus his right to the language. Left stateless, he also lacked other languages, such as Hebrew or the indigenous languages of the Algerian population, Arabic and Berber. His title, *Monolingualism of the Other*, refers to this divided sense of possession: he has only one language that he feels to be his; it does not belong to him.

Testifying in the language of the other

Jacques Derrida (reprinted from *Monolingualism of the Other, or, the Prosthesis of Origin*, Stanford: Stanford University Press, 1998: pp. 19–27).

Under this heading, the monolingualism of the other, let us exercise our imagination. Let us sketch out a figure. It will have only a vague *resemblance* to myself and to the kind of autobiographical anamnesis that always appears like the thing to do when one exposes oneself in the space of *relation*. Let us understand 'relation' in the sense of narration, the narration of the genealogical narrative, for example, but more generally as well, in the sense that Edouard Glissant [1990] imprints upon the expression when he speaks of *Poetics of Relation* [*Poétique de la Relation*], just as one could also speak of a politics of relation.

I therefore venture to present myself to you here, *ecce homo*, in parody, as the exemplary Franco-Maghrebian, but disarmed, with accents that are more naïve, less controlled, and less polished. *Ecce homo*, and do not smile, for a 'passion' would indeed appear to be at stake here, the martyrdom of the Franco-Maghrebian who from birth, since his birth but also from his birth on the other coast, his coast, has, at bottom, chosen and understood nothing, and who still suffers and testifies.

As regards so enigmatic a value as that of attestation, or even of exemplarity in testimony, here is a first question, the most general one, without the shadow of a doubt. What happens when someone resorts to describing an allegedly uncommon 'situation,' mine, for example, by testifying to it in terms that go beyond it, in a language whose generality takes on a value that is in some way structural, universal, transcendental, or ontological? When anybody who happens by infers the following: 'What holds for me, irreplaceably, also applies to all. Substitution is in progress; it has already taken effect. Everyone can say the same thing for themselves and of themselves. It suffices to hear me; I am the universal hostage.'

How does one describe this time, then; how does one designate this unique time? How does one determine this, an uncommon this whose uniqueness stems from testimony alone, from the fact that certain individuals in certain situations testify to the features of a structure nevertheless universal, revealing it, showing it, and allowing it to be read 'more vividly,' more vividly as one says, and because, above all, one says it about an injury, more vividly and *better than others*, and sometimes alone in their category? And what makes it more unbelievable is that they are alone in a genre which becomes in turn a universal example, thus interbreeding and accumulating the two logics, that of exemplarity and that of the host as hostage.

Jacques
Derrida

– That is not what surprises me most. For one can *testify* only to the unbeliev-able. To what can, at any rate, only be believed; to what appeals only to belief and hence to the given word, since it lies beyond the limits of proof, indication, certi-fied acknowledgment [*le constat*], and knowledge. Whether we like it or not, and whether we know it or not, when we ask others to take our word for it, we are already in the order of what is merely believable. It is always a matter of what is offered to faith and of appealing to faith, a matter of what is only 'believable' and hence as unbelievable as a miracle. Unbelievable because *merely* 'credible.' The order of attestation itself testifies to the miraculous, to the unbelievable believable: to what must be believed all the same, whether believable or not. Such is the truth to which I am appealing, and which must be believed, even, and especially, when I am lying or betraying my oath. Even in false testimony, this truth presupposes veracity – and not the reverse.

– Yes, and as I was saying, what makes it more unbelievable is that such indi-viduals testify this way in a language they speak, of course, one that they agree to speak in a certain way and up to a certain point . . .

– . . . in a certain way and up to a certain point, as one ought to say about any practice of language . . .

– . . . but one which they speak by presenting it, *in that very language, as the language of the other*. Such will have been, this time, the experience of the majority of us when we were speaking English at that meeting. But how would I do it, on this very spot, by speaking to you in French? By what right?

Here is an example. What did I do a short while ago by uttering a maxim such as 'I have only one language, yet it is not mine,' or 'we only ever speak one language'? What did I wish to do by continuing in approximately the following manner: 'Therefore there is no such thing as bilingualism or plurilingualism'? Or still, and multiplying the contradictions in this manner, 'We never speak only one language', therefore, 'There is nothing but plurilingualism'? So many apparently contradictory assertions (there is no such thing as *x*, there is nothing but *x*), so many claims of which I indeed believe, however, that, given the time, I would be capable of demon-strating the universal value. Anyone should be able to say 'I only have one language (yet, but, henceforth, lastingly [*à demeure*]) it is not mine.'

An immanent structure of promise or desire, an expectation without a horizon of expectation, informs all speech. As soon as I speak, before even formulating a promise, an expectation, or a desire *as such*, and when I still do not know what will happen to me or what awaits me at the end of a sentence, neither *who* nor *what* awaits whom or what, I am within this promise or this threat – which, from then on, gathers the language together, the promised or threatened language, promising all the way to the point of threatening and *vice versa*, thus gathered together in its very dissemi-nation. Since subjects competent in several languages *tend* to speak only one language, even where the latter is dismembering itself, and because it can only promise and

D

promise itself by threatening to dismember itself, a language can only speak itself of itself. One cannot speak of a language except in that language. Even if to place it outside itself.

Far from sealing off anything, this solipsism conditions the address to the other, it gives its word, or rather it gives the possibility of giving its word, it gives the given word in the ordeal of a threatening and threatened promise: monolingualism and tautology, the absolute impossibility of metalanguage. The impossibility of an absolute metalanguage, at least, for some *effects* of metalanguage, effects or relative phenomena, namely, relays of metalanguage 'within' a language, already introduce into it some translation and some objectification in progress. At the horizon, visible and miraculous, spectral but infinitely desirable, they allow the mirage of another language to tremble.

– What I am having some difficulty understanding is this entire vocabulary of having, habit, and possession of a language that would or would not be one's own – yours, for example. As if the possessive pronoun and adjective were, as far as language goes, proscribed here by language.

– On the part of one who speaks or writes the aforementioned language, this experience of monolingual solipsism is never one of belonging, property, power of mastery, pure 'ipseity' (hospitality or hostility) of whichever kind. Though the 'non-mastery . . . of an appropriated language' of which Glissant [1990] speaks qualifies, above all, more literally and more sensitively, some situations of 'colonial' alienation or historical servitude, this definition, so long as it is imprinted with the requisite inflections, also carries well beyond these determinate conditions. It also holds for what would be called the language of the master, the *hospes*, or the colonist.

Quite far from dissolving the always relative specificity, however cruel, of situations of linguistic oppression or colonial expropriation, this prudent and differentiated universalization must account, and I would even say that it is the only way one can account, for the *determinable* possibility of a subservience and a hegemony. And even account for a terror inside languages (inside languages there is a terror, soft, discreet, or glaring; that is our subject). For contrary to what one is often most tempted to believe, the master is nothing. And he does not have exclusive possession of anything. Because the master does not possess exclusively, and *naturally*, what he calls his language, because, whatever he wants or does, he cannot maintain any relations of property or identity that are natural, national, congenital, or ontological, with it, because he can give substance to and articulate [*dire*] this appropriation only in the course of an unnatural process of politico-phantasmatic constructions, because language is not his natural possession, he can, thanks to that very fact, pretend historically, through the rape of a cultural usurpation, which means always essentially colonial, to appropriate it in order to impose it as 'his own.' That is his belief; he wishes to make others share it through the use of force or cunning; he wants to make others believe it, as they do a miracle, through rhetoric, the school, or the army. It suffices for him, through whatever means there is, to make himself understood, to have his 'speech act' work, to create conditions for that, in order that he may be 'happy' ('felicitous' – which means, in this code, efficacious, productive, efficient, generative of the expected event, but sometimes anything but 'happy') and the trick is played, a *first trick* will have, at any rate, been played.

Liberation, emancipation, and revolution will necessarily be the second trick. It will provide freedom from the first while confirming a heritage by internalizing it, by reappropriating it – but only up to a certain point, for, as my hypothesis shows, there is never any such thing as absolute appropriation or reappropriation. Because there is no natural property of language, language gives rise only to appropriative madness, to jealousy without appropriation. Language speaks this jealousy; it is nothing but jealousy unleashed. It takes its revenge at the heart of the law. The law that, moreover, language itself is, apart from also being mad. Mad about itself. Raving mad.

(As this goes without saying and does not deserve any overly long development here, let us recall briefly, in passing, that this discourse on the ex-appropriation of language, more precisely, of the 'mark,' opens out onto a politics, a right, and an ethics: let us even go so far as to say that it is the only one with the power to do it, whatever the risks are, precisely because the undecidable ambiguity runs those risks and therefore appeals to the decision where it conditions, prior to any program and even any axiomatics, the right and the limits of a right to property, a right to hospitality, a right to *ipseity* in general, to the 'power' of the *hospes* himself, the master and possessor, particularly of himself – *ipse, compos, ipsissimus, despotes, potior, possidere*, to cite in no particular order a chain reconstructed by Benveniste of which we were speaking earlier.)

So much so that 'colonialism' and 'colonization' are only high points [*reliefs*], one traumatism over another, an increasing buildup of violence, the jealous rage of an essential *coloniality* and *culture*, as shown by the two names. A coloniality of culture, and, without a doubt, also of hospitality when the latter conditions and auto-limits itself into a law, however 'cosmopolitan' – as the Kant of perpetual peace and universal right wanted.

Consequently, anyone should be able to declare under oath: I have only one language and it is not mine; my 'own' language is, for me, a language that cannot be assimilated. My language, the only one I hear myself speak and agree to speak, is the language of the other.

This abiding 'alienation' [*aliénation à demeure*] appears, like 'lack,' to be constitutive. But it is neither a lack nor an alienation; it lacks nothing that precedes or follows it, it alienates no *ipseity*, no property, and no self that has ever been able to represent its watchful eye. Although this injunction issues a summons, lastingly [*mette en demeure à demeure*], nothing else 'is there' ever to watch over its past or future. This structure of alienation without alienation, this inalienable alienation, is not only the origin of our responsibility, it also structures the peculiarity [*le propre*] and property of language. It institutes the *phenomenon* of hearing-oneself-speak in order to mean-to-say [*pour vouloir dire*]. But here, we must say the *phenomenon* as *phantasm*. Let us refer for the moment to the semantic and etymological affinity that associates the phantasm to the *phainesthai*, to phenomenality, but also to the spectrality of the phenomenon. *Phantasma* is also the phantom, the double, or the ghost. We are there.

– Do you mean we belong among them?

– Who, upon reading and understanding us properly, here . . .

– Here?

– . . . or there, will dare to have someone believe the opposite? Who would dare claim to prove it? Being here in an element of which the spectral phantasmaticity cannot, under any circumstances, be reduced does not imply that political and historical terror is alleviated on that account, quite the contrary. For there are situations, experiences, and subjects who are, precisely, in a *situation* (but what does *situating* mean in this case?) to testify exemplarily to them. This exemplarity is no longer reducible to that of an example in a series . . . Rather, it would be the exemplarity – remarkable and remarking – that allows one to read in a more dazzling, intense, or even *traumatic* manner the truth of a universal necessity. The structure appears in the experience of the injury, the offense, vengeance, and the lesion. In the experience of terror. It is a traumatic event because at stake here are blows and injuries, scars, often murders, and sometimes collective assassinations. It is reality itself, the scope [*portée*] of any *férance*, of any reference as différance.

That being the case, what status must be assigned to this exemplarity of re-mark? How do we interpret the history of an example that allows the re-inscription of the structure of a universal law upon the body of an irreplaceable singularity in order to render it thus remarkable?

Already, this is an abyssal problem that we cannot treat here in its classical form. Even so, one must, still from the abyss, take note of a chance that is bound to complicate the deal or the folding, and involve the fold in dissemination, *as* dissemination. For it is in the form of a thinking of the unique, precisely, and not of the plural, as it was too often believed, that a thought of dissemination formerly introduced itself as a folding thought of the fold – and as a folded thought of the fold. Because the fold of such a *re-mark* is there, the replica or re-application of the quasi-transcendental or quasi-ontological within the phenomenal, ontical, or empirical example, and within the phantasm itself where the latter presupposes the trace in language, we are justifiably obliged to say at once that 'we only ever speak one language,' and 'we never speak only one language' or 'I only speak one language, (and, but, yet) it is not mine.'

For is the experience of language (or rather, before any discourse, the experience of the mark, the re-mark or the margin) not precisely what makes this *articulation* possible and necessary? Is that not what *gives rise* to this articulation between transcendental or ontological universality, and the exemplary or testimonial singularity of *martyred* existence? While evoking apparently abstract notions of the mark or the re-mark here, we are also thinking of scars. Terror is practiced at the expense of wounds inscribed on the body. We speak here of martyrdom and passion in the strict and quasi-etymological sense of these terms. And when we mention the body, we are naming the body of language and writing, as well as what makes them a thing of the body. We therefore appeal to what is, so hastily, named the body proper, which happens to be affected by the same ex-appropriation, the same 'alienation' without alienation, without any property that is forever lost or to be ever reappropriated.

Do you hear this word, *jamais*, in our language? And what about *sans*? Do you hear without ever understanding? That is what must, henceforth, be demonstrated in the scene thus created.

In what respect, therefore, can the passion of a Franco-Maghrebian martyr testify to this universal destiny which assigns us to a single language while prohibiting us from appropriating it, given that such an interdiction is linked to the very essence of language, or rather writing, to the very essence of the mark, the fold, and the re-mark?

Activity

Issues to consider

❏ Think about the form of the extract. Why might Derrida have chosen to write this supposedly autobiographical text in the form of a dialogue? What does this do to the idea of his text as a form of testimony? Think about how certain forms of language are used to make testimony believable. You might want to consider news reports or other autobiographical texts where someone is claiming to offer an account of her or his experience. Does Derrida's text differ from these kinds of witnessing, and if so, how?

❏ Much of this passage is concerned with the notion of exemplarity. Examples have a strange logic, in that they are always unique, but are always supposed to demonstrate a more generally applicable law (they are always an example *of* something). Think about how examples are used in language study. How have we used them in this book? What happens to ideas of context, intention, and the idea of text being authorised because of who speaks, when extracts and statements are taken as examples?

❏ Derrida mentions the 'absolute impossibility of metalanguage'. What do you think this means? Why might metalanguage be impossible? What consequences might this impossibility have for the study of language or for linguistics?

❏ There is currently a great deal of discussion of the relationship between language and the body. This applies not only to a consideration of 'race', but also of gender, class, age, and so on. What do you think this relationship is? Is it different in the cases of writing and speaking? What social, historical or cultural factors might influence this relationship? Think of examples both of how language is used by certain groups, and also of how those groups are represented in language.

SOCIETY

D3

Theodor W. Adorno

The work of Theodor W. Adorno, a leading member of the Frankfurt School, brought a powerful combination of German philosophy, Marxism and psychoanalysis to bear on a range of topics, including philosophy, art and literature, sociology, political theory and what he called the 'culture industry'. In this extract he offers a reading of one of Samuel Beckett's most extraordinary plays, *Endgame*. Or rather, he offers an explanation of why the play is in some respects unintelligible, and proposes that, in particular, it cannot be understood by philosophy. He argues instead that we must attempt to figure out 'the meaning of the fact that it has no meaning', as a way of thinking through the play's relation to social reality.

Understanding unintelligibility

Theodor W. Adorno (Reprinted from 'Trying to Understand *Endgame*', in *Notes to Literature*, vol. 1, New York: Columbia University Press, 1991, pp. 241–75).

Beckett's oeuvre has many things in common with Parisian existentialism. It is shot through with reminiscences of the categories of absurdity, situation, and decision or the failure to decide, the way medieval ruins permeate Kafka's monstrous house in the suburbs. Now and then the windows fly open and one sees the black, starless sky of something like philosophical anthropology. But whereas in Sartre the form – that of the *pièce à thèse* – is somewhat traditional, by no means daring, and aimed at effect, in Beckett the form overtakes what is expressed and changes it. The impulses are raised to the level of the most advanced artistic techniques, those of Joyce and Kafka. For Beckett absurdity is no longer an 'existential situation' diluted to an idea and then illustrated. In him literary method surrenders to absurdity without preconceived intentions. Absurdity is relieved of the doctrinal universality which in existentialism, the creed of the irreducibility of individual existence, linked it to the Western pathos of the universal and lasting. Beckett thereby dismisses existentialist conformity, the notion that one ought to be what one is, and with it easy comprehensibility of presentation. What philosophy Beckett provides, he himself reduces to cultural trash, like the innumerable allusions and cultural tidbits he employs, following the tradition of the Anglo-Saxon avant-garde and especially of Joyce and Eliot.

[. . . I]nterpretation of *Endgame* cannot pursue the chimerical aim of expressing the play's meaning in a form mediated by philosophy. Understanding it can mean only understanding its unintelligibility, concretely reconstructing the meaning of the fact that it has no meaning. Split off, thought no longer presumes, as the Idea once did, to be the meaning of the work, a transcendence produced and vouched for by the work's immanence. Instead, thought transforms itself into a kind of second-order material, the way the philosophical ideas expounded in Thomas Mann's *Magic Mountain* and *Doctor Faustus* have their fate as material does, a fate that takes the place of the sensuous immediacy that dwindles in the self-reflective work of art. Until now this transformation of thought into material has been largely involuntary, the plight of works that compulsively mistook themselves for the Idea they could not attain;

Theodor W. Adorno

Beckett accepts the challenge and uses thoughts *sans phrase* as clichés, fragmentary materials in the *monologue intérieur* that spirit has become, the reified residues of culture. Pre-Beckettian existentialism exploited philosophy as a literary subject as though it were Schiller in the flesh. Now Beckett, more cultured than any of them, hands it the bill: philosophy, spirit itself, declares itself to be dead inventory, the dreamlike leavings of the world of experience, and the poetic process declares itself to be a process of wastage.

[. . .]

Exhorted to play along, he responds with parody, parody both of philosophy, which spits out his dialogues, and of forms. Existentialism itself is parodied; nothing remains of its invariant categories but bare existence. The play's opposition to ontology, which outlines something somehow First and Eternal, is unmistakable in the following piece of dialogue, which involuntarily caricatures Goethe's dictum about *das alte Wahre*, what is old and true, a notion that deteriorates to bourgeois sentiment:

> HAMM: Do you remember your father.
> CLOV (wearily): Same answer. (Pause.) You've asked me these questions millions of times.
> HAMM: I love the old questions. (With fervor.) Ah, the old questions, the old answers, there's nothing like them!

Thoughts are dragged along and distorted, like the residues of waking life in dreams, *homo homini sapienti sat*. This is why interpreting Beckett, something he declines to concern himself with, is so awkward. Beckett shrugs his shoulders at the possibility of philosophy today, at the very possibility of theory. The irrationality of bourgeois society in its late phase rebels at letting itself be understood; those were the good old days, when a critique of the political economy of this society could be written that judged it in terms of its own *ratio*. For since then the society, has thrown its *ratio* on the scrap heap and replaced it with virtually unmediated control. Hence interpretation inevitably lags behind Beckett. His dramatic work, precisely by virtue of its restriction to an exploded facticity, surges out beyond facticity and in its enigmatic character calls for interpretation. One could almost say that the criterion of a philosophy whose hour has struck is that it prove equal to this challenge.

[. . .] Meaning nothing becomes the only meaning. The deadliest fear of the characters in the drama, if not of the parodied drama itself, is the fear, disguised as humour, that they might mean something.

> HAMM: We're not beginning to . . . to . . . mean something?
> CLOV: Mean something! You and I, mean something! (Brief laugh.) Ah that's a good one! (32–33)

With the disappearance of this possibility, which has long since been suppressed by the superior power of an apparatus in which individuals are interchangeable or superfluous, the meaning of language disappears as well. Irritated by the degenerate

Theodor W.
Adorno

clumsiness of the impulse of life in his parents' trashcan conversation and nervous because 'it doesn't end,' Hamm asks, 'What do they have to talk about? What does anyone still have to 'talk about?' (23). The play lives up to that question. It is built on the foundation of a prohibition of language, and it expresses that taboo in its own structure. But it does not escape the aporia of expressionist drama: that even where language tends to reduce itself to pure sound, it cannot divest itself of its semantic element, cannot become purely mimetic or gestural, just as forms of painting that are emancipated from objective representation cannot completely free themselves of resemblance to material objects. Once definitively separated from the values of signification, mimetic values become arbitrary and accidental and ultimately turn into a second-order convention. The way *Endgame* deals with this distinguishes it from *Finnegans Wake*. Instead of trying to liquidate the discursive element in language through pure sound, Beckett transforms it into an instrument of its own absurdity, following the ritual of the clown, whose babbling becomes nonsense by being presented as sense. The objective decay of language, that bilge of self-alienation, at once stereotyped and defective, which human beings' words and sentences have swollen up into within their own mouths, penetrates the aesthetic arcanum. The second language of those who have fallen silent, an agglomeration of insolent phrases, pseudo-logical connections, and words galvanized into trademarks, the desolate echo of the world of the advertisement, is revamped to become the language of a literary work that negates language [. . .]

A short dialogue follows:

CLOV: Do this, do that, and I do it. I never refuse. Why?
HAMM: You're not able to.
CLOV: Soon I won't do it any more.
HAMM: You won't be able to any more. (Exit Clov.) Ah the creatures, the creatures, everything has to be explained to them. (43)

Every day millions of bosses beat the fact that 'everything has to be explained to them' into their subordinates. Through the nonsense it is supposed to justify in that passage, however – Hamm's explanation negates his own command – the line not only casts a harsh light on the craziness of the cliché, which habit obscures, but also expresses what is deceptive about dialogue: the fact that those who are hopelessly estranged from one another can no more reach one another by conversing than the two old cripples in the trashcans. Communication, the universal law of the cliché, proclaims that there is no communication any more. The absurdity of talk does not unfold in opposition to realism but rather develops out of it. For by its very syntactic form – its logicity, its deductive relationships, its fixed concepts – communicative language postulates the law of sufficient cause. But this requirement is scarcely ever satisfied any more: when human beings converse with one another they are motivated in part by their psychology, the prelogical unconscious, and in part they pursue ends which, as ends of mere self-preservation, deviate from the objectivity whose illusory image is reflected in logical form.

Theodor W.
Adorno

[. . .]

The final history of the subject is made the theme of an intermezzo that can allow itself its symbolism because it reveals its own inadequacy and thereby the inadequacy of its meaning. The hybris of idealism, the enthronement of human meaning as the creator at the center of his creation, has entrenched itself in that 'bare interior' like a tyrant in his last days. There, with an imagination reduced to the smallest proportions, Hamm recapitulates what men once wanted to be, a vision of which they were deprived as much by the course of society as by the new cosmology, and which they nevertheless cannot let go of. Clov is his male nurse. Hamm has him push him in his wheelchair to the middle of the room, the room which the world has become and which is at the same time the interior of his own subjectivity:

HAMM: Take me for a little turn. (Clov goes behind the chair and pushes it forward.) Not too fast! (Clov pushes chair.) Right round the world! (Clov pushes chair.) Hug the walls, then back to the center again. (Clov pushes chair.) I was right in the center, wasn't I? (25)

The loss of a center which that parodies, because that center was already a lie, becomes the pitiful object of a nagging and impotent pedantry:

CLOV: We haven't done the round.
HAMM: Back to my place. (Clov pushes chair back to center.) Is that my place?
CLOV: I'll measure it.
HAMM: More or less! More or less!
CLOV (moving chair slightly): There!
HAMM: I'm more or less in the center?
CLOV: I'd say so.
HAMM: You'd say so! Put me right in the center!
CLOV: I'll go and get the tape.
HAMM: Roughly! Roughly! (Clov moves chair slightly.) Bang in the center! (26–7)

But what is being requited in this stupid ritual is not something the subject has done. Subjectivity itself is at fault; the fact that one exists at all. Heretically, original sin is fused with creation. Being, which existential philosophy trumpets as the meaning of being, becomes its antithesis. Panic fear of the reflex movements of the living not only serves as an incitement to indefatigable domination of nature; it is directed to life itself, as the cause of the catastrophe life has become.

HAMM: All those I might have helped. (Pause.) Helped! (Pause.) Saved. (Pause.) Saved! (Pause.) The place was crawling with them! (Pause. Violently.) Use your head, can't you, use your head, you're on earth, there's no cure for that! (68)

From which he draws the conclusion: 'The end is in the beginning and yet you go on' (69). The autonomous moral law reverses itself antinomically; pure domination of nature becomes the duty to exterminate, which was always lurking behind it.

> HAMM: More complications! (Clov gets down.) Not an underplot, I trust. (Clov moves ladder nearer window, gets up on it, turns telescope on the without.)

[In the German edition to which Adorno refers, the dialogue continues as follows:

> CLOV: Oi, oi, oi, oi!
> HAMM: A leaf? A flower? A toma . . . (he yawns) . . . to?
> CLOV (looking):   You'll get your tomatoes right away! Someone! There's someone there!
> HAMM   (stops yawning): Well, go wipe him out. (Clov gets down from the ladder. Softly.) Someone! (with trembling voice.) Do your duty! (78)]

A question addressed by Clov, the frustrated rebel, to his frustrated master passes judgment on the idealism from which this totalitarian concept of duty is derived:

> CLOV: Any particular sector you fancy? Or merely the whole thing? (73)

That sounds like a test of Benjamin's idea that a single cell of reality, truly contemplated, counterbalances the whole rest of the world. The totality, a pure positing by the subject, is the void. No statement sounds more absurd than this most rational of statements, which reduces 'everything' to an 'only,' the mirage of a world that can be dominated anthropocentrically. As rational as this utmost *Absurdum* may be, however, it is not possible to argue away the absurd aspect of Beckett's play solely because hasty apologetics and a desire for labels have appropriated it. *Ratio*, which has become completely instrumental, devoid of self-reflection and reflection on what it has disqualified, must inquire after the meaning that it itself has expunged. But in the state that makes this question necessary there is no answer left but the void that the question, as pure form, already is. The historical inevitability of this absurdity makes it seem ontological: that is the delusoriness of history itself. Beckett's drama demolishes it. The immanent contradiction of the absurd, the nonsense in which reason terminates, opens up the emphatic possibility of something true that cannot even be conceived of anymore. It undermines the absolute claim of the status quo, that which simply is the way it is. Negative ontology is the negation of ontology: it was history alone that produced what the mythical power of the timeless and eternal has appropriated. The historical fiber of situation and language in Beckett does not concretize, *more philosophico*, something ahistorical – precisely this practice on the part of existentialist dramatists is as alien to art as it is philosophically backward. Rather, what is eternal and enduring for Beckett is the infinite catastrophe; it is only

Theodor W.
Adorno

the fact that 'the earth is extinguished, though I never saw it lit' (81) that justifies Clov's answer to Hamm's question, 'Do you not think this has gone on long enough?': 'I've always thought so' (45). Prehistory lives on; the phantasm of eternity is only its curse. After Clov has told Hamm, who is completely paralyzed, what he has seen of the earth, which the latter ordered him to look at (72), Hamm confides to him, as though confiding his secret:

CLOV (absorbed):   Mmm.
HAMM: Do you know what it is?
CLOV (as before):   Mmm.
HAMM: I was never there. (74)

No one has ever set foot on the earth; the subject is not yet a subject. Determinate negation takes dramatic form through its consistent inversion. The two partners qualify their understanding that there is no nature anymore with the bourgeois phrase 'you exaggerate' (11). Presence of mind is the proven means of sabotaging reflection. It occasions the melancholy reflection:

CLOV (sadly):   No one that ever lived ever thought so crooked as we. (11)

Where they come closest to the truth, they sense, with double comedy, that their consciousness is false; this is how a situation that can no longer be reached by reflection is reflected. But the whole play is constructed by means of this technique of reversal. It transfigures the empirical world into what it had already been called in the late Strindberg and Expressionism. 'The whole house stinks of corpses . . . The whole universe' (46). Hamm, who responds, 'To hell with the universe,' is just as much a descendant of Fichte, who despises the world because it is nothing but raw materials and products, as he is the one who has no hope but the cosmic night, which he supplicates with poetic quotations. Absolute, the world becomes hell: nothing exists but it. Beckett uses typography to emphasize Hamm's statement: 'Beyond is the . . . [OTHER] hell' (26; capitals omitted in the English version). He lets a twisted secular metaphysics shine through, with a Brechtian commentary:

CLOV: Do you believe in the life to come?
HAMM: Mine was always that. (Exit Clov.) Got him that time! (49)

In this conception Benjamin's notion of dialectics at a standstill comes into its own:

HAMM: It will be the end and there I'll be, wondering what can have
          brought it on and wondering what can have . . . (he hesitates) . . .
          why it was so long coming. (Pause.) There I'll be, in the old
          refuge, alone against the silence and . . . (he hesitates) . . . the
          stillness. If I can hold my peace, and sit quiet, it will be all over,
          with sound, and motion, all over and done with. (69)

That stillness is the order that Clov allegedly loves and that he defines as the goal of his activities:

> CLOV: A world where all would be silent and still and each thing in its
>   last place, under the last dust. (57)

The Old Testament 'dust thou shalt become' is translated into: filth. Excretions become the substance of a life that is death. But the imageless image of death is an image of indifference, that is, a state prior to differentiation. In that image the distinction between absolute domination – the hell in which time is completely confined within space, in which absolutely nothing changes any more – and the messianic state in which everything would be in its right place, disappears. The last absurdity is that the peacefulness of the void and the peacefulness of reconciliation cannot be distinguished from one another. Hope skulks out of the world, which cannot conserve it any more than it can pap and bon-bons, and back to where it came from, death. From it the play draws its only consolation, a stoic one:

> CLOV: There are so many terrible things now.
> HAMM: No, no, there are not so many now. (44)

Consciousness gets ready to look its own end in the eye, as though it wanted to survive it the way these two have survived the destruction of their world. Proust, about whom Beckett wrote an essay in his youth, is said to have tried to record his own death throes; the notes were to be inserted into the description of Bergotte's death. *Endgame* carries out this intention as though it were a mandate bequeathed it in a will.

Issues to consider

☆ Activity

- ❏ It is common in both linguistic and literary study to look for meaning in a 'positivist' way. So examining questions of the relation between language and society might look for the way in which the world is described, or for a text's 'message'. This is what Adorno refers to when he mentions Jean-Paul Sartre's *pièce à thèse*, which means a work that wants to present an argument. What Beckett is doing, according to Adorno, is something rather different. What, then, is the nature of the relation between the text and the world that Adorno sees in Beckett's play? How is this communicated (if that is the right word) by the language of the text?
- ❏ Adorno claims that 'Beckett shrugs his shoulders at the possibility of philosophy today, at the possibility of theory'. Try to work out the argument that lies behind this idea. You may want to look at the play, to read about Beckett, or to read more Adorno to see where this idea fits. What are the consequences for a book such as this one, or for any theoretical project?
- ❏ One aspect of the play, and of Adorno's reading of it, is the significance of Beckett's use of quotation and cliché. How does quotation work, either in literary works or in speech, and what is it used for? How can we tell the difference between a quotation and a cliché?

❑ Bearing in mind that Beckett's text is a playscript, what account has Adorno taken of the form of the piece? Is genre or convention important in the determination of meaning? What might be added by a consideration of performance conditions? Does the question of genre or convention have significance for a linguistic analysis of a text?

PERFORMATIVITY

Influenced by speech act theory, it is common now to see certain kinds of language use as having a direct influence on the world. In the following extract from Judith Butler (1997), the connections between law and language are explored through limit cases such as 'hate speech' or 'fighting words'. Butler comes at these questions from both ends, as it were, asking how non-verbal signs such as a burning cross can be said to make a statement, and how speeches can be thought of as acts. At stake in such debates is the right to free speech, but also the right to live free from threats, verbal or non-verbal. At stake also, then, is the political, legal and cultural status of language.

The performance of the law

Judith Butler (reprinted from *Excitable Speech*, London: Routledge, 1997: pp. 52–60, 64–5).

In two recent cases, the Supreme Court has reconsidered the distinction between protected and unprotected speech in relation to the phenomenon of 'hate speech.' Are certain forms of invidious speech to be construed as 'fighting words,' and if so, are they appropriately considered to be a kind of speech unprotected by the first Amendment? In the first case, *R.A.V. v. St. Paul*, 112 S. Ct. 2538, 120 L. Ed. 2d 305 (1992), the ordinance in question was one passed by the St. Paul City Council in 1990, and read in part as follows:

> Whoever places on public or private property a symbol, object, appellation, characterization or graffiti, including, but not limited to, a burning cross or Nazi swastika, which one knows or has reasonable grounds to know arouses anger, alarm, or resentment in others, on the basis of race, color, creed, religion or gender commits disorderly conduct and shall be guilty of a misdemeanor.
>
> [St Paul City Council 1990]

A white teenager was charged under this ordinance after burning a cross in front of a black family's house. The charge was dismissed by the trial court but reinstated by the Minnesota State Supreme Court; at stake was the question whether the ordinance itself was 'substantially overbroad and impermissably content based.' The defense contended that the burning of the cross in front of the black family's house was to be construed as an example of protected speech. The State Supreme Court overturned the decision of the trial court, arguing first that the burning of the cross could not be construed as protected speech because it constituted 'fighting words' as defined in *Chaplinsky v. New Hampshire*, 315 U.S. 568, 572 (1942), and second, that the reach of the ordinance was permissible considering the 'compelling government interest in protecting the community against bias-motivated threats to public safety and order.' *In Re Welfare of R.A.V.*, 464 N.W.2 507, 510 (Minn[esota], 1991).

The United States Supreme Court reversed the State Supreme Court decision, reasoning first that the burning cross was not an instance of 'fighting words' but a 'viewpoint' within the 'free marketplace of ideas' and that such 'viewpoints' are categorically protected by the first Amendment. The majority on the High Court (Scalia, Rehnquist, Kennedy, Souter, Thomas) then offered a *second* reason for declaring the ordinance unconstitutional, a judicially activist contribution which took many jurists by surprise: the justices severely restricted the possible doctrinal scope of 'fighting words' by claiming it unconstitutional to impose prohibitions on speech solely on the basis of the 'content' or 'subjects addressed' in that speech. In order to determine whether words are fighting words, there can be no decisive recourse to the content and the subject matter of what is said.

One conclusion on which the justices appear to concur is that the ordinance imposed overbroad restrictions on speech, given that forms of speech *not* considered to fall within the parameters of fighting words would nonetheless be banned by the ordinance. But while the Minnesota ordinance proved too broad for all the justices, Scalia, Thomas, Rehnquist, Kennedy, and Souter took the opportunity of this review to severely restrict any future application of the fighting words doctrine. At stake in the majority opinion is not only when and where 'speech' constitutes some component of an injurious act such that it loses its protected status under the first Amendment, but what constitutes the domain of 'speech' itself.

According to a rhetorical reading of this decision – distinguished from a reading that follows established conventions of legal interpretation – the court might be understood as asserting its state-sanctioned linguistic power to determine what will and will not count as 'speech' and, in the process, enacting a potentially injurious form of juridical speech. What follows, then, is a reading which considers not only the account that the Court gives of how and when speech becomes injurious, but considers as well the injurious potential of the account itself as 'speech' considered in a broad sense. Recalling Cover's [1986] claim that legal decisions can engage the nexus of language and violence, consider that the adjudication of what will and will not count as protected speech will itself be a kind of speech, one which implicates the state in the very problem of discursive power with which it is invested to regulate, sanction, and restrict such speech.

In the, following, then, I will read the 'speech' in which the decision is articulated against the version of 'speech' officially circumscribed as protected content in the decision. The point of this kind of reading is not only to expose a contradictory

Judith
Butler

set of rhetorical strategies at work in the decision, but to consider the power of that discursive domain which not only produces what will and will not count as 'speech' but which regulates the political field of contestation through the tactical manipulation of that very distinction. Furthermore, I want to argue that the very reasons that account for the injuriousness of such acts, construed as speech in a broad sense, are precisely what render difficult the prosecution of such acts. Lastly, I want to suggest that the court's speech carries with it its *own* violence and that the very institution that is invested with the authority to adjudicate the problem of hate speech recirculates and redirects that hatred in and as its own highly consequential speech, often by coopting the very language that it seeks to adjudicate.

The majority opinion, written by Scalia, begins with the construction of the act, the burning of the cross; and one question at issue is whether or not this act constitutes an injury, whether it can be construed as 'fighting words' or whether it communicates a content which is, for better or worse, protected by first Amendment precedent. The figure of burning will be repeated throughout the opinion, first in the context in which the burning cross is construed as the free expression of a viewpoint within the marketplace of ideas, and, second, in the example of the burning of the flag, which could be held illegal were it to violate an ordinance prohibiting outside fires, but which could not be held to be illegal if it were the expression of an idea. Later Scalia will close the argument through recourse to yet another fire: 'Let there be no mistake about our belief that burning a cross in someone's front yard is reprehensible.' 'But,' Scalia continued, 'St. Paul has sufficient means at its disposal to prevent such behavior without adding the first Amendment to the fire.' *R.A.V v. St. Paul*, 112 S. Ct. at 2550, 120 L. Ed. 2d at 326.

Significantly, Scalia here aligns the act of cross-burning with those who defend the ordinance, since both are producing fires, but whereas the cross-burner's fire is constitutionally protected speech, the ordinance-maker's language is figured as the incineration of free speech. The analogy suggests that the ordinance is itself a kind of cross-burning, and Scalia then draws on the very destructive implications of cross-burning to underscore his point that the ordinance itself is destructive. The figure thus affirms the destructiveness of the cross-burning that the decision itself effectively denies, the destructiveness of the act that it has just elevated to the status of protected verbal currency within the marketplace of ideas.

The Court thus transposes the place of the ordinance and the place of the cross-burning, but also figures the first Amendment in an analogous relation to the black family and its home which in the course of the writing has become reduced to 'someone's front yard.' The stripping of blackness and family from the figure of the complainant is significant, for it refuses the dimension of social power that constructs the so-called speaker and the addressee of the speech act in question, the burning cross. And it refuses as well the racist history of the convention of cross-burning by the Ku Klux Klan which marked, targeted, and, hence, portended a further violence against a given addressee. Scalia thus figures himself as quenching the fire which the ordinance has lit, and which is being stoked with the first Amendment, apparently in its totality. Indeed, compared with the admittedly 'reprehensible' act of burning a cross in 'someone's' front yard, the ordinance itself appears to conflagrate in much

Judith
Butler

greater dimensions, threatening to burn the book which it is Scalia's duty to uphold; Scalia thus champions himself as an opponent of those who would set the constitution on fire, cross-burners of a more dangerous order.

The lawyers arguing for the legality of the ordinance based their appeal on the fighting words doctrine. This doctrine, formulated in *Chaplinsky v. New Hampshire*, 315 U.S. 568, 572 (1942), argued that speech acts unprotected by the Constitution are those which are not essential to the communication of ideas: 'such utterances are no essential part of any exposition of ideas, and are of such slight social value as a step to truth that any benefit that may be derived from them is clearly outweighed by the social interest in order and morality.' Scalia takes this phrasing to legitimate the following claim: 'the unprotected features of the words are, despite their verbal character, essentially a "non-speech" element of communication.' *R.A.V v. St. Paul*, 112 S. Ct. at 2545, 120 L. Ed. 2d at 319. In his efforts to protect all contents of communication from proscription, Scalia establishes a distinction between the content and the vehicle of that expression; it is the latter which is proscribable, and the former which is not. He continues, 'fighting words are thus analogous to a noisy sound truck.' *Id.* What is injurious, then, is the sound, but not the message, indeed, 'the government may not regulate use based on hostility – or favoritism – towards the underlying message expressed.' *Id.*

The connection between the signifying power of the burning cross and Scalia's regressive new critical distinction between what is and is not a speech element in communication is nowhere marked in the text. Scalia assumes that the burning cross is a message, an expression of a viewpoint, a discussion of a 'subject' or 'content': in short, that the act of burning the cross is fully and exhaustively translatable into a *constative* act of speech; the burning of the cross which is, after all, on the black family's lawn, is thus made strictly analogous – and morally equivalent – to an individual speaking in public on whether or not there ought to be a fifty-cent tax on gasoline. Significantly, Scalia does not tell us what the cross would say if the cross could speak, but he does insist that what the burning cross is doing is expressing a viewpoint, discoursing on a content which is, admittedly, controversial, but for that very reason, ought not to be proscribed. Thus the defense of cross-burning as free speech rests on an unarticulated analogy between that act and a public constation. This speech is not a doing, an action or an injury, even as it is the enunciation of a set of 'contents' that might offend. The injury is thus construed as one that is registered at the level of sensibility, which is to say that it is an offense that is one of the risks of free speech.

That the cross burns and thus constitutes an incendiary destruction is not considered as a sign of the intention to reproduce that incendiary destruction at the site of the house or the family; the historical correlation between cross-burning and marking a community, a family, or an individual for further violence is also ignored. How much of that burning is translatable into a declarative or constative proposition? And how would one know exactly what constative claim is being made by the burning cross? If the cross is the expression of a viewpoint, is it a declaration as in, 'I am of the opinion that black people ought not to live in this neighborhood' or even, 'I am of the opinion that violence ought to be perpetrated against black people,' or is it a perlocutionary performative, as in imperatives and commands which take the form of 'Burn!' or 'Die!'? Is it an injunction that works its power metonymically not only in the sense that the fire recalls prior burnings which have served to mark black people as targets for violence, but also in the sense that the fire is understood to be transferable from the cross to the target that is marked by the cross? The relation between cross-burning and torchings of both persons and properties is historically established. Hence, from this perspective, the burning cross assumes the status of a direct address and a *threat* and, as such, is construed either as the incipient moment of injurious action *or* as the statement of an intention to injure.

Although Justice Stevens agreed with the decision to strike down the Minnesota ordinance, he takes the occasion to rebuke Scalia for restricting the fighting words doctrine. Stevens reviews special cases in which conduct may be prohibited by special rules. Note in the following quotation how the cross-burning is nowhere mentioned, but the displacements of the figure of fire appear in a series of examples which effectively transfer the need for protection *from racist speech* to the need for protection *from public protest against racism*. Even within Stevens's defense of proscribing conduct, a phantasmatic figure of a menacing riot emerges:

> Lighting a fire near an ammunition dump or a gasoline storage tank is especially dangerous; such behavior may be punished more severely than burning trash in a vacant lot. Threatening someone because of her race or religious beliefs may cause particularly severe trauma or touch off a riot, and threatening a high public official may cause substantial social disruptions; such threats may be punished more severely than threats against someone based on, say, his support of a particular athletic team.
> (*R.A.V. v. St. Paul*, 112 S. Ct. at 2561, 120 L Ed. 2d at 340)

Absent from the list of fires above is the burning of the cross in question. In the place of that prior scene, we are asked first to imagine someone who would light a fire near a gas tank, and then to imagine a more innocuous fire in a vacant lot. But with the vacant lot, we enter the metaphor of poverty and property, which appears to effect the unstated transition to the matter of blackness introduced by the next line, 'threatening someone because of her race or religious beliefs . . .': *because* of her race is not the same as 'on the basis of' her race and leaves open the possibility that the race causally induces the threat. The threat appears to shift mid-sentence as Stevens continues to elaborate a second causality: this threat 'may cause particularly severe trauma or touch off a riot' at which point it is no longer clear whether the threat which warrants the prohibition on conduct refers to the 'threatening someone because of her race or religious beliefs' or to the riot that might result therefrom. What immediately follows suggests that the limitations on rioters has suddenly become more urgent to authorize than the limitation on those who would threaten this 'her' 'because of her race. . . .' After 'or touch off a riot,' the sentence continues, 'and threatening a high official may cause substantial social disruption . . .,' as if the racially marked trauma had already led to a riot and an attack on high officials.

This sudden implication of the justices themselves might be construed as a paranoid inversion of the original cross-burning narrative. That original narrative is nowhere mentioned, but its elements have been redistributed throughout the examples; the fire which was the original 'threat' against the black family is relocated first as an incendiary move against industry, then as a location in a vacant lot, and then reappears tacitly in the riot which now appears to follow from the trauma and threaten public officials. The fire which initially constituted the threat against the black family becomes metaphorically transfigured as the threat that blacks in trauma now wield against high officials. And though Stevens is on record as endorsing a construction of 'fighting words' that would include cross-burning as *un*protected speech, the language in which he articulates this view deflects the question to that of the state's right to circumscribe conduct to protect itself against a racially motivated riot.

The circumscription of content explicitly discussed in the decision appears to emerge through a production of semantic excess in and through the metonymic chain of anxious figuration. The separability of content from sound, for instance, or of content from context, is exemplified and illustrated through figures which signify in excess of the thesis which they are meant to support. Indeed, to the extent that, in the Scalia analysis, 'content' is circumscribed and purified to establish its protected status, that content is secured through the production and proliferation of 'dangers' from which it calls to be protected. Hence, the question of whether or not the black family in Minnesota is entitled to protection from public displays such as cross-burnings is displaced onto the question of whether or not the 'content' of free speech is to be protected from those who would burn it. The fire is thus displaced from the cross to the legal instrument wielded by those who would protect the family from the fire, but then to the black family itself, to blackness, to the vacant lot, to rioters in Los Angeles who explicitly oppose the decision of a court and who now represent the incendiary power of the traumatized rage of black people who would burn the judiciary itself. But, of course, that construal is already a reversal of the narrative in which a court delivers a decision of acquittal for the four policemen indicted for the brutal beating of Rodney King, a decision that might be said to 'spark' a riot which calls into question whether the claim of having been injured can be heard and countenanced by a jury and a judge who are extremely susceptible to the suggestion that a black person is always and only endangering, but never endangered. And so the High Court might be understood in its decision of June 22, 1992, to be taking its revenge on Rodney King, protecting itself against the riots in Los Angeles and elsewhere which appeared to be attacking the system of justice itself. Hence, the justices identify with the black family who sees the cross burning and takes it as a threat, but they substitute themselves for that family, and reposition blackness as the agency behind the threat itself.

The decision enacts a set of metonymic displacements which might well be read as anxious deflections and reversals of the injurious action at hand; indeed, the original scene is successively reversed in the metonymic relation between figures such that the fire is lit by the ordinance, carried out by traumatized rioters on the streets of Los Angeles, and threatens to engulf the justices themselves.

[. . .]

Two remarks of qualification: first, some critical race theorists such as Charles Lawrence [see Matsuda *et al.* 1993] will argue that cross burning is speech, but that not all speech is to be protected, indeed, not all speech *is* protected, and that racist speech conflicts with the Equal Protection Clause because it hinders the addressed subject from exercising his/her rights and liberties. Other legal scholars in critical race studies, such as Richard Delgado, will argue for expanding the domain of the fighting words restriction on first Amendment rights. Matsuda and MacKinnon [see MacKinnon 1993], following the example of sex discrimination jurisprudence, will argue that it is impossible to distinguish between conduct and speech, that hateful remarks are injurious actions. Oddly enough, this last kind of reasoning has reappeared in the recent policy issued on gays in the military; where the statement 'I am a homosexual' is considered to be a 'homosexual act.' [. . .] According to this policy, the act of coming out is implicitly construed as fighting words. Here it seems that one must be reminded that the prosecution of hate speech in a court runs the risk of giving that court the opportunity to impose a further violence of its own. And if the court begins to decide what is and is not violating speech, that decision runs the risk of constituting the most binding of violations.

For, as in the case with the burning cross, it was not merely a question of whether the court knows how to read the threat contained in the burning cross, but whether the court itself signifies along a parallel logic. For this has been a court that can only imagine the fire engulfing the first Amendment, sparking the riot which will fray its own authority. And so it protects itself against the imagined threat of that fire by protecting the burning cross, allying itself with those who would seek legal protection from a spectre wrought from their own fantasy. Thus the court protects the burning cross as free speech, figuring those it injures as the site of the true threat, elevating the burning cross as a deputy for the court, the local protector and token of free speech: with so much protection, what do we have to fear?

 Activity

Issues to consider

❏ In Judith Butler's discussion, much turns on the distinction between protected and unprotected speech. What do you think should be in each of these categories? Butler's example is taken from a specific location. You may wish to do some research on the kinds of speech protected (or not) in your own country or state.

❏ Think about the ways in which non-verbal objects may be said to make a statement or to have the power to speak. How can this power be accounted for, in speech act or some other kind of linguistic theory? Where does the agency of such a 'statement' lie? You may wish to read the rest of Butler's *Excitable Speech*, which takes up this question.

❏ Butler questions here the conclusions reached by the different US courts, challenging their understanding of the pragmatics of performativity. Of course, she does not challenge the right of those courts to have an opinion, since *as courts* the felicity condition that allows them to perform the speech act of judgement is satisfied. Do you think this acceptance is acceptable? In many airport security areas there are now signs which say: 'Statements made in jest will be taken seriously', and travellers have been arrested and detained for making jokes, which were obviously insincere, about carrying bombs. Performativity in speech act theory usually refers to the felicity conditions of the *speaker* being appropriate for a successful perlocution; in these cases, though, a third agency is claiming the power to arbitrate on the force of another's utterance. How would you feel if a company took your mild expression of interest as a serious intention to buy; or if a builder regarded your collection of a quotation for work as a signal to proceed to knock down your kitchen walls; or if a fundamentalist religious group took your ironic statement in a novel as an act of blasphemy and called on others to assassinate you?

❏   Though it is unlikely in reality, it is possible to imagine the racist cross-burner in Butler's example as a conceptual performance artist who intended his act as an 'ironic' comment on the iconography of Christianity, American fundamentalist Christianity, and the institutionalisation of racism. How would a theory of language based on speech acts and performativity handle the notion of irony?

INTENTION   D5

Few things have attracted more attention in literary theory in recent years than the debate about authorship. Central to these debates have been two essays, Roland Barthes's journalistic but provocative 'The death of the author', and Michel Foucault's more measured but no less controversial 'What is an author?'. Foucault's answer to his own question is primarily a sociological or historical one, analysing what he describes as the 'author function'. Consequently he examines the author as a legal entity, endowed with rights of ownership over his texts, but also made responsible for those texts. Contrary to the usual notion of the author as the originator of a text, however, Foucault's author is a necessary 'ideological figure', a product of our need for someone or something to perform a certain function.

What is an author?

Michel Foucault (reprinted from Paul Rabinow (ed.) *The Foucault Reader*, Harmondsworth: Penguin, 1994: pp. 108–13, 117–20).

Let us analyze this 'author function' as we have [. . .] described it. In our culture, how does one characterize a discourse containing the author function? In what way is this discourse different from other discourses? If we limit our remarks to the author of a book or a text, we can isolate four different characteristics.

First of all, discourses are objects of appropriation. The form of ownership from which they spring is of a rather particular type, one that has been codified for many years. We should note that, historically, this type of ownership has always been subsequent to what one might call penal appropriation. Texts, books, and discourses really began to have authors (other than mythical, 'sacralized' and 'sacralizing' figures) to the extent that authors became subject to punishment, that is, to the extent that discourses could be transgressive. In our culture (and doubtless in many others), discourse was not originally a product, a thing, a kind of goods; it was essentially an act – an act placed in the bipolar field of the sacred and the profane, the licit and the illicit, the religious and the blasphemous. Historically, it was a gesture fraught with risks before becoming goods caught up in a circuit of ownership.

Once a system of ownership for texts came into being, once strict rules concerning author's rights, author-publisher relations, rights of reproduction, and related matters were enacted – at the end of the eighteenth and the beginning of the nineteenth century – the possibility of transgression attached to the act of writing took on, more and more, the form of an imperative peculiar to literature. It is as if the author, beginning with the moment at which he was placed in the system of property that characterizes our society, compensated for the status that he thus acquired by rediscovering the old bipolar field of discourse, systematically practicing transgression and thereby restoring danger to a writing which was now guaranteed the benefits of ownership.

The author function does not affect all discourses in a universal and constant way, however. This is its second characteristic. In our civilization, it has not always been the same types of texts which have required attribution to an author. There was a time when the texts that we today call 'literary' (narratives, stories, epics, tragedies, comedies) were accepted, put into circulation, and valorized without any question about the identity of their author; their anonymity caused no difficulties since their ancientness, whether real or imagined, was regarded as a sufficient guarantee of their status. On the other hand, those texts that we now would call scientific – those dealing with cosmology and the heavens, medicine and illnesses, natural sciences and geography – were accepted in the Middle Ages, and accepted as 'true,' only when marked with the name of their author. 'Hippocrates said,' 'Pliny recounts,' were not really formulas of an argument based on authority; they were the markers inserted in discourses that were supported to be received as statements of demonstrated truth.

A reversal occurred in the seventeenth or eighteenth century. Scientific discourses began to be received for themselves, in the anonymity of an established or always redemonstrable truth; their membership in a systematic ensemble, and not the reference to the individual who produced them, stood as their guarantee. The author function faded away, and the inventor's name served only to christen a theorem, proposition, particular effect, property, body, group of elements, or pathological syndrome. By the same token, literary discourses came to be accepted only when endowed with the author function. We now ask of each poetic or fictional text: From where does it come, who wrote it, when, under what circumstances, or beginning with what design? The meaning ascribed to it and the status or value accorded it depend on the manner in which we answer these questions. And if a text should be discovered in a state of anonymity – whether as a consequence of an accident or the author's explicit wish – the game becomes one of rediscovering the author. Since literary anonymity is not tolerable, we can accept it only in the guise of an enigma. As a result, the author function today plays an important role in our view of literary works. (These are obviously generalizations that would have to be refined insofar as recent critical practice is concerned.)

The third characteristic of this author function is that it does not develop spontaneously as the attribution of a discourse to an individual. It is, rather, the result of a complex operation which constructs a certain rational being that we call 'author.' Critics doubtless try to give this intelligible being a realistic status, by discerning, in the individual, a 'deep' motive, a 'creative' power, or a 'design,' the milieu in which writing originates. Nevertheless, these aspects of an individual which we designate as making him an author are only a projection, in more or less psychologizing terms, of the operations that we force texts to undergo, the connections that we make, the traits that we establish as pertinent, the continuities that we recognize, or the exclusions that we practice. All these operations vary according to periods and types of discourse. We do not construct a 'philosophical author' as we do a 'poet,' just as, in the eighteenth century, one did not construct a novelist as we do today. Still, we can find through the ages certain constants in the rules of author construction.

It seems, for example, that the manner in which literary criticism once defined the author – or, rather, constructed the figure of the author beginning with existing texts and discourses – is directly derived from the manner in which Christian tradition authenticated (or rejected) the texts at its disposal. In order to 'rediscover' an author in a work, modern criticism uses methods similar to those that Christian exegesis employed when trying to prove the value of a text by its author's saintliness. In *De viris illustribus*, Saint Jerome explains that homonymy is not sufficient to identify legitimately authors of more than one work: different individuals could have had the same name, or one man could have, illegitimately, borrowed another's patronymic. The name as an individual trademark is not enough when one works within a textual tradition.

How, then, can one attribute several discourses to one and the same author? How can one use the author function to determine if one is dealing with one or several individuals? Saint Jerome proposes four criteria: (1) if among several books attributed to an author one is inferior to the others, it must be withdrawn from the list of the author's works (the author is therefore defined as a constant level of value); (2) the same should be done if certain texts contradict the doctrine expounded in the author's other works (the author is thus defined as a field of conceptual or theoretical coherence); (3) one must also exclude works that are written in a different style, containing words and expressions not ordinarily found in the writer's production (the author is here conceived as a stylistic unity); (4) finally, passages quoting statements that were made or mentioning events that occurred after the author's death must be regarded as interpolated texts (the author is here seen as a historical figure at the crossroads of a certain number of events).

Modern literary criticism, even when – as is now customary – it is not concerned with questions of authentication, still defines the author the same way: the author provides the basis for explaining not only the presence of certain events in a work, but also their transformations, distortions, and diverse modifications (through his biography, the determination of his individual perspective, the analysis of his social position, and the revelation of his basic design). The author is also the principle of a certain unity of writing – all differences having to be resolved, at least in part, by the principles of evolution, maturation, or influence. The author also serves to neutralize the contradictions that may emerge in a series of texts: there must be – at a certain level of his thought or desire, of his consciousness or unconscious – a point where contradictions are resolved, where incompatible elements are at last tied together or organized around a fundamental or originating contradiction. Finally, the author is a particular source of expression that, in more or less completed forms, is manifested equally well, and with similar validity, in works, sketches, letters, fragments, and so on. Clearly, Saint Jerome's four criteria of authenticity (criteria which seem totally insufficient for today's exegetes) do define the four modalities according to which modern criticism brings the author function into play.

But the author function is not a pure and simple reconstruction made second-hand from a text given as passive material. The text always contains a certain number of signs referring to the author. These signs, well known to grammarians, are personal pronouns, adverbs of time and place, and verb conjugation. Such elements do not play the same role in discourses provided with the author function as in those lacking it. In the latter, such 'shifters' refer to the real speaker and to the spatio-temporal coordinates of his discourse (although certain modifications can occur, as in the operation of relating discourses in the first person). In the former, however, their role is more complex and variable. Everyone knows that, in a novel narrated in the first person, neither the first-person pronoun nor the present indicative refers exactly either to the writer or to the moment in which he writes, but rather to an alter ego whose distance from the author varies, often changing in the course of the work. It would be just as wrong to equate the author with the real writer as to equate him with the fictitious speaker; the author function is carried out and operates in the scission itself, in this division and this distance.

One might object that this is a characteristic peculiar to novelistic or poetic discourse, a 'game' in which only 'quasi-discourses' participate. In fact, however, all discourses endowed with the author function do possess this plurality of self. The self that speaks in the preface to a treatise on mathematics – and that indicates the circumstances of the treatise's composition – is identical neither in its position nor in its functioning to the self that speaks in the course of a demonstration, and that appears in the form of 'I conclude' or 'I suppose.' In the first case, the 'I' refers to an individual without an equivalent who, in a determined place and time, completed a certain task; in the second, the 'I' indicates an instance and a level of demonstration which any individual could perform provided that he accepted the same system of symbols, play of axioms, and set of previous demonstrations. We could also, in the same treatise, locate a third self, one that speaks to tell the work's meaning, the obstacles encountered, the results obtained, and the remaining problems; this self is situated in the field of already existing or yet-to-appear mathematical discourses. The author function is not assumed by the first of these selves at the expense of the other two, which would then be nothing more than a fictitious splitting in two of the first one.

On the contrary, in these discourses the author function operates so as to effect the dispersion of these three simultaneous selves.

No doubt analysis could discover still more characteristic traits of the author function. I will limit myself to these four, however, because they seem both the most visible and the most important. They can be summarized as follows: (1) the author function is linked to the juridical and institutional system that encompasses, determines, and articulates the universe of discourses; (2) it does not affect all discourses in the same way at all times and in all types of civilization; (3) it is not defined by the spontaneous attribution of a discourse to its producer, but rather by a series of specific and complex operations; (4) it does not refer purely and simply to a real individual, since it can give rise simultaneously to several selves, to several subjects – positions that can be occupied by different classes of individuals.

[. . .]

To conclude, I would like to review the reasons why I attach a certain importance to what I have said.

First, there are theoretical reasons. On the one hand, an analysis in the direction that I have outlined might provide for an approach to a typology of discourse. It seems to me, at least at first glance, that such a typology cannot be constructed solely from the grammatical features, formal structures, and objects of discourse: more likely there exist properties or relationships peculiar to discourse (not reducible to the rules of grammar and logic), and one must use these to distinguish the major categories of discourse. The relationship (or nonrelationship) with an author, and the different forms this relationship takes, constitute – in a quite visible manner – one of these discursive properties.

On the other hand, I believe that one could find here an introduction to the historical analysis of discourse. Perhaps it is time to study discourses not only in terms of their expressive value or formal transformations, but according to their modes of existence. The modes of circulation, valorization, attribution, and appropriation of discourses vary with each culture and are modified within each. The manner in which they are articulated according to social relationships can be more readily understood, I believe, in the activity of the author function and in its modifications than in the themes or concepts that discourses set in motion.

It would seem that one could also, beginning with analyses of this type, reexamine the privileges of the subject. I realize that in undertaking the internal and architectonic analysis of a work (be it a literary text, philosophical system, or scientific work), in setting aside biographical and psychological references, one has already called back into question the absolute character and founding role of the subject. Still, perhaps one must return to this question, not in order to reestablish the theme of an originating subject, but to grasp the subject's points of insertion, modes of functioning, and system of dependencies. Doing so means overturning the traditional problem, no longer raising the questions: How can a free subject penetrate the substance of things and give it meaning? How can it activate the rules of a language from within and thus give rise to the designs which are properly its own? Instead, these questions will be raised: How, under what conditions, and in what forms can something like a subject appear in the order of discourse? What place can it occupy in each type of discourse, what functions can it assume, and by obeying what rules? In short, it is a matter of depriving the subject (or its substitute) of its role as originator, and of analyzing the subject as a variable and complex function of discourse.

Second, there are reasons dealing with the 'ideological' status of the author. The question then becomes: How can one reduce the great peril, the great danger with which fiction threatens our world? The answer is: one can reduce it with the author. The author allows a limitation of the cancerous and dangerous proliferation of significations within a world where one is thrifty not only with one's resources and riches, but also with one's discourses and their significations. The author is the principle of thrift in the proliferation of meaning. As a result, we must entirely reverse the traditional idea of the author. We are accustomed, as we have seen earlier, to saying that the author is the genial creator of a work in which he deposits, with infinite wealth and generosity, an inexhaustible world of significations. We are used to thinking that the author is so different from all other men, and so transcendent with regard to all languages that, as soon as he speaks, meaning begins to proliferate, to proliferate indefinitely.

The truth is quite the contrary: the author is not an indefinite source of significations which fill a work; the author does not precede the works; he is a certain functional principle by which, in our culture, one limits, excludes, and chooses; in short, by which one impedes the free circulation, the free manipulation, the free composition, decomposition, and recomposition of fiction. In fact, if we are accustomed to presenting the author as a genius, as a perpetual surging of invention, it is because, in reality, we make him function in exactly the opposite fashion. One can say that the author is an ideological product, since we represent him as the opposite of his historically real function. (When a historically given function is represented in a figure that inverts it, one has an ideological production.) The author is therefore the ideological figure by which one marks the manner in which we fear the proliferation of meaning.

In saying this, I seem to call for a form of culture in which fiction would not be limited by the figure of the author. It would be pure romanticism, however, to imagine a culture in which the fictive would operate in an absolutely free state, in which fiction would be put at the disposal of everyone and would develop without passing through something like a necessary or constraining figure. Although, since the eighteenth century, the author has played the role of the regulator of the fictive, a role quite characteristic of our era of industrial and bourgeois society, of individualism and private property, still, given the historical modifications that are taking place, it does not seem necessary that the author function remain constant in form, complexity, and even in existence. I think that, as our society changes, at the very moment when it is in the process of changing, the author function will disappear, and in such a manner that fiction and its polysemous texts will once again function according to another mode, but still with a system of constraint – one which will no longer be the author, but which will have to be determined or, perhaps, experienced.

All discourses, whatever their status, form, value, and whatever the treatment to which they will be subjected, would then develop in the anonymity of a murmur. We would no longer hear the questions that have been rehashed for so long: Who really spoke? Is it really he and not someone else? With what authenticity or original-ity? And what part of his deepest self did he express in his discourse? Instead, there would be other questions, like these: What are the modes of existence of this discourse? Where has it been used, how can it circulate, and who can appropriate it for himself? What are the places in it where there is room for possible subjects? Who can assume these various subject functions? And behind all these questions, we would hear hardly anything but the stirring of an indifference: What difference does it make who is speaking?

Michel Foucault

Issues to consider

☐ Foucault's argument is primarily a historical one. Does the author still function in the way that he describes? What changes if any might there be to the author function as new forms of textuality, such as electronic texts, become more common? Can the anonymity that Foucault mentions towards the end of his essay be detected yet?

☐ At several points in this book, we have found ourselves asking whether and how people might be held accountable for the things that they say or write. What would Foucault's discussion add to this debate?

☐ In the light of the discussions in Units B5 and D5, is there a 'translator func-tion'? How would you define it? What are, or should be, a translator's rights and responsibilities?

☐ Central to Barthes's essay is the role of the reader. Foucault, in comparison, makes relatively little of this. How would you rethink Foucault's discussion if you were to focus on a 'reader function'?

✪ Activity

COGNITION

D6

In their book, *Philosophy in the Flesh* – from which the following extract is taken – Lakoff and Johnson (1999) complete the journey begun with their influential 1980 book *Metaphors We Live By*. In the earlier work, conceptual metaphors underlying much of our everyday language and embodied perception were set out. In the later book, this principle is applied to the tradition of the philosophy of language. In the following extract, Lakoff and Johnson argue that the metaphorical basis of theorising about language does not have to lead either to a conceptual relativism or to an aban-donment of the possibility of theory. Theirs is a positivist view that takes empirical work from cognitive science and psychology and uses it to set the limits of language theories.

George
Lakoff and
Mark
Johnson

How philosophical theories work

George Lakoff and Mark Johnson (reprinted from *Philosophy in the Flesh*, New York: Basic Books, 1999: pp. 541–8).

Philosophy rests on shared conceptual metaphors

Philosophers use the same cognitive resources that everyone else does when they think and reason. They operate with the same general metaphors and metonymies that define our various folk theories, that populate the cognitive unconscious, and that are the shared property of whole cultures and traditions. We have seen that philosophers employ a relatively small number of conceptual metaphors that form the core of their central doctrines in fields ranging from metaphysics and epistemology to ethics and political theory. It is these metaphors, taken for granted throughout the body of a philosopher's work, that make the philosophy a unified theory and not a mere laundry list of concepts and claims. Such core metaphorical mappings define the inference patterns common throughout the philosopher's reasoning and reveal the generalizations that link a philosopher's key doctrines.

Whenever a philosophical theory seems intuitive to us, it is primarily because it is based on metaphors that are deeply embedded in our cognitive unconscious and are widely shared within a culture. A theory will resonate for us just insofar as it orchestrates many of the conceptual metaphors that make up our everyday folk theories. Nobody would understand Kant's moral theory at all if it didn't make use, albeit creatively, of the same metaphors that underlie our cultural models of morality.

Metaphysics as metaphor

From Thales to Heraclitus, Plato to Aristotle, Descartes to Kant, Russell to Quine, it is the core metaphors at the heart of each philosopher's thought that define its metaphysics. Each of those source-to-target mappings project the ontology of a given source domain to form the ontology of the relevant target domain. For example, since the Pythagoreans took the Being Is Number metaphor as foundational, they projected the ontology of mathematical objects onto Being in general. They thought of numbers as chunks of space with distinctive shapes, and so they saw the world as made up of concatenations of such shapes. Or, when Descartes appropriated the Understanding Is Seeing metaphor, he thereby accepted an ontology of the mental realm that required mental counterparts to visible objects, people who see, natural light sources, and so forth. His metaphysics of mind is populated with metaphorical counterparts to these entities, and he reasons about them using patterns of inference imported from the domain of vision to the domain of mind and thought.

Metaphorical metaphysics of this sort is not some quaint product of antiquated and naive philosophical views. Rather, it is a characteristic of *all* philosophies, because it is a characteristic of all human thought. Thus, as we saw in our account of mind, most of analytic philosophy is defined by an interweaving of several metaphors (Thought Is Language, Thinking Is Mathematical Calculation, The Mind Is A Machine, etc.) that are shared within our culture. Any contemporary philosophical view that employs the Thinking Is Mathematical Calculation metaphor thereby appropriates its distinct ontology, in which all thoughts must be unitary entities, just as numbers are conceived to be. Just as much for Quine as for Thales, metaphysics stems from metaphors.

George Lakoff and Mark Johnson

Philosophical innovation

There is nothing deflationary about this view of the metaphoric nature of philosophical theories. Showing that philosophies are built up from metaphors, metonymies, and image schemas does not diminish their importance. On the contrary, it reveals just how marvellous such philosophical systems really are. Philosophers are not simply logic-choppers who fine-tune what their culture already knows in its bones. Instead, they are the poets of systematic thought. Philosophy at its best is creative and synthetic. It helps us put our world together in a way that makes sense to us and that helps us deal with the problems that confront us in our lives. When philosophers do this well they are using our ordinary conceptual resources in very extraordinary ways. They see ways of putting ideas together to reveal new systematic connections between different aspects of our experience. They sometimes give us the means for criticizing even our most deeply rooted concepts. They show us ways to extend our metaphors and other imaginative structures to deal with newly emerging situations and problems. Thus, Kant, almost single-handedly, generated the notion of moral autonomy (and its metaphors) that has become a defining feature of the modern view of moral responsibility.

Constrained philosophical imagination

To set out the defining metaphors of a philosophy is not necessarily to critique it. Many philosophers with a traditional view of language and meaning mistakenly believe that discovering the metaphorical underpinnings of a theory somehow undermines it. This is just false. It is based on an objectivist, literalist view of language and mind that does not, and cannot, recognize the existence of conceptual metaphor.

Two decades ago, Paul de Man [see de Man 1996] attracted considerable philosophical attention with his analyses of metaphors lying at the heart of philosophical theories. This was thought to be disturbing, because it denied the literalist view of concepts and meaning, and also because de Man held a view of metaphor as unstable and indeterminate in meaning. De Man's analyses of Locke's view of mind and language and Kant's treatment of judgment do, indeed, challenge the literalist view. However, de Man was mistaken in claiming that metaphor is destabilizing and indeterminate. He expresses this view of the indeterminacy and unreliability of metaphor in his remarks on metaphors in Kant's philosophy:

> The considerations about the possible danger of uncontrolled metaphors, focused on the cognate figures of support, ground, and so forth, reawaken the hidden uncertainty about the rigor of a distinction that does not hold if the language in which it is stated reintroduces the elements of indetermination its sets out to eliminate.
>
> [de Man 1996: 48]

George
Lakoff and
Mark
Johnson

De Man is wrong to claim that such metaphors destabilize philosophical theories. We have seen how conceptual metaphors ground abstract concepts through cross-domain mappings using aspects of our embodied experience and how they establish the inferential structures within philosophies. As our analyses show, conceptual metaphors are anything but loci of indeterminateness and uncertainty. Metaphors are the very means by which we can understand abstract domains and extend our knowledge into new areas. Metaphor, like any other embodied, imaginative structure, is not a philosophical liability. Rather, it is a remarkable gift – a tool for understanding things in a way that is tied to our embodied, lived experience. Identifying philosophers' metaphors does not belittle them. Instead, it helps us understand the power of philosophical theory to make sense of our lives. The extended analyses of philosophers' conceptual metaphors that we have given in this book show that it is the metaphors that unify their theories and give them the explanatory power they have. There is no philosophy without metaphor.

Only two things are denied by the presence of conceptual metaphor in philosophy: (1) There is no philosophy built up solely from literal concepts that could map directly onto the mind-independent world. (2) There is no transcendent, disembodied, literal reason that is fully accessible to consciousness. Neither of these things is necessary in order to do philosophy. On the contrary, a belief in them is an obstacle to cognitively realistic, empirically responsible philosophical views that have a bearing on our lives.

How philosophy is changed

What difference does any of this cognitive analysis make for our understanding of philosophy? Plenty. Let us consider some examples of how we might think differently about a particular philosophical view once we have studied it from the perspective of second-generation cognitive science.

We saw how several of Aristotle's most famous doctrines are the consequence of his weaving together of conceptual metaphors. Take, for instance, his fateful view of logic as purely formal. This view emerges in the following way. Predications Are Categories. That is, to predicate an attribute of a thing is to place it within a category. Categories are understood metaphorically as abstract containers. Syllogisms, as forms of deductive reasoning, work via a container logic (e.g., *A* is in *B*, and *B* is in *C*, so *A* is in *C*). We saw also that Aristotle's founding metaphor was Ideas Are Essences. To conceptualize a thing is to categorize it, which is to state its essence, the defining attributes that make it the kind of thing it is. For Aristotle, then, the essences of things in the world, since they are what constitute ideas, can actually be *in* the mind. And for the essence to be in the mind, it cannot be the substance or matter of a thing; rather, it must be its *form*: Essences Are Forms. So, if our ideas are the forms of things, and we reason with the forms of things, then logic is purely formal, abstracting away from any content.

Seeing these tight connections among the metaphors explains for us the logic of Aristotle's arguments and shows us why he has the doctrines he has. Once we see this, we see also that there is no absolute necessity about this particular view of things. It is a view based on a metaphorical logic that uses one particular set of conceptual

George
Lakoff and
Mark
Johnson

metaphors. However, there are other possible metaphors for understanding logic and reasoning in ways inconsistent with the metaphors Aristotle used to characterize 'logic.'

The fact that the same patterns of inference occur with different content was taken by Aristotle to be empirical verification of his view that logic is a matter of form. From the perspective of cognitive semantics, of course, there is a very different explanation for the same empirical observations. Via the metaphor that Categories Are Containers (that is, bounded regions in space), the logic of containers is mapped onto all categories conceptualized in the cognitive unconscious in terms of containment, that is, of bounded regions of space. *Modus ponens* and *modus tollens* are examples of the logic of containment:

> Embodied *Modus Ponens*: If Container A is inside Container B and X is inside Container A, then X is inside Container B.
> Embodied *Modus Tollens*: If Container A is inside Container B and X is outside Container B, then X is outside Container A.

Here X is either another container or a specific entity. Apply the Categories Are Containers metaphor, and we get the equivalent of the Aristotelian principles.

The general applicability of these principles to any such categories, regardless of the specific content of the categories, is an instance of embodied content: the concept of containment and the Categories Are Containers metaphor. Symbolic logic is disembodied and therefore an inaccurate, misleading way to characterize such embodied principles of human logic. Symbolic logic involves the manipulation of meaningless symbols and therefore misses the embodied character of these forms of human reason.

Once we use the tools and methods of second-generation cognitive science to understand Aristotle's logic, we may need to rethink his logic and see another, more cognitively realistic, view of logic. The alternative to formal, disembodied reason is an embodied, imaginative reason.

The same situation holds for Descartes' conception of mind and his idea of self-reflection. That conception is built on the Understanding Is Seeing metaphor, with all of its many submappings: Ideas Are Objects, Reason Is Light, Knowers Are Seers, Intelligence Is Visual Acuity, and so on. Somehow Reason is supposed to shine its light on its own internal operations, even as they are occurring. In this way Self-Knowledge Is Self-Reflection.

Some of these metaphors may be apt or not in various contexts. However, cognitive science suggests that the particular metaphor of self-reflection is cognitively unrealistic. It ignores the pervasive and indispensable workings of the cognitive unconscious. Thus, we have strong reasons for questioning the adequacy of the entire system of metaphors that jointly give rise to the notion of direct self-reflection.

Finally, recall the set of metaphors that together make up the Language of Thought metaphor that underlies so much of contemporary analytic philosophy. We saw that these metaphors, such as Thought Is Language, Thinking Is Mathematical Calculation, Ideas Are Objects, and The Mind Is A Machine (nowadays, a computer), are all deeply embedded in our cultural folk model of mind, thought, and language.

George
Lakoff and
Mark
Johnson

They are then brought together in a unique way by contemporary analytic philosophers to form the Language of Thought metaphor, in which, for example, ideas are symbols (of a language of thought) that get their meaning via the Fregean metaphor that such symbols correspond to things in the world.

We cannot emphasize strongly enough just how pervasive and widely influential such metaphors have been in defining the goals and methods of analytic philosophy. Because of this, it is worth reviewing once more those entailments of our everyday metaphors for the mind that appear prominently in one or another version of analytic philosophy.

THOUGHT AS LANGUAGE

Thought has the properties of a language.
Thought is external and public.
The structure of thought is accurately representable as a linear sequence of
      written symbols of the sort that constitute a written language.
Every thought is expressible in language.

THE MIND AS BODY SYSTEM

Thoughts have a public, objective existence independent of any thinker.
Thoughts correspond to things in the world.

THOUGHT AS MOTION

Rational thought is direct, deliberate, and step-by-step.

THOUGHT AS OBJECT MANIPULATION

Thinking is the manipulation of mental objects.
Thoughts are objective. Hence, everyone can have the same thoughts; that
      is, thought is universal.
Communicating is sending ideas to other people via language.
Thoughts have a structure, just as objects do.
The structure of thoughts can be uniquely and correctly analyzed, just as the
      structure of an object can.

THOUGHT AS MATHEMATICAL CALCULATION

Just as numbers can be accurately represented by sequences of written
      symbols, so thoughts can be adequately represented by sequences of
      written symbols.
Just as mathematical calculation is mechanical (i.e., algorithmic), so rational
      thought is.
Just as there are systematic universal principles of mathematical calculation
      that work step-by-step, so there are systematic universal principles of
      reason that work step-by-step.

George
Lakoff and
Mark
Johnson

Just as numbers and mathematics are universal, so thoughts and reason are
    universal.

THE MIND AS MACHINE

Each complex thought has a structure imposed by mechanically putting
    together simple thoughts in a regular, describable, step-by-step fashion.

In addition, much of analytic philosophy has also inherited some important
metaphorical entailments from Aristotle. Although analytic philosophy eschews
Aristotle's central metaphor, Ideas Are Essences, it accepts many of the entailments
of that metaphor within the Aristotelian worldview. Here are some examples:

First, concepts (what the mind 'grasps') are defined by inherent characteristics
of things in the world.

Second, there is Aristotle's definition of definition: 'A definition is a phrase signifying a thing's essence' (*Topics* 102a). That is, a definition is a set of necessary and
sufficient conditions for something to be the kind of thing it is. Thus, a definition of
a concept is a collection of necessary and sufficient conditions through which we can
grasp the inherent characteristics of kinds of things in the world.

In other words, all concepts are literal, defined directly in terms of the features
of kinds of things in the world. The meaning of concepts is therefore literal, defined
in terms of the properties of kinds of things in the world in itself.

A third entailment of Aristotle's metaphors is Logic Is Formal [. . .].

A fourth is Aristotle's theory of metaphor: Metaphor is not conceptual, since it
is not literal; it is therefore a matter of the use of words. Moreover, it is not the
proper use of words (which is literal), and so it is an improper use of words, appropriate to rhetoric and poetry rather than ordinary speech. Metaphors, to be
comprehensible at all, must be based on similarity (the principal relationship between
concepts). Moreover, the similarity must be an objective feature of the external
world, since concepts are defined in terms of such features.

These entailments of Aristotle's metaphors are widely accepted without question
by a great many Anglo-American philosophers. The same is true of many of the entailments of Descartes' metaphors:

Thought is essentially disembodied, and all thought is conscious.

We can, just by thinking about our own ideas and the operations of our own
    minds, with care and rigor, come to understand the mind accurately and
    with absolute certainty.

Nothing about the body, neither imagination, nor emotion, nor perception,
    nor any detail of the biological nature of the body, need be known in
    order to understand the nature of the mind.

Finally, certain of Kant's principal moral theses, which are entailments of his
metaphors, have also been widely adopted within Anglo-American philosophy. They
are:

George Lakoff and Mark Johnson

There are universal moral laws.

We can know these universal moral laws through reason alone, reflecting on itself.

Therefore, no empirical facts can have any bearing on what we *ought* to do. ('You can't get an *ought* from an *is*.')

Universal Reason is what gives us freedom – freedom to choose our own moral ends – and hence makes us morally independent, that is 'autonomous.'

Though Anglo-American philosophers are by no means all Kantians, these entailments of Kant's moral metaphors are commonplace in much of Anglo-American moral theory.

It is sobering to realize that students studying Anglo-American philosophy are taught all (or at least most) of these metaphorical entailments as truths. They collectively define the core of the Anglo-American philosophical worldview. Yet there is nothing sacred or absolute about these metaphorical entailments. As it happens, all of them are at odds with the view of mind and language emerging from second-generation cognitive science. These are metaphorical entailments that ignore the embodiment of our concepts and reasoning. They ignore the cognitive unconscious that operates via conceptual metaphors, metonymies, and image schemas. Even though they have been massively influential in determining the course of much contemporary analytic philosophy, it may be time to give them up in favor of more cognitively realistic conceptions of the mind, language, and morality.

The cognitive science of philosophy thus does not just describe how philosophies work. It does that, and that is important work. But it also frequently gives us a basis for evaluation and criticism of philosophies. It allows us to bring our empirical understanding of the mind into the study of philosophies old and new.

Activity **Issues to consider**

❑ Lakoff and Johnson offer a view of philosophical theorising as a creative metaphorical process, as 'metaphorising'. You might try to follow their practice of identifying the different metaphorical permutations that underlie the various theories of language set out in this book. If they are right, you should find that similar metaphorical mappings correspond with similar sorts of theories. Is this what you find?

❑ What are Lakoff and Johnson's assumptions about communicativeness? They criticise de Man's view of metaphor as 'unstable and indeterminate in meaning'. How stable and determinate is their view? Do you agree with their analysis of Paul de Man's work?

❑ In listing metaphors for the mind that are used by philosophers of language, can you identify which philosophical frameworks are being attached to each conceptual metaphor? How do you think that practitioners of these other approaches might defend themselves?

❏   The model of metaphorical mapping developed in cognitive linguistics is promi-
    nently information-based. Attributes and content are mapped between domains
    in conceptual metaphors. How might Lakoff and Johnson's view of the cognitive
    unconscious be applied to aesthetics?

CREATIVITY

In recent work, Ronald Carter has revisited the notion of 'literary language' and 'literariness' first theorised by the Russian Formalists in the 1920s. Drawing on examples
of real language collected in context through the CANCODE (Cambridge and
Nottingham Corpus of Discourse in English) project, Carter has identified the extraordinary extent of creativity and 'poetic-ness' in everyday language. These findings
are feeding back into thinking about creativity in high art such as literature, as well
as reshaping our understanding of creativity as a central feature of language use. The
following extract is taken from a journal article which preceded Carter's (2004) book,
Language and Creativity, in which many of these ideas are further developed.

On literary language

Ronald Carter (reprinted from 'Common language: corpus, creativity and cognition'
Language and Literature (Sage Publications, 1999), 8 (3): 195–216).

Literary language: a brief history of definitions
Two main models for definition can be discerned and these can be grouped, rather
loosely, into *inherence* and *socio-cultural* models, although the division is by no means
a clear-cut one. We shall begin with the more formalist inherency definitions because
they are both historically antecedent and more overtly observable.

INHERENCY MODELS; DEVIATION THEORY AND SELF-REFERENTIALITY
Inherency definitions are predicated on a division between poetic and practical
language. According to deviation theory literariness or poeticality inheres in the
degrees to which language use departs or deviates from expected configurations and
normal patterns of language and thus defamiliarizes the reader. Literary language use
is therefore different because it makes strange, disturbs, upsets our routinized
'normal' view of things and thus generates new or renewed perceptions. In a much
quoted poetic example, Dylan Thomas's 'a grief ago' would be poetic by virtue of
its departure from semantic selection restrictions which state that only temporal nouns
such as *week* or *month* can occur in such a sequence. As a result, however, grief comes
to be perceived as a temporal process.

Ronald Carter

Another influential 'inherency' definition is particularly associated with Roman Jakobson. In a famous paper (Jakobson, 1960) he articulated a theory of poetic language which stressed the *self-referentiality* of poetic language. Thus, in the examples:

I hate horrible Harry

or

I like Ike

the verbs *hate* and *like* are selected rather than, for example, *loathe* or *support* because they establish a reinforcing phonaesthetic patterning. The examples cited (the latter is Jakobson's own and is a specific slogan in favour of the former American president Dwight Eisenhower, whose nickname was Ike) demonstrate that poeticality can *inhere* in such everyday language as political advertising slogans. Jakobson's definition is, like definitions of deviation theory, founded in an assumed distinction between 'poetic' and 'pragmatic' language. According to Jakobson, in non-literary discourse the signifier is a mere vehicle for the signified. In literary discourse it is brought into a much more active and reinforcing relationship serving, as it were, to symbolize or represent the signified as well as to refer to it.

This emphasis on patternings and parallelisms and on the self-referential and representational nature of literary discourse is valuable; but it should be pointed out that (1) Jakobson's criteria work rather better in respect of poetry than of prose and; (2) he supplied no clear criteria for determining the *degrees* of poeticality or 'literariness' in his examples, and does not seem to want to answer his own question as to what exactly makes some messages more unequivocally aesthetic examples than others; and (3) like deviation theorists, Jakobson stresses too much the *production* of effects, neglecting in the process the recognition and reception of such effects. The reader or receiver (or listener) of the message and his or her socio-cultural position tend to get left out of account.

SOCIO-CULTURAL MODELS

Initial accounts of literary language which attempt more boldly to underscore the role of the reader or receiver interacting in a socio-linguistic context with the sender of a verbal message have been generally termed *speech act theories* of literary discourse. One of their main proponents was Richard Ohmann.

Ohmann's basic proposition is that the kinds of conditions which normally attach to speech acts such as insulting, questioning and promising do not obtain in literary contexts. Instead we have quasi- or mimetic speech acts. As Ohmann puts it:

> A literary work is a discourse whose sentences lack the illocutionary forces that would normally attach to them . . . specifically, a literary work purportedly imitates (or reports) a series of speech acts, which in fact have no other existence . . . Since the quasi-speech acts of literature are not carrying on the world's business – describing, urging, contracting, etc., the reader may well attend to them in a non-pragmatic way and thus allow them to realize their emotive potential.

> (Ohmann 1971: 2)

Thus, the literary speech act is typically a different kind of speech act – one which involves (on the part of the reader) a suspension of the normal pragmatic functions words may have in order for the reader to regard them as in some way representing or displaying the actions they would normally perform.

Ohmann's theory, like all inherency models, again suffers from an essentialist opposition between literary and non-literary which careful (historical) consideration does not really bear out. Pratt (1977), for example, has convincingly demonstrated that non-fictional, non-pragmatic, mimetic, disinterested, playful speech acts routinely occur outside what is called literature. Hypothesizing, telling white lies, pretending, playing devil's advocate, imagining, fantasizing, relating jokes or anecdotes, even using illustrations to underscore a point in scholarly argument, are then, by Ohmann's definition, literary. For more recent studies see Kuiper and Haggo (1984) and McCarthy and Carter (1994, ch. 4).

In a more extreme version of these arguments, Eagleton (1983: 10) argues that 'anything can be literature' and that it is all a matter of how we choose (or are chosen) to read a text. Because texts are extremely varied and the social and cultural positions from which readers read texts even more varied, a definition of literature can only be relative to specific contexts. In certain institutionalized contexts such as a department of literature in a school or university, definitions of literature will be made by the selection of texts for study which will in turn do no more than reflect the 'interests', predispositions and theories of those teachers, publishing houses or examination boards which make the prescription.

[. . .]

PRESENTATIONALITY

Anders Petterson's work (1990) develops another socio-cultural definition of literature by locating linguistic analysis within more established domains of literary and cultural theory. Petterson demonstrates that what constitutes literary language and literariness is historically and culturally variable and that many of the issues to do with the deviancy and self-reflexivity of literary language belong more comfortably within the 20th century and within modernist accounts of literary formations. Petterson's main conclusion is that literature (in its most central contemporary sense) in most historical and most western cultural settings is a verbal composition which is especially marked by its presentationality. For Petterson literature differs from other categories he explores such as functionally informative and directive discourse because 'to verbally understand serious literature is . . . to understand that it is presentational and to apprehend it in the intended manner is to seek to obtain emotional, cognitive or formal aesthetic satisfaction from it' (Petterson 1990: 256).

Petterson's position finds general support in studies devoted to more universalist and *cognitive* preoccupations with aesthetic functions. Bauman (1977, 1986), for example, stresses the 'designed for performance' aspect of literary presentation, drawing many examples from more oral-based cultures and arguing that 'aesthetic' satisfaction may simply result from a display and appropriate evaluation of verbal skill, the evaluation being based on a judgement of the extent to which clear public rules for the performance have been adhered to. (See also established work on 'verbal duelling'/'flyting'.) Bever (1986) points out that aesthetic satisfaction is produced not simply by straightforward arousal but rather by the *pleasure* which ensues when difficulty is followed by resolution, a good example being when a complex narrative is resolved by an ingenious plot outcome or in which a specific moral problem is addressed and solutions proposed. Parallelism [. . .] is another example in which the first part is resolved by the reinstatement of a related pattern in the second part, a process which serves as a kind of psychological closure or completion.

In earlier studies Berlyne (1971) had gone even further, and with an apparent recognition of the demands of many modernist texts, had argued that a presentation of aesthetic arousal can be autonomous and that, indeed, complexity need not be resolved and may even be all the more pleasurable for remaining so. Cognitive anthropologists in this tradition are, however, less concerned with specific textual functions than with the universal, non-culture-specific character of verbal art. Fabb (1997) reviews this ground lucidly.

PRELIMINARY CONCLUSIONS

The above definitions are largely based on a recognition of the social and cultural nature of literary language as discourse and rightly situate speakers and listeners (as well as writers and readers) as essential constituents of the definition. The definitions assume the *inherently* distinctive nature of literary language and establish that such distinctiveness is relative to social and cultural contexts and to the assignment of such distinctiveness by human subjects. This assignment of distinctiveness assumes, however, that 'literary' language can only be measured against the norms of 'ordinary' discourse and therefore assumes by omission that ordinary discourse cannot be literary. The explanatory models discussed so far do not, however, account adequately for the kinds of cognitive-affective or psycholinguistic responses to literary language suggested by them.

In relation to examples [. . .] given earlier can we account for the *pattern-reforming* and *pattern-reinforcing* tendencies of the (largely) socially symmetrical spoken [. . .] discourse in terms of providing pleasure? Can we say that the (aesthetic) pleasure results mainly from the registering of new morphologies, extended idiomatic constructions and convergent parallelisms, or are there more dynamic 'problem-solving' processes at work? Do listeners co-construct a discourse so that both speakers and listeners achieve greater mutuality? Is the interaction more or less successful if precise interpretation is not achieved? Answers to such questions demand greater attention to psychological and psycholinguistic factors.

For a long time the field of poetics and stylistics has relied for its inspiration on inherency and socio-cultural explanatory models. Their adequacy is, however, not accepted by a growing and ever more influential body of work in the field of psycholinguistics and of literary study within the explanatory models and paradigms of cognitive science. Such models have started from studies of the endemically figurative character of language.

[. . .]

All language is literary language

Ronald
Carter

The opposition of literary to non-literary language is an unhelpful one and the notion of literary language as a yes/no category should be replaced by one which sees literary language as a continuum, a cline of literariness in language use with some uses of language being marked as more literary than others, broadly following the main outlines of the argument advanced in Carter and Nash (1990: ch. 2). Although the most immediate focus is on text-intrinsic linguistic features, it should not be forgotten that whether the reader (or listener) *chooses* to 'read' or respond to a text (spoken or written) in a literary way, as a poetic text as it were, is one crucial determinant of its literariness.

Such a position is echoed in the writings of many 20th century literary theorists and philosophers, beginning with pre-modernist thinkers such as Nietzsche. In *What Is Literary Language?* Tambling (1988) points out that for Nietzsche all language is literary language because even supposedly referential language has no original reference point and because even a referential statement is a rhetorical device, one which is designed to persuade the listener or reader to act or to think in a particular way. The position is close to that of Derrida's discussions of textuality in which for him, as Tambling argues:

> 'Literary language' is a pleonasm . . . all language is literary, because it is all mere writing (the earlier meaning of 'literary'), and it can all be read for the guileful, ambiguous and indeterminate uses of language that literature employs . . . 'what is literary language?' is not a question to be asked merely by those who study 'literature': it affects those who write history, philosophy, political science or science itself.
>
> (Tambling, 1988: 74)

Lecercle (1990) adopts a not dissimilar line, arguing that many models of language this century have been impoverished by a failure properly to examine the more creative 'remainder' of language. The 'remainder', as he terms it, is necessarily ignored by more formalist inspired models which idealize language systems and which, following the lead of Saussure in particular, focus on *langue* to the exclusion of *parole*. The 'remainder' only comes to our notice when we examine real uses of conversational language or investigate it diachronically or look at particular forms such as poetry or explore everyday metaphors, puns, riddles and verbal games. Lecercle questions whether such uses of language can ever be fully formalized but he argues that linguistic systems would be all the richer for recognizing their existence, pointing out in the process that the preoccupation of much modern linguistics with invented data, sentence-level grammar and a narrowly truth-condition-determined semantics does not allow any direct engagement with such data and their associated issues.

PLEASURE AND VERBAL PLAY: RISKS AND REWARDS

Several of the above-mentioned commentators on 'literary' creative and non-literal discourses have pointed to the pleasure conferred by and derived from verbal play.

Ronald Carter

The notion that ordinary language users regularly and typically communicate in ways from which pleasure may be derived has gained considerable ground in recent years and correspondingly the assumption that pleasure is the sole preserve of the highest forms of artistic encounter may need to be re-inspected.

Activity

Issues to consider

- ❏ Is artistic creativity and everyday creativity really the same thing? Is the difference simply one of culturally assigned prestige value? Is artistic creativity homogenous? You might like to consider the different ways in which creativity has been conceptualised, analysed and valued through history.

- ❏ Are there degrees of creativity, as Carter suggests? How might you start to formulate a scale on which one event was more or less creative than another? You will have to decide on your own criteria for creativity in order to establish any principles here.

- ❏ You might read Carter's (2004) book and Attridge's (2004) book, excerpted in C7. How do these two writers agree in their conception of creativity, and how does their understanding differ?

- ❏ What do you think is the relationship between creativity and the aesthetic pleasure derived from the artistic enterprise? How are your feelings on encountering a piece of high art different from your feelings confronted by a particularly clever or witty advertising hoarding?

- ❏ Taking this strand (7) and the thread on interpretation (9) together, what is the creative role of reading? How would you draw the different emphases on producer and receiver in the communicative process?

D8

FIGURATION

The question of figuration, as we have seen in Units A8 and B8, is the question of how to acknowledge the ways in which language can appear to offer more than one 'meaning' simultaneously. What this raises, of course, is the matter of reading. In a justly famous example of 'rhetorical' reading, Barbara Johnson examines not only the fictional consequences of different modes of reading in Herman Melville's novella *Billy Budd*, but also extends this concern to the relation between reading, law and judgement. Consequently, she opens up the political dimensions of how we read 'evidence'.

Judging, reading

Barbara
Johnson

Barbara Johnson (Extract from 'Melville's Fist: The Execution of *Billy Budd*', in *The Critical Difference: Essays in the Contemporary Rhetoric of Reading*, Baltimore: Johns Hopkins University Press, 1980: pp. 79–109).

Three readings of reading

It is no doubt significant that the character around whom the greatest critical dissent has revolved is neither the good one nor the evil one but the one who is explicitly presented as a *reader*, Captain Vere. On some level, readers of *Billy Budd* have always testified to the fact that reading, as much as killing, is at the heart of Melville's story. But how is the act of reading being manifested? And what, precisely, are its relations with the deadliness of the spaces it attempts to comprehend?

As we have noted, critical readings of *Billy Budd* have generally divided themselves into two opposing groups, the 'testament of acceptance' school on the one hand and the 'testament of resistance' or 'irony' school on the other. The first is characterized by its tendency to take at face value the narrator's professed admiration of Vere's sagacity and the final benediction of Vere uttered by Billy. The second group is characterized by its tendency to distance the reader's point of view from that of any of the characters, including the narrator, so that the injustice of Billy's execution becomes perceptible through a process of reversal of certain explicit pronouncements within the tale. This opposition between 'acceptance' and 'irony' quite strikingly mirrors [. . .] the opposition within the story between Billy's naiveté and Claggart's paranoia. We will therefore begin our analysis of Melville's study of the nature of reading with an examination of the way in which the act of reading is manifested in the confrontation between these two characters.

It seems evident that Billy's reading method consists of taking everything at face value, while Claggart's consists of seeing a mantrap under every daisy. Yet in practice, neither of these methods is rigorously upheld. The naive reader is not naive enough to forget to edit out information too troubling to report. The instability of the space between sign and referent, normally denied by the naive reader, is called upon as an instrument whenever that same instability threatens to disturb the content of meaning itself. Billy takes every sign as transparently readable as long as what he reads is consistent with transparent peace, order, and authority. When this is not so, his reading clouds accordingly. And Claggart, for whom every sign can be read as its opposite, neglects to doubt the transparency of any sign that tends to confirm his own doubts: 'the master-at-arms *never suspected the veracity*' (p. 357) of Squeak's reports. The naive believer thus refuses to believe any evidence that subverts the transparency of his beliefs, while the ironic doubter forgets to suspect the reliability of anything confirming his own suspicions.

Naiveté and irony thus stand as symmetrical opposites blinded by their very incapacity to see anything but symmetry. Claggart, in his antipathy, 'can really form no conception of an *unreciprocated* malice' (p. 358). And Billy, conscious of his own blamelessness, can see nothing but pleasantness in Claggart's pleasant words: 'Had the fore-topman been conscious of having done or said anything to provoke the ill-will of the official, it would have been different with him, and his sight might have been purged if not sharpened. As it was, innocence was his blinder' (p. 366). Each character sees the other only through the mirror of his own reflection. Claggart, looking at Billy, mistakes his own twisted face for the face of an enemy, while Billy, recognizing in Claggart the negativity he smothers in himself, strikes out.

The naive and the ironic readers are thus equally destructive, both of themselves and of each other. It is significant that both Billy and Claggart should die. Both readings do violence to the plays of ambiguity and belief by forcing upon the text the applicability of a universal and absolute law. The one, obsessively intent on preserving peace and eliminating equivocation, murders the text; the other, seeing nothing but universal war, becomes the spot on which aberrant premonitions of negativity become truth.

But what of the third reader in the drama, Captain Vere? What can be said of a reading whose task is precisely to read the *relation* between naiveté and paranoia, acceptance and irony, murder and error?

For many readers, the function of Captain Vere has been to provide 'complexity' and 'reality' in an otherwise 'oversimplified' allegorical confrontation:

> Billy and Claggart, who represent almost pure good and pure evil, are too simple and too extreme to satisfy the demands of realism; for character demands admixture. Their all but allegorical blackness and whiteness, however, are functional in the service of Vere's problem, and Vere, goodness knows, is real enough.
>
> [William York Tindall, quoted in Stafford 1969: 187]

> *Billy Budd* seems different from much of the later work, less 'mysterious,' even didactic. . . . Its issues seem somewhat simplified, and, though the opposition of Christly Billy and Satanic Claggart is surely diagrammatic, it appears almost melodramatic in its reduction of values. Only Captain Vere seems to give the story complexity, his deliberations acting like a balance wheel in a watch, preventing a rapid, obvious resolution of the action. . . . It is Vere's decision, and the debatable rationale for it, which introduces the complexity of intimation, the ambiguity.
>
> [Seelye 1970: 162]

As the locus of complexity, Captain Vere then becomes [in the words of various critics] the 'balance wheel' not only in the clash between good and evil but also in the clash between 'accepting' and 'ironic' interpretations of the story. Critical opinion has pronounced the captain 'vicious' and 'virtuous,' 'self-mythifying' and 'self-sacrificing,' 'capable' and 'cowardly,' 'responsible' and 'criminal,' 'moral' and 'perverted,' 'intellectual' and 'stupid,' 'moderate' and 'authoritarian.' But how does the same character provoke such diametrically opposed responses? Why is it the judge that is so passionately judged?

In order to analyze what is at stake in Melville's portrait of Vere, let us first examine the ways in which Vere's reading differs from those of Billy Budd and John Claggart:

1. While the naive/ironic dichotomy was based on a symmetry between *individuals*, Captain Vere's reading takes place within a social *structure*: the rigidly hierarchical structure of a British warship. While the naive reader (Billy) destroys the other in order to defend the self, and while the ironic reader (Claggart) destroys the self by projecting aggression onto the other, the third reader (Vere) subordinates both self and other, and ultimately sacrifices both self and other, for the preservation of a political order.

2. The apparent purpose of both Billy's and Claggart's readings was to determine character; to preserve innocence or to prove guilt. Vere, on the other hand, subordinates character to action, being to doing. 'A martial court,' he tells his officers, 'must needs in the present case confine its attention to the *blow's consequence*, which consequence justly is to be deemed not otherwise than as the *striker's deed*' (p. 384).

3. In the opposition between the metaphysical and psychoanalytical readings of Billy's deed, the deciding question was whether the blow should be considered accidental or (unconsciously) motivated. But in Vere's courtroom reading, both these alternatives are irrelevant: 'Budd's intent or non-intent is nothing to the purpose' (p. 389). What matters is not the cause but the consequences of the blow.

4. The naive or literal reader takes language at face value and treats signs as *motivated*; the ironic reader assumes that the relation between sign and meaning can be *arbitrary* and that appearances are made to be reversed. For Vere, the functions and meanings of signs are neither transparent nor reversible but fixed by socially determined *convention*. Vere's very character is determined not by a relation between his outward appearance and his inner being but by the 'buttons' that signify his position in society. While both Billy and Claggart are said to owe their character to 'nature,' Vere sees his actions and being as meaningful only within the context of a contractual allegiance:

> Do these buttons that we wear attest that our allegiance is to Nature? No, to the King. Though the ocean, which is inviolate Nature primeval, though this be the element where we move and have our being as sailors, yet as the King's officers lies our duty in a sphere correspondingly natural? So little is that true, that in receiving our commissions we in the most important regards ceased to be natural free agents. When war is declared are we the commissioned fighters previously consulted? We fight at command. If our judgments approve the war, that is but coincidence. (p. 387)

Judgment is thus for Vere a function neither of individual conscience nor of absolute justice but of 'the rigor of martial law' (p. 387) operating *through* him.

5. While Billy and Claggart read spontaneously and directly, Vere's reading often makes use of precedent (historical facts, childhood memories), allusions (to the Bible, to various ancient and modern authors), and analogies (Billy is like Adam, Claggart

Barbara
Johnson

is like Ananias). Just as both Billy and Claggart have no known past, they read without memory; just as their lives end with their reading, they read without foresight. Vere, on the other hand, interrogates both past and future for interpretative guidance.

6. While Budd and Claggart thus oppose each other directly, without regard for circumstance or consequence, Vere reads solely in function of the attending historical situation; the Nore and Spithead mutinies have created an atmosphere 'critical to naval authority' (p. 380), and, since an engagement with the enemy fleet is possible at any moment, the *Bellipotent* cannot afford internal unrest.

The fundamental factor that underlies the opposition between the metaphysical Budd/Claggart conflict on the one hand and the reading of Captain Vere on the other can be summed up in a single word: history. While the naive and the ironic readers attempt to impose upon language the functioning of an absolute, timeless, universal law (the sign as either motivated or arbitrary), the question of *martial* law arises within the story precisely to reveal the law as a historical phenomenon, to underscore the element of contextual mutability in the conditions of any act of reading. Arbitrariness and motivation, irony and literality, are parameters between which language constantly fluctuates, but only historical context determines which proportion of each is perceptible to each reader. Melville indeed shows history to be a story not only of events but also of fluctuations in the very functioning of irony and belief:

> The event *converted into irony for a time* those spirited strains of Dibdin. . . .
> (p. 333)

> Everything is *for a term venerated* in navies. (p. 408)

The opposing critical judgments of Vere's decision to hang Billy are divided, in the final analysis, according to the place they attribute to history in the process of justification. For the ironists, Vere is misusing history for his own self-preservation or for the preservation of a world safe for aristocracy. For those who accept Vere's verdict as tragic but necessary, it is Melville who has stacked the historical cards in Vere's favor. In both cases, the conception of history as an interpretive instrument remains the same: it is its *use* that is being judged. And the very direction of *Billy Budd* criticism itself, historically moving from acceptance to irony, is no doubt itself interpretable in the same historical terms.

Evidence can be found in the text for both pro-Vere and anti-Vere judgments:

> Full of disquietude and misgiving, the surgeon left the cabin. Was Captain Vere suddenly affected in his mind? (p. 378)

> Whether Captain Vere, as the surgeon professionally and privately surmised, was really the sudden victim of any degree of aberration, every one must determine for himself by such light as this narrative may afford. (pp. 379–80)

> That the unhappy event which has been narrated could not have happened at a worse juncture was but too true. For it was close on the heel of the

> suppressed insurrections, an aftertime very critical to naval authority, demanding from every English sea commander two qualities not readily interfusable – prudence and rigor. (p. 380)

Barbara Johnson

> Small wonder then that the *Bellipotent*'s captain . . . felt that circumspection not less than promptitude was necessary. . . . Here he may or may not have erred. (p. 380)

The effect of these explicit oscillations of judgment within the text is to underline the importance of the act of judging while rendering its outcome undecidable. Judgment, however difficult, is clearly the central preoccupation of Melville's text, whether it be the judgment pronounced *by* Vere or *upon* him.

There is still another reason for the uncertainty over Vere's final status, however: the unfinished state of the manuscript at Melville's death. According to editors Hayford and Sealts [see Melville 1962: 34–5], it is the 'late pencil revisions' that cast the greatest doubt upon Vere; Melville was evidently still fine-tuning the text's attitude toward its third reader when he died. The ultimate irony in the tale is thus that our final judgment of the very reader who takes history into consideration is made problematic by the intervention of history; by the historical accident of the author's death. History here affects interpretation not only within the content of the narration but also within the very production of the narrative. And what remains suspended by this historical accident is nothing less than the exact signifying value of history. Clearly, the meaning of 'history' as a feature distinguishing Vere's reading from those of Claggart and Budd can in no way be taken for granted.

Issues to consider

- ❑ In attempting to justify the invasion of Iraq in 2003, Western politicians made much of Iraq's supposed possession of Weapons of Mass Destruction, even though none could be found by UN inspectors. In the light of Johnson's essay, how would you characterise the modes of reading evidence employed?
- ❑ It is common to speak of a reading 'doing justice' to a text. How would you differentiate between a just and an unjust reading?
- ❑ In B8 and C8 we considered the possibilities that certain figurative patterns become naturalised, and thus the text enacts a certain view of the world upon the reader. To what extent does the reader have responsibilities for the outcome of such reading? Does a reader have to enter into the figurative landscape of a text in order to read it, or can readers keep a sort of filtering distance from the metaphors that they run through their minds during reading?
- ❑ If the readerly resolutions of figurative patterns in text are partly determined by cultural factors, which shape our idealised cognitive models, how far can two differently cultured readers ever understand each other? In other words, are texts-with-readings culture-specific, or can readers wilfully project their minds and reading practices into another culture and read as the other?

INTERPRETATION

Michael Toolan's *Total Speech*, from which the following extract is taken, is subtitled 'An integrational linguistic approach to language'. In the book, Toolan sets his own view against *segregationist* approaches in linguistics, explicitly attacking relevance theory (B9), schema theory (B9), cognitive linguistics (B8 and D6), and the notion of interpretive communities (A9). He accuses most segregationist linguistics of 'mentalism'. Toolan's work – even if you do not agree with it – forces students of language to question all their assumptions about the practice of linguistics.

Meaning, mind and use

Michael Toolan (reprinted from *Total Speech*, Durham, NC: Duke University Press, 1996: pp. 169–79).

If integrational linguistics owes a debt to Wittgenstein's philosophy of language (particularly in the later works), still there are numerous distinct interpretations of those philosophical investigations, tending to divergent conclusions. Some may challenge the emphasis, here, on intentionality, on linguistic meaning as an individualized, memory-enabling filtering of countless experiences of integrated language-in-context occasions, and on individualized mental modeling as still too mentalist. My account wishes to give room to both (mental) intention and public use; but some Wittgensteinians emphasize use and everyday or commonsense practices with the language while remaining deeply skeptical of the need to speculate about mental processing in relation to what, for them, is an entirely public activity. Speculations about brain activity or mental processes as, or as if these were, the crucial underpinnings of language behavior amounts, in the latter view, to a disastrous category mistake.

A standard case posed as a counterargument to mentalist intentionalist theory is the later Wittgenstein's commentary on individuals' use of the word *pain*. A person may declare that he has a certain pain, but, it is argued, there is absolutely no way in which any other individual can adequately inspect that pain, let alone feel it or know it in its specificity. Just what the mental or body-internal activity is that goes on within the person such as to prompt him to describe it by saying 'I have a pain' is beyond the reach of others. What is within the reach of others, however, is the person's use of the word *pain*, in expected contexts, accompanying standard symptoms, and so on. Those are the everyday criteria by which we judge whether a person is using the word *pain* correctly (i.e., appropriately) and, by extension, the criteria by which we judge whether she or he knows the meaning of the word *pain*. The meaning of the word *pain* is revealed in its appropriate or nonproblematic use, monitored and backed not only by dictionaries but also by off-the-cuff paraphrases in context and other in situ means of displaying that the appropriate use of a word is known. Appropriate or nonproblematic use is the best criterion of correct understanding. The most glaring problem with this view, however, is that it is no sooner formulated than it self-destructs: the phrase *appropriate or nonproblematic use* advertises its own roots in collectivist homogeneity, in which each knows the (single, determinate, code-like) language perfectly. In practice, all these homogenized singularities

Michael
Toolan

strive to conceal pluralities. There is almost never a single appropriate and nonproblematic use of any particular word but always a great number of ways of using it
appropriately or inappropriately, problematically or nonproblematically. And, on each
distinct occasion of use, it will be some of those endlessly varied judgments of appropriateness that will be displayed by interlocutors in situ. To invoke dictionaries in
support of the singularist view of appropriateness is merely to increase the huffing
and puffing, to pull rank in a situation where this may seem effective only because
rank and source of authority were the issue all along.

These caveats notwithstanding, the radical corollary of the thesis that meaning is
displayed in established public use is that all commentary on the mental machinery,
associations, and effects sometimes claimed to be going on in the individual, behind
or beneath the actual public inspectable use, is redundant and distracting: in
Wittgenstein's analogy, it is a wheel that turns without engaging with the rest of the
mechanism. What we mean by the meaning of an expression is essentially a paraphrase – typically a representation, as one or more propositions – of what we judge
to be the use to which that expression is or has been standardly put. And here the
tendency to treat stretches of linguistic activity as abstractable and recurrent items –
expressions – has a deep influence [. . .]. So too has our tendency to judge that our
own use of any expression is only a tiny part of the bulk of uses of the expression
throughout the speech community; as a result, there is a strong impulse for individual
language users to subordinate their own uses and meaning paraphrases of expressions
to ones that are more widely established.

Extensive attention to normative tendencies in language use is therefore a significant need, from an integrational linguistic point of view. What get abstracted and
labeled *utterance meanings* are constantly, and with good reason, a function of
community judgments about how those utterances are used and to be used. The fact
that there are indeed foundational public understandings of utterances like 'I have a
pain' is confirmed by the variety of activities in which we frequently engage that
appeal to that understanding.

Although Wittgenstein's example of *pain* is one in which uninspectability of
private mental response is particularly dramatized, the larger point is that, mutatis
mutandis, the same uninspectability – and the same alleged irrelevance of private
response to meaning, when the latter is construed entirely in terms of evident appropriate use – applies to much less speaker-internal language. By *less speaker-internal
language* is intended language that purports to refer to phenomena potentially in plain
view of the speaker and addressee, such as observable physical events, states, and
entities. Thus, even language with humdrum external reference, as in such utterances
as 'I have two feet' and 'Seattle is rainy,' the same verificationist issue – or misdi-
rection – can arise if we let it. And that verificationist issue concerns the inspectability
of the actual mental activity that might underlie the declaration 'I have a pain' in the
one case and 'Seattle is rainy' in the other. Although the distinctly different verificationist issue of whether in fact the speaker is in pain and whether in fact Seattle is
rainy is clearly more or less easy to resolve in particular cases, it is not the focus of
interest here. What is of interest, as indicated, is the nature of the putative mental
activity accompanying particular utterances, particularly when those utterances make

Michael
Toolan

reference to private and seemingly uninspectable experiences, for in those cases we are tempted to judge that the fittingness of the utterance itself depends directly on the occurrence of a particular kind of accompanying mental activity. The mental experience of pain – and this alone – seems to be the wheel engaged with the machinery so as to warrant the public utterance 'I have a pain.' But the temptation to travel, qua linguists, along this theoretical cul-de-sac must be resisted. To so travel would be to subscribe to a version of 'communicational skepticism' and in the face of this to require 'a mental criterion of understanding' (Taylor 1990: 132); in themselves, neither of these moves is warranted, and, if adopted, they are soon found to bring neither theoretical relief nor resolution.

The questions, What is meaning? and, What is linguistic meaning? are problematic from the outset – as I have hoped to show [. . . in this book]. It is not evident that they can or should be answered prior to consideration of arguably more foundational questions such as, What is language? and, How does language emerge, function, and change? And it is these latter questions that have been my implicit focus. When [earlier] it was argued that individuals derive meanings of utterance partly by recourse to extensive but schematically ordered memories of past situations in which they have encountered language embedded within purposeful interaction (memories in which, then, linguistic forms are remembered as they were experienced, integrated within specific contexts), the whole argument was geared not to the subordinate question, What is the nature and function of literal meaning in language communication? but a more comprehensive one: What has been assumed to be the nature and function of language communication, such that a characterization and role has been assigned to literal meaning within it?

Nevertheless, many social-normativist theorists want to preserve – at all costs, it sometimes seems – the sensibleness of such everyday remarks as 'What does *egregious* mean?' 'I bet you don't know what *egregious* means,' and 'What's the opposite of *egregious*?' All these straightforward uses of language would become problematic, they suggest, if meaning had no singular existence at all and was at best a reflex of complex reticulations of diverse and uninspectable private knowledge in the minds of individuals. While accepting the Wittgensteinian argument against private language as an argument against the notion that language meanings are in the mind/brain, they are unwilling to abandon the notion of shared meaning itself. If shared meaning is not sourced 'in' the individual, it is concluded, it must be established, shared, and sustained by the community.

But to invest such absolute power in the community is to escape cognitive-mechanist determinism only to become enmeshed in social determinism. A social-determinist view of language asserts that what is said and what is meant by what is said are factors fixed in advance for the entire community and binding on all members. By virtue of being a member of that community, you necessarily use the community's language, into which you have been inducted, in just the ways that prevail. What such social-determinist accounts have no explanation for is the fact that an individual's experience of language use is nothing like this. Our experience as individuals is that what we say and how we say it and what it will mean or be taken to mean varies with each succeeding case and that, when we use language, it is first and foremost on our own behalf: each of us is individually responsible and accountable for what he or she says. The importance of the various everyday language games in which we quiz each other over word and sentence meanings needs acknowledging; but, despite the charm of their everyday commonsensicality, these are a potentially misleading activity. They are misleading, that is, if they are taken to constitute adequate grounds for theorizing about language. Distinct from the extremes of both cognitive and social determinism, then, is the kind of local determination, negotiated by individual speakers and hearers (and subsequently potentially ratified by other language users), emphasized here.

Michael
Toolan

[. . .]

The appeal for a place for mentalism (in the sense of memory and imagination) in theorizing about language can never finally be adjudicated by methods of proof or disproof; it is finally about commitments and varieties of faith. Social-determinist language theorists subscribe to the view that the collective language-shaping forces of the community are incontestably sovereign. Cognitive determinists locate an equally fixed and uniform program controlling language competence within each individual's mind-brain. The view here has tried to give due attention to cognitive factors that, at the very least, can be said to be hard to conceive of as purely determinist – particularly the faculties that we summarize as memory and imagination. Those cognitive factors, it is argued, work in conjunction with aspects of an individual's reaction to and use of language that are unquestionably nondeterminist, no matter how constrained they may on occasion be owing to societal pressures to conform. The individual's active and reflective part in language use is characterized by speakers' unequivocal habitual sense that they are personally and severally responsible for what they say and for the effects that their uses of language have. Moral judgment is directly involved in language use, then, including, as it were, the morality of using language publicly in a way that diverges from established social norms. Morality is involved since, in practice, language is always in use within human purposeful activities, and those are inescapably value laden, choice implicating, preference and assumption reflecting, reflecting and articulating judgments about what is right and wrong, desirable and undesirable, correct and incorrect. Part of the standard linguistic depiction of the language user has entailed a theoretically absolute separation of this value ladenness, this concern for correctness, that is implicit and explicit in everyday language use from 'the language proper,' 'the language itself.' But this contrived separation of the language itself, 'as a system,' from language in use, shaped by unpredictable group and individual preferences, prescriptions, prejudices, and affiliations, continues to unravel as the allegedly autonomous structural-systematic 'core' is reexamined. If speaker intuitions – one of the preferred instruments of autonomous linguistic theory – are to be trusted, where lies the boundary between the autonomous core and the normatively shaped, value-expressive supplementary specifics? Where can we place a border between the purely structural and the partly functional? Is it even coherently conceivable that a sharp transition exists between two components or levels of such intrinsically distinct character?

Activity ✪   **Issues to consider**

- ❏ Even if integrationism is right in theory, does it matter in practice? In other words, it might be absolutely true that absolute iterability is impossible in language, but since people act as if repetition has occurred, should that be taken into account as part of an overall theory of language? Put another way, consider whether the differences between a fifth and sixth iteration are significant enough to affect the meaningfulness, force or power of an utterance.

- ❏ Integrationism denies the separation of text from context, arguing that any exploration of communicativeness relies on the integration of both. Are all investigations of language investigations of communicativeness? Should they be? Is there really no value at all in 'pure' semantics, syntax, lexicology or phonetics?

- ❏ How do you think integrationism might handle non-communicativeness?

- ❏ Can there be any accommodation between a socially-determined view of language and a cognitive-perceptual view? Are they necessarily two ends of the theoretical spectrum, or merely two aspects of the same approach? How might you integrate, say, cognitive models of language with socially situated perspectives?

FURTHER READING

Listed below are suggestions for further reading. This list includes both introductory texts and more advanced material. Texts that are particularly useful for those new to the area are marked with an asterisk (*).

General introductions

Barry, P. (1995) *Beginning Theory*, Manchester: Manchester University Press.

*Bennett, A. and Royle, N. (2004) *An Introduction to Literature, Criticism and Theory*, 3rd edn, Harlow: Pearson.

Chapman, S. (2000) *Philosophy for Linguists: An Introduction*, London: Routledge.

*Culler, J. (1997) *Literary Theory: A Very Short Introduction*, Oxford: Oxford University Press.

Eagleton, T. (1983) *Literary Theory: An Introduction*, Oxford: Blackwell.

*Green, K. and LeBihan, J. (1996) *Critical Theory and Practice: A Coursebook*, London: Routledge.

Herrnstein-Smith, B. (1988) *Contingencies of Value: Alternative Perspectives for Critical Theory*, Chicago: University of Chicago Press.

Joseph, J., Love, N. and Taylor, T. (2001) *Landmarks in Linguistic Thought II*, London: Routledge.

*Leitch, V.B. *et al.* (eds) (2001) *The Norton Anthology of Theory and Criticism*, New York: W.W. Norton.

Macey, D. (2000) *The Penguin Dictionary of Critical Theory*, Harmondsworth: Penguin.

Selden, R., Widdowson, P. and Brooker, P. (1997) *A Reader's Guide to Contemporary Literary Theory*, 4th edn, Brighton: Harvester Wheatsheaf.

Taylor, T. and Harris, R. (1997) *Landmarks in Linguistic Thought I*, London: Routledge.

Widdowson, P. (2000) *Literature*, London: Routledge.

1 Gender

Bergvall, V.L., Bing, J.M. and Freed, A.F. (eds) (1996) *Rethinking Language and Gender Research: Theory and Practice*, London: Longman.

*Cameron, D. (ed.) (1998) *The Feminist Critique of Language: A Reader*, 2nd edn, London: Routledge.

McQuillan, M. (ed.) (2003) 'Reading Cixous Writing', *Oxford Literary Review* 24: special issue.

*Mills, S. (1995a) *Feminist Stylistics*, London: Routledge.

Mills, S. (1995b) *Language and Gender*, London: Longman.
*Moi, T. (1985) *Sexual/Textual Politics: Feminist Literary Theory*, London: Methuen.
Sellers, S. (1996) *Hélène Cixous: Authorship, Autobiography and Love*, Cambridge: Polity Press.
Shiach, M. (1991) *Hélène Cixous: A Politics of Writing*, London: Routledge.
*Talbot, M. (1998) *Language and Gender: An Introduction*, Cambridge: Polity Press.
Walsh, C. (2005) *Language and Power: A Resource Book for Students*, London: Routledge.
Wodak, R. (ed.) (1997) *Gender and Discourse*, London: Sage.

2 Race

Bhabha, H.K. (ed.) (1990) *Nation and Narration*, London: Routledge.
*Gates, Jr, H.L. (ed.) (1986) *'Race', Writing, and Difference*, Chicago: University of Chicago Press.
Loomba, A. (1998) *Colonialism/Postcolonialism*, London: Routledge.
*McLeod, J. (2000) *Beginning Postcolonialism*, Manchester: Manchester University Press.
Said, E.W. (1993) *Culture and Imperialism*, London: Chatto & Windus.
Spivak, G.K. (1996) *The Spivak Reader* (eds D. Landry and G. MacLean), London: Routledge.
Thomas, G. (1991) *Linguistic Purism*, London: Longman.
Walder, D. (1998) *Post-Colonial Literatures in English: History, Language, Theory*, Oxford: Blackwell.
Young, R. (1999) *Postcolonialism: A History*, Oxford: Blackwell.

3 Society

Adorno, T.W. (1991) *The Culture Industry: Selected Essays on Mass Culture* (ed. J.M. Bernstein), London: Routledge.
Barthes, R. (1972) *Mythologies* (trans. Annette Lavers), London: Jonathan Cape.
Eagleton, T. (ed.) (1994) *Ideology*, London: Longman.
Hawkes, D. (1996) *Ideology*, London: Routledge.
Mulhern, F. (ed.) (1992) *Contemporary Marxist Literary Criticism*, London: Longman.
*Thomas, L., Wareing, S., Thornborrow, J., *et al.* (1999) *Language, Society and Power: An Introduction*, London: Routledge.
Williams, R. (1961) *Culture and Society 1780–1950*, Harmondsworth: Penguin.
*Williams, R. (1977) *Marxism and Literature*, Oxford: Oxford University Press.
Žižek, S. (1989) *The Sublime Object of Ideology*, London: Verso.
Žižek, S. (ed.) (1994) *Mapping Ideology*, London: Verso.

4 Performativity

Austin, J.L. (1979) *Philosophical Papers*, 3rd edn, Oxford: Clarendon Press.
Cavell, S. (1995) *Philosophical Passages: Wittgenstein, Emerson, Austin, Derrida*, Oxford: Blackwell.
*Culler, J. (1997) *Literary Theory: A Very Short Introduction*, Oxford: Oxford University Press, pp. 95–109.

Johnson, B. (1980) 'Poetry and Performative Language: Mallarmé and Austin', in *The Critical Difference: Essays in the Contemporary Rhetoric of Reading*, Baltimore: Johns Hopkins University Press.

Parker, A. and Sedgwick, E.K. (eds) (1995) *Performativity and Performance*, London: Routledge.

Searle, J.R. (1969) *Speech Acts: An Essay in the Philosophy of Language*, Cambridge: Cambridge University Press.

5 Intention

Bennett, A. (ed.) (1995) *Readers and Reading*, London: Longman.

Burke, S. (1992) *The Death and Return of the Author: Criticism and Subjectivity in Barthes, Foucault and Derrida*, Edinburgh: Edinburgh University Press.

*Burke, S. (ed.) (1995) *Authorship: From Plato to the Postmodern: A Reader*, Edinburgh: Edinburgh University Press.

Clark, T. (1997) *The Theory of Inspiration: Composition as a Crisis of Subjectivity in Romantic and Post-Romantic Writing*, Manchester: Manchester University Press.

Gibbs, R. (1999) *Intentions in the Experience of Meaning*, Cambridge: Cambridge University Press.

Kamuf, P. (1988) *Signature Pieces: On the Institution of Authorship*, Ithaca: Cornell University Press.

Miller, J.H. (1987) *The Ethics of Reading*, New York: Columbia University Press.

Syrotinski, M. and Maclachlan, I. (eds) (2001) *Sensual Reading: New Approaches to Reading and Its Relations to the Senses*, London: Associated University Presses.

6 Cognition

Gavins, J. and Steen, G. (eds) (2003) *Cognitive Poetics in Practice*, London: Routledge.

Langacker, R. (1987) *Foundations of Cognitive Grammar, Vol. I: Theoretical Prerequisites*, Stanford: Stanford University Press.

Langacker, R. (1991) *Foundations of Cognitive Grammar, Vol. II: Descriptive Application*, Stanford: Stanford University Press.

Semino, E. and Culpeper, J. (eds) (2002) *Cognitive Stylistics*, Amsterdam: Benjamins.

*Stockwell, P. (2002) *Cognitive Poetics: An Introduction*, London: Routledge.

Turner, M. (1996) *The Literary Mind: The Origins of Thought and Language*, Oxford: Oxford University Press.

*Ungerer, F. and Schmid, H-J. (1996) *An Introduction to Cognitive Linguistics*, London: Longman.

Werth, P. (1999) *Text Worlds: Representing Conceptual Space in Discourse*, London: Longman.

7 Creativity

Attridge, D. (2004) *The Singularity of Literature*, London: Routledge.

Bohm, D. and Nichol, L. (eds) (1998) *On Creativity*, London: Routledge.

*Carter, R. (2004) *Language and Creativity: The Art of Common Talk*, London: Routledge.

Kearney, R. (1998) *The Wake of Imagination: Ideas of Creativity in Western Culture*, London: HarperCollins.

*Nash, W. (1998) *Language and Creative Illusion*, London: Longman.

Pope, R. (1994) *Textual Intervention: Critical and Creative Strategies for Literary Studies*, London: Routledge.

*Pope, R. (2004) *Creativity*, London: Routledge.

Steiner, G. (2002) *Grammars of Creation*, London: Faber.

8 Figuration

Aristotle (1984) *Poetics* and *Rhetoric*, in *The Complete Works of Aristotle* (ed. Jonathan Barnes), 2 vols, Princeton: Princeton University Press. [Both texts are in Volume 2.]

Chase, C. (1986) *Decomposing Figures: Rhetorical Readings in the Romantic Tradition*, Baltimore: Johns Hopkins University Press.

Kövecses, Z. (2000) *Metaphor and Emotion: Language, Culture, and Body in Human Feeling*, Cambridge: Cambridge University Press.

Lakoff, G. and Johnson, M. (1999) *Philosophy in the Flesh: The Embodied Mind and Its Challenge to Western Thought*, New York: Basic Books.

*Ortony, A. (ed.) (1993) *Metaphor and Thought*, 2nd edn, Cambridge: Cambridge University Press.

Richards, I.A. (1965) *The Philosophy of Rhetoric*, Oxford: Oxford University Press.

Sacks, S. (ed.) (1979) *On Metaphor*, Chicago: University of Chicago Press.

Vickers, B. (1988) *In Defence of Rhetoric*, Oxford: Oxford University Press.

9 Interpretation

Cavallo, G. and Chartier, R. (eds) (1999) *A History of Reading in the West*, Cambridge: Polity.

Eco, U. (1990) *The Limits of Interpretation*, Bloomington: Indiana University Press.

Gadamer, H-G. (1989) *Truth and Method* (trans. J. Weinsheimer and D. Marshall), 2nd edn, New York: Crossroad Press.

Harris, R. (1998) *Introduction to Integrational Linguistics*, Oxford: Pergamon.

Lecercle, J.-J. (1999) *Interpretation as Pragmatics*, London: Macmillan.

Lentricchia, F. and Dubois, A. (eds) (2003) *Close Reading: The Reader*, Durham, NC: Duke University Press.

Toolan, M. (1996) *Total Speech: An Integrational Linguistic Approach to Language*, Durham, NC: Duke University Press.

REFERENCES

Adorno, T.W. (1991) 'Trying to Understand *Endgame*', in *Notes to Literature*, vol. 1, New York: Columbia University Press, pp. 241–75.

Althusser, L. (1994) 'Ideology and Ideological State Apparatuses (Notes Towards an Investigation)', in S. Žižek (ed.) *Mapping Ideology*, London: Verso.

Aristotle (1995) *The Complete Works of Aristotle* (ed. J. Barnes), 2 vols, Princeton: Princeton University Press.

Attridge, D. (2004) *The Singularity of Literature*, London: Routledge.

Austin, J.L. (1976) *How to Do Things with Words*, 2nd edn, Oxford: Oxford University Press.

Austin, J.L. (1979) *Philosophical Papers*, 3rd edn, Oxford: Clarendon Press.

Barthes, R. (1989) *The Rustle of Language* (trans. R. Howard), Berkeley, CA: University of California Press.

Bauman, R. (1977) *Verbal Art as Performance*, Boston, MA: Newbury House.

Bauman, R. (1986) *Story, Performance and Event: Contextual Studies of Oral Narrative*, Cambridge: Cambridge University Press.

Beckett, S. (1958) *Endgame*, New York: Grove Press.

Benjamin, W. (1992) *Illuminations* (trans. H. Zohn), London: Fontana.

Berger, J. (1984) *And Our Faces, My Heart, Brief as Photos*, New York: Vintage.

Berlyne, D. (1971) *Aesthetics and Psychobiology*, New York: Appleton-Century-Crofts.

Bever, T.G. (1986) 'The aesthetic basis for cognitive structures', in M. Brand and R. Harnish (eds) *The Representation of Knowledge and Belief*, Tucson: University of Arizona Press, pp. 314–56.

Brooks, C. (1947) *The Well Wrought Urn*, New York: Harcourt Brace.

Butler, J. (1990) *Gender Trouble: Feminism and the Subversion of Identity*, London: Routledge.

Butler, J. (1993) *Bodies That Matter: On the Discursive Limits of 'Sex'*, London: Routledge.

Butler, J. (1997) *Excitable Speech*, London: Routledge.

Cameron, D. (1995) *Verbal Hygiene*, London: Routledge.

Carter, R. (1999) 'Common language: corpus, creativity and cognition', *Language and Literature* 8(3): 195–216.

Carter, R. (2004) *Language and Creativity: The Art of Common Talk*, London: Routledge.

Carter, R. and Nash, W. (1990) *Seeing Through Language: Styles of English Writing*, Oxford: Blackwell.

Chomsky, N. (1957) *Syntactic Structures*, The Hague: Mouton.

Chomsky, N. (1964) *Current Issues in Linguistic Theory*, The Hague: Mouton.

Chomsky, N. (1965) *Aspects of the Theory of Syntax*, Cambridge, MA: MIT Press.

Chomsky, N. (1981) *Lectures on Government and Binding*, Dordrecht: Foris.

Chomsky, N. (1988) *Language and Problems of Knowledge*, Cambridge, MA: MIT Press.

Chomsky, N. (1992) *A Minimalist Program for Linguistic Theory*, Cambridge, MA: MIT Working Papers in Linguistics.

Cixous, H. and Clément, C. (1986) *The Newly Born Woman* (trans. B. Wing), Minneapolis: University of Minnesota Press.

Cockcroft, R. (2002) *Renaissance Rhetoric: Reconsidered Passion – The Interpretation of Affect in Early Modern Writing*, London: Palgrave.

Conrad, J. (2000) *Heart of Darkness*, in *The Norton Anthology of English Literature*, 7th edn, Vol. 2, New York: W.W. Norton, pp. 1958–2017.

Cook, G. (1994) *Discourse and Literature*, Oxford: Oxford University Press.

Cover, R.M. (1986) 'Violence and the Word', *Yale Law Journal* 96.

Culler, J. (1983) *On Deconstruction: Theory and Criticism after Structuralism*, London: Routledge.

Culler, J. (1997) *Literary Theory: A Very Short Introduction*, Oxford: Oxford University Press.

de Man, P. (1979) *Allegories of Reading: Figural Language in Rousseau, Nietzsche, Rilke, and Proust*, New Haven, CT: Yale University Press.

de Man, P. (1986) *The Resistance to Theory*, Minneapolis: University of Minnesota Press.

de Man, P. (1996) *Aesthetic Ideology*, Minneapolis: University of Minnesota Press.

Derrida, J. (1982) *Margins of Philosophy* (trans. A. Bass), Hemel Hempstead: Harvester.

Derrida, J. (1989) *Mémoires for Paul de Man* (rev. edn, trans. C. Lindsay and others), New York: Columbia University Press

Derrida, J. (1995) *On the Name* (ed. T. Dutoit), Stanford, CA: Stanford University Press.

Derrida, J. (1998) *Monolingualism of the Other, or, the Prosthesis of Origin* (trans. P. Mensah), Stanford, CA: Stanford University Press.

Derrida, J. (2002) *Negotiations: Interventions and Interviews 1971–2001* (ed. and trans. E. Rottenberg), Stanford, CA: Stanford University Press.

Dolan, C. (1994) 'Translating the Bible into suitable Klingon stirs cosmic debate', *Wall Street Journal*, 13 June 1994.

Donne, J. (1983) *The Complete English Poems*, Harmondsworth: Penguin.

Eagleton, T. (1983) *Literary Theory: An Introduction*, Oxford: Blackwell.

Eagleton, T. (1991) *Ideology: An Introduction*, London: Verso.

Ellison, R. (1965) *Invisible Man*, Harmondsworth: Penguin.

Fabb, N. (1997) *Linguistics and Literature*, Oxford: Blackwell.

Fairclough, N. (1989) *Language and Power*, London: Longman.

Fairclough, N. (1992) *Discourse and Social Change*, Cambridge: Polity.

Fairclough, N. (1995) *Critical Discourse Analysis: The Critical Study of Language*, London: Longman.

Fanon, F. (1986) *Black Skin, White Masks* (trans. C.L. Markmann), London: Pluto.

Felman, S. (2003) *The Scandal of the Speaking Body: Don Juan with J.L. Austin, or Seduction in Two Languages*, Stanford, CA: Stanford University Press.

Fish, Stanley (1980) *Is There a Text in this Class?* Cambridge, MA: Harvard University Press.

Fodor, J. (1979) *The Language of Thought*, Cambridge, MA: Harvard University Press.

Foucault, M. (1989) *The Order of Things*, London: Routledge.

Foucault, M. (1994) *The Foucault Reader* (ed. P. Rabinow), Harmondsworth: Penguin.

Freud, S. (1990) *Art and Literature: The Penguin Freud Library 14* (ed. A. Dickson), Harmondsworth: Penguin.

Freud, S. (2003) *The Uncanny* (trans. D. McLintock), Harmondsworth: Penguin.

Gadamer, H.-G. (1989) *Truth and Method* (trans. J. Weinsheimer and D. Marshall, 2nd edn, from *Wahrheit und Methode*, 1960), New York: Crossroad Press.

Gates, Jr, H.L. (ed.) (1986) *'Race', Writing, and Difference*, Chicago: University of Chicago Press.

Gibbs, R. (2003) 'Prototypes in dynamic meaning construal', in J. Gavins and G. Steen (eds) *Cognitive Poetics in Practice*, London: Routledge, pp. 27–40.

Glissant, E. (1990) *Poétique de la Relation*, Paris: Gallimard.

Grice, H.P. (1975) 'Logic and conversation', in P. Cole and J.L. Morgan (eds) *Syntax and Semantics 3: Speech Acts*, New York: Academic Press.

Habermas, J. (1998) *The Philosophical Discourse of Modernity* (trans. F. Lawrence), Cambridge: Polity.

Harris, R. (1998) *Introduction to Integrational Linguistics*, Oxford: Pergamon.

Heidegger, M. (1971) *Poetry, Language, Thought* (trans. A. Hofstadter), New York: Harper.

Hirsch, E.D. (1976) *Validity in Interpretation*, New Haven, CT: Yale University Press.

Huck, G. and Goldsmith, J. (1995) *Ideology and Linguistic Theory: Noam Chomsky and the Deep Structure Debates*, London: Routledge.

Ingarden, R. (1973) *The Literary Work of Art: An Investigation on the Borderlines of Ontology, Logic, and Theory of Literature* (trans. G. Grabowics), Evanston, IL: Northwestern University Press.

Iser, W. (1974) *The Implied Reader: Patterns of Communication in Prose Fiction from Bunyan to Beckett*, Baltimore, MD: Johns Hopkins University Press.

Iser, W. (1978) *The Act of Reading: A Theory of Aesthetic Response*, Baltimore, MD: Johns Hopkins University Press.

Jakobson, R. (1960) 'Linguistics and poetics', in T. Sebeok (ed.) *Style in Language*, Cambridge, MA: MIT Press, pp. 350–77.

Johnson, B. (1980a) *The Critical Difference: Essays in the Contemporary Rhetoric of Reading*, Baltimore, MD: Johns Hopkins University Press.

Johnson, B. (1980b) 'Melville's Fist: The Execution of *Billy Budd*', in *The Critical Difference: Essays in the Contemporary Rhetoric of Reading*, Baltimore, MD: Johns Hopkins University Press, pp. 79–109.

Joyce, J. (1977) *A Portrait of the Artist as a Young Man*, in *The Essential James Joyce*, London: Grafton, pp. 175–365.

Kant, I. (1998) *Groundwork of the Metaphysics of Morals* (ed. M. Gregor), Cambridge: Cambridge University Press.

Knowlson, J. (1996) *Damned to Fame: The Life of Samuel Beckett*, London: Bloomsbury.

Kuiper, K. and Haggo, D. (1984) 'Livestock auctions, oral poetry, and ordinary language', *Language in Society* 13: 205–34.

Lacan, J. (1968) *The Language of the Self* (trans. A. Wilden), New York: Dell.

Lacan, J. (1977) *Écrits: A Selection* (trans. A. Sheridan), London: Tavistock.

Lakoff, G. (1987) *Women, Fire and Dangerous Things: What Categories Reveal About the Mind*, Chicago: University of Chicago Press.

Lakoff, G. and Johnson, M. (1999) *Philosophy in the Flesh*, New York: Basic Books.

Lakoff, G. and Turner, M. (1989) *More Than Cool Reason: A Field Guide to Poetic Metaphor*, Chicago: University of Chicago Press.

Lawrence, D.H. (1998) *Women in Love* (ed. D. Bradshaw), Oxford: Oxford University Press.

Lawson, N. (2001) *Nigella Bites*, London: Chatto & Windus.

Lecercle, J.J. (1990) *The Violence of Language*, London: Routledge.

Le Guin, U. (1974) *The Compass Rose*, London: Gollancz.

Leitch, V.B. *et al.* (eds) (2001) *The Norton Anthology of Theory and Criticism*, New York: W.W. Norton.

Levinas, E. (1996) *Basic Philosophical Writings* (ed. A.T. Peperzak, S. Critchley and R. Bernasconi), Bloomington, IN: Indiana University Press.

McCarthy, M. and Carter, R. (1994) *Language as Discourse*, London: Longman.

MacKinnon, C. (1993) *Only Words*, Cambridge, MA: Harvard University Press.

Marotti, A. (1986) *John Donne, Coterie Poet*, Madison: University of Wisconsin Press.

Marx, K. (1992) *Surveys from Exile: Political Writings: Volume 2* (ed. D. Fernbach), Harmondsworth: Penguin.

Matsuda, M.J., Lawrence, C.R., Delgado, R., *et al.* (eds) (1993) *Words that Wound: Critical Race Theory, Assaultive Speech and the First Amendment*, Boulder, CO: Westview Press.

Melville, Herman (1967) *Billy Budd, Sailor, and Other Stories* (ed. Harold Beaver), New York: Penguin.

Miller, J.H. (2001) *Speech Acts in Literature*, Stanford, CA: Stanford University Press.

Morrison, T. (1988) *Beloved*, London: Picador.

Mulhern, F. (ed.) (1992) *Contemporary Marxist Literary Criticism*, London: Longman.

Ngũgĩ wa Thiong'o (1986) *Decolonising the Mind: The Politics of Language in African Literature*, London: James Currey.

Nietzsche, F. (1996) *On the Genealogy of Morals* (trans. Douglas Smith), Oxford: Oxford University Press.

Nietzsche, F. (1999) *The Birth of Tragedy and Other Writings* (eds R. Geuss and R. Speirs), Cambridge: Cambridge University Press.

Noon, J. (1998) *Pixel Juice*, London: Doubleday.

Ohmann, R. (1971) 'Speech acts and the definition of literature', *Philosophy and Rhetoric* 4: 1–19.

Orwell, G. (1948) *Nineteen Eighty-Four*, London: Secker & Warburg.

Orwell, G. (2000) 'Politics and The English Language', in *The Norton Anthology of English Literature*, 7th edn, Vol. 2, New York: W.W. Norton, pp. 2462–71.

Patai, R. (1969) *Golden River to Golden Road: Society, Culture, and Change in the Middle East*, 3rd edn, Philadelphia, PA: University of Pennsylvania Press.

Petterson, A. (1990) *A Theory of Literary Discourse in Aesthetics 2*, Lund: Lund University Press.

Phillips, A. (1996) *Monogamy*, London: Faber and Faber.

Plato (1989) *The Collected Dialogues of Plato, Including the Letters* (eds E. Hamilton and H. Cairns), Princeton: Princeton University Press.

Pratt, M.L. (1977) *Towards a Speech Act Theory of Literary Discourse*, Bloomington, IN: Indiana University Press.

Putnam, H. (1990) *Realism with a Human Face*, Cambridge, MA: Harvard University Press.

Quintilian (1953) *Institutio Oratoria* (trans. H.E. Butler), 4 vols, London: William Heinemann.

Rancière, J. (1998) *Disagreement: Politics and Philosophy* (trans. J. Rose), Minneapolis: University of Minnesota Press.

Ronen, R. (1994) *Possible Worlds in Literary Theory*, Cambridge: Cambridge University Press.

Royle, N. (2003) *The Uncanny*, Manchester: Manchester University Press.

Ryan, M.L. (1991) *Possible Worlds: Artificial Intelligence and Narrative Theory*, Bloomington, IN: Indiana University Press.

Said, E. (1983) *The World, the Text, and the Critic*, London: Faber & Faber.

Said, E. (2003) *Orientalism*, Harmondsworth: Penguin.

St Paul City Council (1990) St Paul Bias Motivated Crime Ordinance, Section 292.02 Minn. Legis. Code.

Sapir, E. (1921) *Language*, New York: Harcourt, Brace.

Searle, J.R. (1969) *Speech Acts: An Essay in the Philosophy of Language*, Cambridge: Cambridge University Press.

Seelye, J. (1970) *Melville: The Ironic Diagram*, Evanston, IL: Northwestern University Press.

Semino, E. (1997) *Language and World Creation in Poems and Other Texts*, London: Longman.

Sperber, D. and Wilson, D. (1986) *Relevance: Communication and Cognition*, Oxford: Blackwell.

Stafford, W.T. (ed.) (1969) *'Billy Budd' and the Critics*, Belmont, CA: Wadsworth.

Steen, G. (1992) *Metaphor in Literary Reception*, Amsterdam: Vrije Universiteit.

Steen, G. (1994) *Understanding Metaphor in Literature*, London: Longman.

Stockwell, P. (2000) *The Poetics of Science Fiction*, London: Longman.

Stockwell, P. (2002) *Cognitive Poetics: An Introduction*, London: Routledge.

Tambling, J. (1988) *What is Literary Language?* Milton Keynes: Open University Press.

Taylor. T. (1990) 'Normativity and linguistic form', in H. Davis and T. Taylor (eds) *Redefining Linguistics*, London: Routledge.

Toolan, M. (1996) *Total Speech: An Integrational Linguistic Approach to Language*, Durham, NC: Duke University Press.

Turner, M. (1987) *Death is the Mother of Beauty: Mind, Metaphor, Criticism*, Chicago: University of Chicago Press.

Turner, M. (1996) *The Literary Mind: The Origins of Thought and Language*, Oxford: Oxford University Press.

Ungerer, F. and Schmid, H.-J. (1996) *An Introduction to Cognitive Linguistics*, London: Longman.

Vološinov, V.N. (1996) *Marxism and the Philosophy of Language* (trans. L Matejka and I.R. Titunik), Cambridge, MA: Harvard University Press.

Werth, P. (1999) *Text Worlds: Representing Conceptual Space in Discourse*, London: Longman.

Williams, R. (1983) *Keywords: A Vocabulary of Culture and Society*, London: Flamingo.

Wittgenstein, L. (2001) *Philosophical Investigations* (trans. G.E.M. Anscombe), Oxford: Blackwell.

Žižek, S. (ed.) (1994) *Mapping Ideology*, London: Verso.

Žižek, S. (1989) *The Sublime Object of Ideology*, London: Verso.

GLOSSARIAL INDEX

Where there is a definition or clear usage given in context, the word is indexed in **bold**. Other page references are to places in the book where the term is also used.

eBooks – at www.eBookstore.tandf.co.uk

A library at your fingertips!

eBooks are electronic versions of printed books. You can store them on your PC/laptop or browse them online.

They have advantages for anyone needing rapid access to a wide variety of published, copyright information.

eBooks can help your research by enabling you to bookmark chapters, annotate text and use instant searches to find specific words or phrases. Several eBook files would fit on even a small laptop or PDA.

NEW: Save money by eSubscribing: cheap, online access to any eBook for as long as you need it.

Annual subscription packages

We now offer special low-cost bulk subscriptions to packages of eBooks in certain subject areas. These are available to libraries or to individuals.

For more information please contact webmaster.ebooks@tandf.co.uk

We're continually developing the eBook concept, so keep up to date by visiting the website.

www.eBookstore.tandf.co.uk